The Mentally Retarded Child

IDENTIFICATION, ACCEPTANCE, AND CURRICULUM

The Mentally Retarded Child

IDENTIFICATION, ACCEPTANCE, AND CURRICULUM

By

ROY DeVERL WILLEY, Ph.D.

Professor of Education
University of Nevada
Reno, Nevada

and

KATHLEEN BARNETTE WAITE, M.Ed.

Visiting Lecturer
University of Nevada
Reno, Nevada

CHARLES C THOMAS • PUBLISHER

Springfield • Illinois • U.S.A.

Published and Distributed Throughout the World by

CHARLES C THOMAS • PUBLISHER

BANNERSTONE HOUSE

301-327 East Lawrence Avenue, Springfield, Illinois, U.S.A.

NATCHEZ PLANTATION HOUSE

735 North Atlantic Boulevard, Fort Lauderdale, Florida, U.S.A.

With THOMAS BOOKS careful attention is given to all details of manufacturing and design. It is the Publisher's desire to present books that are satisfactory as to their physical qualities and artistic possibilities and appropriate for their particular use. THOMAS BOOKS will be true to those laws of quality that assure a good name and good will.

Printed in the United States of America
C-1

Dedication

To my son
Blair Young Willey

To my daughter
Rulan K. Waite

Preface

THIS volume was specifically designed for those adults who work or plan to work with mentally retarded children. It is hoped, too, that school superintendents, principals, supervisors, and school counselors can gain valuable information from this book concerning the planning and organization of an educational or training program for mentally retarded individuals.

The authors attempt to present practical, easily understood methods for teaching reading, spelling, oral and written language, social studies, health, and the fine arts. The reader will find a more detailed and comprehensive treatment of the subject than is found to date in textbooks designed for adult use.

Section One clarifies concepts, defines terms, relates the history of mental retardation, and describes in detail the characteristics of the mentally retarded child. A discussion of the etiology of mental deficiency is also included. Section Two contains the practical side of the volume and deals specifically with the education and training of the mentally retarded child. The reader will be especially interested in the chapter discussing the education of the severely (trainable) mentally retarded. Section Three discusses mentally retarded children and their environment. This chapter will be particularly interesting and useful to parents.

One of the authors is currently teaching a class of mentally retarded youngsters and has had college experience in training teachers for this area of special education. The other author is a university professor who teaches classes in the education of exceptional children. The present volume thus deals adequately with theoretical coverage of the education of mentally retarded children as well as practical, down-to-earth, methods of teaching.

K. B. W.

R. D. W.

Contents

SECTION TWO
EDUCATION AND TRAINING OF THE MENTALLY RETARDED

SECTION THREE
THE MENTALLY RETARDED AND THEIR ENVIRONMENT

The Mentally Retarded Child

IDENTIFICATION, ACCEPTANCE, AND CURRICULUM

Section One

MENTAL RETARDATION

The first three chapters of this book are concerned with definitions, history, characteristics, symptoms, and causes. Chapter One considers the term "Mental Retardation" and its application to the child. Presented, too, is a general description of mentally retarded children and treatment in contrast to that of the era preceding the nineteenth century. Chapter Two is particularly concerned with the characteristics of mentally retarded children. Chapter Three examines some symptoms and some causes of mental retardation.

CHAPTER ONE

The Mentally Retarded Child

THE "New Look" including modern trends and issues in Mental Retardation is beginning to appear in contemporary education. It blends ideas both new and old and hopefully forecasts a brighter future for all mentally retarded people. Recent changes are reflected in new modes of expression which indicate alteration in thinking and values. As the term "feebleminded" gave place to "Mental Deficiency" so this in turn has changed to "Mental Retardation." These changes in terminology indicate a tendency to depart from precise clinical diagnosis toward a more general appraisal of the child as a person in "softer" words and with more generally descriptive evaluation of total aptitudes.

THE TERM "MENTAL RETARDATION"

Many attempts have been made to define precisely what is meant by the concept of "mental retardation," not only in terms of the intelligence quotient, but more adequately in consideration of many additional factors, such as the nature of the intellectual development of the child, and the manifold conditions that affect the rate of his development, as well as the specific manifestations at any given period. The broadest definition of mentally retarded children is: those human beings who, because of limited mental capacities, are without special assistance, incapable of adapting to their environment. These include children for whom special efforts must be made to enable them to live a reasonably normal, self-sufficient, productive life in our society. They may not always be able to respond to these special efforts and may even, despite such training, require lifelong care and supervision.

Among the more acceptable definitions of mental retardation are the following:

> E. A. Doll describes this condition as one of "social incompetence due to subnormal intellectual powers which have been

arrested in development,"[1] and in a more explicit statement, develops his definition further; ". . . six criteria by statement or implication have been generally considered essential to an adequate definition and concept. These are: 1) social incompetence; 2) due to mental subnormality; 3) which has been developmentally arrested; 4) which obtains at maturity; 5) is of constitutional origin, and 6) is essentially incurable."[2]

Doll's definition of social incompetence "which obtains at maturity" implies a permanent kind of inferiority or handicap which is of constitutional origin and cannot be cured. This may be due either to heredity or to damage from disease, deprivation or trauma. Maturity is taken to mean that age, somewhere between fifteen and twenty-five, at which physical and intellectual development have reached the height of their growth and the individual has reached his peak biologically, physically and intellectually. Beyond this point, any growth that occurs, takes place in the realms of wisdom, mechanical skills and social awareness.

It should be noted that the ultimate criteria stressed are those of competence and the ability to adapt and adjust to the demands of society. In these respects the behavioral reaction of the mentally retarded child is the product of many interesting forces. The home environment, the attitude of the child's parents and siblings toward him, his acceptance by neighbors and friends, his classmates, as well as his lowered intellectual potential—all influence the child's reactions. In coping with these behavioral reactions, it is essential to understand primarily the underlying reasons; that is, to adopt a dynamic approach to these problems.

A. F. Tredgold defines mental retardation as:

"A state of incomplete mental development of such a kind and degree that the individual is incapable of adapting himself to the normal environment of his fellows in such a way as to maintain existence independent of supervision, control or external support."[3]

S. E. Perry describes the dynamic approach as follows:

". . . It requires a complete reassessment of the nature of mental

---

[1] E. A. Doll: Definition. *Training School Bulletin, 37*:163-164, 1941.

[2] E. A. Doll: The essentials of an inclusive concept of mental deficiency. *American Journal of Mental Deficiency, 46*:214-219, 1941.

[3] A. F. Tredgold: *A Textbook of Mental Deficiency.* Baltimore, William Wood and Co., 1937.

deficiency. . . . Each mentally defective person must be considered, not as belonging to a homogeneous category called deficiency, but as an individual; his subnormal intellectual functioning must be considered, not as constitutionally or organically determined, but as an interdependent complex of constitutional or physiological processes, interpersonal processes, and sociocultural processes; and from a research standpoint the mentally defective must be approached, not with an assumption of irreversibility and permanence, but with the assumption that benevolent intervention may lead to a reversibility or improvement of the conditions."[4]

The modern approach to the problem is to view the intelligence test score as one phase of appraisal, an integral part of the child's total personality and ability to function, but to give equal importance to many other factors that compose the total personality picture.

Thomas E. Jordan states:

"Mental retardation is the condition which accounts for the lower end of the curve of intellectual abilities, and the study of mental retardation illustrates the extent to which one human being can differ in intellectual characteristics from his fellows."[5]

Gunnar Dybwad says:

"Mental retardation is a condition which originates during the developmental period and is characterized by markedly subaverage intellectual functioning, resulting to some degree in social inadequacy."[6]

Definition by Rick Heber:

"Mental retardation refers to subaverage general intellectual functioning which originates during the developmental period and is associated with impairment in one or more of the following: 1) maturation; 2) learning; 3) social adjustment."[7]

---

[4] S. E. Perry: Some theoretical problems of mental deficiency and their action implications. *Psychiatry*, 17:46, 1954.

[5] Thomas E. Jordan: *The Mentally Retarded*. Columbus, Ohio, Charles E. Merrill Books, Inc., 1961, p. 1.

[6] Gunnar Dybwad: Mental retardation. In Jerome H. Rothstein: *Mental Retardation—Readings and Resources*. New York, N. Y., Holt, Rinehart and Winston, Inc., 1961, p. 5.

[7] Rick Heber: Definition of mental retardation. In Jerome H. Rothstein: *Mental Retardation—Readings and Resources*. New York, N. Y., Holt, Rinehart and Winston, Inc., 1961, pp. 9-10.

Sub-average refers to performance which is greater than one standard deviation below the population mean of the age group involved on measures of general intellectual functioning.

This level of general intellectual functioning may be assessed by performance on one or more of the various objective tests which have been developed for that purpose. Though the upper age limit of the developmental period can not be precisely specified, it may be regarded, for practical purposes, as being at approximately sixteen years. This criterion is in accord with the traditional concept of mental retardation with respect to age and serves to distinguish mental retardation from other disorders of human behavior.

The definition specifies that the subaverage intellectual functioning must be reflected by impairment in one or more of the following aspects of adaptive behavior: 1) maturation; 2) learning, and 3) social adjustment. These three aspects of adaptation assume different importance as qualifying conditions of mental retardation for different age groups.

Rate of maturation refers to the rate of sequential development of self-help skills of infancy and early childhood such as sitting, crawling, standing, walking, talking, habit training, and interaction with age peers. In the first few years of life adaptive behavior is assessed almost completely in terms of these and other manifestations of sensory-motor development. Consequently, delay in acquisition of early developmental skills is of prime importance as a criterion of mental retardation during the preschool years.

Learning ability refers to the facility with which knowledge is acquired as a function of experience. Learning difficulties are usually manifest in the academic situation and if mild in degree, may not even become apparent until the child enters school. Impaired learning ability is, therefore, particularly important as a qualifying condition of mental retardation during the school years.

Social adjustment is particularly important as a qualifying condition of mental retardation at the adult level where it is assessed in terms of the degree to which the individual is able to maintain himself independently in the community and in gainful employment as well as by his ability to meet and conform to other personal and social responsibilities and standards set by the community. During the preschool and school age years, social adjustment is reflected, in large measure, in the level and manner in which the child relates to parents, other adults, and his age peers.

It is this accompanying deficiency in one or more of these three aspects of adaptation which determines the need of the individual for professional services and for legal action as a mentally retarded person.[7]

Seymour B. Sarason (psycho-social) mental retardation:

". . . refers to the individuals who, for temporary or long standing reasons, function intellectually below the average of their peer groups but whose social adequacy is not in question or, if it is in question, there is the likelihood that the individual can learn to function independently and adequately in the community."[8]

George A. Jervis (medical):

". . . mental deficiency may be defined, from a medical point of view, as a condition of arrested or incomplete mental development induced by disease or injury before adolescence or arising from genetic causes."[9]

Christine P. Ingram (educational):

"The term 'slow-learning' is used by many as a designation for any child who cannot meet average grade academic standards year by year. This group comprises approximately 18 to 20 per cent of the school population. Those who measure approximately 50 to 89 IQ on individual, standardized intelligence scales. Within this classification the terms 'borderline' or 'dull normal' are generally applied by the psychologist to those who measure approximately 75 to 89 IQ. This is the larger group, comprising 16 to 18 per cent of the school population. The terms 'mentally retarded' or 'mentally handicapped' are applied to those who measure approximately 50 to 75 IQ, the lowest 2 per cent of the school population in learning ability."[10]

Stanley D. Porteus and G. R. Corbett (legal):

"Feeble-minded persons are those who by reason of permanently

---

[8] Seymour B. Sarason: Mentally retarded and mentally defective children: major psychological problems. In W. W. Cruickshank: *Psychology of Exceptional Children & Youth.* New York, Prentice-Hall, 1955, pp. 440-442.

[9] Geo. A. Jervis: Medical aspects of mental deficiency. *American Journal of Mental Deficiency,* 57:175, 1952.

[10] Christine P. Ingram: *Education of the Slow Learning Child.* Second Edition. New York, Roland, 1953, p. 4.

retarded or arrested mental development existing from an early age are incapable of independent self-management, and self-support."[11]

E. Paul Benoit (neuropsychological):

". . . Mental retardation may be viewed as a deficit of intellectual function resulting from varied intrapersonal and/or extrapersonal determinants, but having as a common proximate cause a diminished efficiency of the nervous system, thus entailing a lessened general capacity for growth in perceptual and conceptual integration and consequently in environment adjustment."[12]

G. Orville Johnson:

"The mentally handicapped are defined as those children who are so intellectually retarded that it is impossible for them to be adequately educated in the regular classroom. They are however, educable in the sense that they can acquire sufficient knowledge and ability in the academic areas that the skills can and will become useful and useable tools. Further, they have a prognosis of social adequacy and occupational or economic self-sufficiency as adults. They will be able to apply the skills learned during the years of their formal education, toward maintaining an independent social and economic existence as adults."[13]

Edward William Dolch contends that we must distinguish between the mentally retarded and the mentally deficient. He stated:

"Teachers usually define mentally deficient as the children who cannot learn. The assumption is that they cannot, because they do not have the 'brains' with which to learn. It would be more correct to say that these children do not learn. Men who have worked with this type of child tell us that some of these children who do not learn are not hindered by lack of 'brains' but by other things. The result is the same but the causes are very different. If the child is actually mentally deficient, there is noth-

---

[11] Stanley D. Porteus and G. R. Corbett: Statutory definitions of feebleminded in the U.S.A. *The Journal of Psychology*, *35*:103-104, 1953.

[12] E. Paul Benoit: Toward a new definition of mental retardation. *American Journal of Mental Deficiency*, *63*:56, 1959.

[13] Wm. M. Cruickshank and G. Orville Johnson: *Education of Exceptional Children and Youth*. Englewood Cliffs, N. J., Prentice-Hall, Inc., 1958, p. 190.

ing we can do to remedy the deficiency. But if he has been retarded instead, we can overcome the retardation to some extent
at least. So it is wisest, in the case of any particular child, to ask
ourselves whether his apparent mental deficiency may not be
instead a case of mental retardation."[14]

Efforts to define mental retardation have been made by hundreds of people. A descriptive definition proposed by one may not
be better than those which have been proposed by others. It is
doubtful that one single definition can describe all the mental
deficiencies, and several will be needed for the different entities.
However, our lack of success in presenting a perfect definition at
this time should not retard our efforts in applying current knowledge toward a preventive program.

While the lack of agreement on terminology continues to plague
researchers and reviewers, educators and psychologists appear to
be moving toward agreement that mental retardation should be
used as a broad generic term including a wide range of psychological and physical syndromes which have one common base—
subnormal intellectual development.

CLASSIFICATION OF MENTAL RETARDATION

There is no universal agreement as to the classification of children who are mentally retarded. A precise scientific approach has
not been yet developed, and in some respects, classification is an
arbitrary matter. Many of the systems in use currently are based
on different sets of criteria, including the presumed etiology, the
behavioral characteristics of the children, or upon intelligence
test performance.

C. E. Benda has evolved a classification of those children regarded as "intellectually inadequate" (with an intelligence quotient ranging from 50-70) which lists five major categories:

1. Emotionally Disturbed Normal Children: These score low
on intelligence tests because of factors which exist outside of the
intellectual field. Because of their low scores they are thought to
be mentally retarded.[15] However, in this category, it has been

---

[14] Edward Wm. Dolch: *Helping Handicapped Children in School.* Champaign, Ill.,
The Garrard Press, 1948, pp. 220-221.

[15] C. E. Benda: *Developmental Disorders of Mental and Cerebral Palsies.* New
York, Grune and Stratton, 1952.

pointed out by Clarke and Clarke that: an early adverse environment may have a "crippling" effect on mental development. Removal or correction of such environmental factor will improve the apparent intellectual retardation, and result in a higher intelligence score.[16]

This lack of clarity in regard to the relationship between intelligence test scores and behavioral manifestations of intelligence has established the concept of pseudo-feeblemindedness. The change in a child's performance may occur spontaneously, but more often it is the result of active intervention upon the part of the teacher or examiner. This intervention might be the removal of the child to a more positive environment, the use of psychotherapy or medication, or the correction of a sensory defect.

2. Mentally Ill Children with Low Intelligence: These children are unable to cope with the test situation in a successful manner and score low in spite of their adequate intellectual potentials. This is due to a serious emotional disorder, such as childhood schizophrenia, or infantile dementia. The most prevalent picture of a mentally retarded child with severe personality involvement appears to be one in which there are severe withdrawal symptoms and unnatural mannerisms. A serious handicap in treating children in this group is the great difficulty encountered in gaining any access to their thought processes.

3. Biologically, Normal Children with Low Intelligence: These children have no demonstrable biological involvements, but exhibit a low degree of intelligence. They constitute a "normal" part of our population. The subcultural level is composed of this group, to a large extent.

4. Oligoencephaly: These children are considered as being pathological in terms of their over-all constitutional inadequacy.

5. Brain-injured Children: These children are considered by Benda to be more or less "accidental" cases. The injury may result from such causes as birth trauma, infectious diseases, or metabolic disorders. Although Benda constantly refers to the psychological test performance in his classification, he nevertheless includes many additional factors in his final diagnosis.

---

[16] A. D. B. Clarke and A. M. Clarke: Pseudo-feeblemindedness, some implications. *American Journal of Mental Deficiency,* 59:507-509, 1955.

The American Psychiatric Association has postulated a classification consisting of three categories as follows:

1. Mild Deficiency: Children at this level can profit from a simplified school curriculum and make an adequate, though modest, social adjustment. They have a range in intelligence from 66 to 80 and learn to adjust well to varying social situations. With adequate attention and guidance they may even acquire a "social veneer" and can mingle in social groups with some degree of success. The kind of achievement they attain, however, is directly dependent upon the treatment and guidance offered them.

2. Moderate Deficiency: These children need special academic and vocational training and guidance, but do not require institutional care. They range in intelligence from 50 to 65, more or less, but it should be stressed that the intelligence test score in itself does not entirely determine the particular level of deficiency. Here again also, it should be stressed for both of the foregoing groups, that each child is an individual, and differs from the other children in many respects, though each of the groups has some characteristics in common.

3. Severe Deficiency: These children relate to other persons only at the most elementary level. They tend to be totally lost in any but the most elementary social situations, and may require some type of custodial supervision.[17]

Strauss's classification is based upon etiological or causative factors and consists of two major divisions:

1. Exogenous conditions, which are composed essentially of brain-injured children, the damage having occurred before, during or following the birth of the child. However, Strauss excludes from this grouping those children who show signs of gross neurological involvement, and limits their classification to those with no motor disabilities, but whose test performances are indicative of some brain damage.

2. Endogenous conditions, which encompass children with no brain damage, but who are, nevertheless, mentally retarded.[18]

---

[17] National Association for Retarded Children, Inc., New York 16, N. Y., January 1958. (Information through personal correspondence between the association and one of the authors.)

[18] A. A. Strauss and M. A. Lehtinen: *Psychopathology and Education of the Brain-Injured Child.* New York, Grune & Stratton, 1947.

A well trained special education teacher would probably think of this endogenous group as being composed of children whose retardation is due to genetic factors or causes from within the child. These children tend to be more stable emotionally and the educational outlook is better for them. The exogenous results from factors outside the child (environmental) such as damage to the embryo from a virus infection of the mother, or injuries suffered during birth. These children are inclined to have narrow interests, their general adjustment is rigid and conforming but they are usually verbal.

E. O. Lewis has a classification divided into two categories, consisting of the pathological group, or children whose intellectual deficiencies are traced to some organic brain damage, and the subcultural group, or children with no demonstrable brain damage or other physical pathology.[19]

Mental defects determined by multiple genes are classified as "undifferentiated" because they carry no specific physical distinction and are "aclinical" in that they show no clinical manifestation other than intellectual impairment. This group has also been classified by other terms: "Residual" because it is composed of persons who are left after a classification of specific forms; "Subcultural" because so many of these individuals originate from low cultural environments; "Familial" because of the high frequency of the condition in the subjects' families. These cases can be diagnosed only by psychological and social adjustment criteria, differentiation between high-grade morons and dull-normal individuals may be difficult. Sometimes anti-social behavior and psychopathic traits occur in this group but they are far from universal. It has been estimated that undifferentiated mental defects account for 30 to 75 per cent of all the mentally retarded. In all probability, the lower figure is more nearly correct.

The two etiological broad classifications are Primary and Secondary Amentia. Primary, the largest group, makes up approximately 75 per cent of the population of mental defects, the clinical etiology is not clearly traceable to disease or traumatic factors, although these factors may be and often are, present. The secondary classification is composed of mentally deficient individuals

---

[19] E. O. Lewis: Types of mental deficiency and their social significance. *Journal of Mental Science,* 79:298-304, 1933.

whose condition can be more clearly assumed to be due to disease or trauma.

There are still other categories of classification. The traditional method of classifying mentally retarded children has been on the basis of intellectual capacities, and the four major divisions are: idiots, imbecile, moron and borderline. Although the exact limits of each of these categories have not been established, there is a general agreement upon the characteristics of each of these groups. These characteristics are described in Chapter II.

GENERAL DESCRIPTION OF MENTALLY RETARDED STUDENTS

The largest percentage of retarded children has an intelligence quotient ranging from 59-70. These children can dress themselves quite adequately, have normal control of bowel and bladder, can feed themselves, and are fairly attentive to their surroundings. Speech functions, though at a lower level than that of average children, are usually adequate also, and reading and writing are performed at an elementary level. Such children can profit from the experience of special classroom teaching, and are usually capable of learning to do many manual tasks, and with help, can hold a simple job. Given proper training and help, these children can manage to support themselves, but require guidance throughout life.

In the group ranking near borderline level, the range of the intelligence quotient is from 70 to 80. In this group, the principal difficulty is that of academic achievement. The borderline children are slow in learning, exhibit poor reasoning ability, and are not capable of exercising their intelligence. Usually they are allowed to remain in school, and are often promoted solely on the basis of their age and physical size. Such children can profit from specially prepared school programs, geared to their individual needs.

The children who belong in these two categories are not equally slow in all kinds of activities, nor are they abnormal in all of their characteristics. Some may show mechanical ability, or keen artistic sense, and will do well in these areas, even though they may not be able to read well or do arithmetic. In those subjects requiring a high intellectual level for understanding and grasping, the child will show severe limitations. However, retarded children can profit from extended practice, and they require a specially devised and carefully planned curriculum in the academic subjects.

In physical development these children are about as heterogeneous a group as are average children; in matters of health, however, they are more susceptible to various ailments. Defects of hearing and speech, malnutrition, defective tonsils, adenoids, and defects of vision are more common than among average children. Each physical handicap that can be overcome, helps the retarded child to make a better adjustment with what intellectual capacity he has, in addition to contributing to his comfort and happiness.

In areas of personality adjustment the retarded child is more apt to show self-distrust, physical timidity, dependence and deference, and a significant lack of ability to make friends, take the initiative in social activity or engage in activities requiring leadership and competition. He will also show a lack of self-confidence, creativity, self-defense, curiosity and playfulness.

In a series of studies of the adjustment of groups of slow learners as compared to average groups of children, Georgia Lightfoot found that in such attributes as cooperation, selfishness, desire for approbation, gregariousness, defensiveness, and exclusiveness, there was not too great a difference in the reactions of the two groups.[20]

Thus we see that the retarded child is a person very much like the child in the average group. He is a variant of a type, and has more or less of the common characteristics of all other pupils in school; i.e., the same basic needs, the same methods of learning, albeit, at a slower pace; and about the same amount of variability and unevenness of abilities and other resources. Being by definition intellectually less endowed, he does not reason or learn to manage academic subjects as well as the average child. In most other respects, however, the difference between an average child and a retarded child is not too discernible.

EARLY HISTORY OF MENTAL RETARDATION

Should we become discouraged and dissatisfied with our progress in serving the retarded, it would be well to remember that

---

[20] Georgia Lightfoot: *Characteristics of Bright and Dull Children.* New York, Bureau of Publication, Teacher's College, Columbia University, 1951.

professional services to these individuals are less than 150 years old in western civilization, and slightly more than a century old in this country.

The problem of mental deficiency has been met and solved according to the prevailing philosophy of the time. In ancient times, the Spartan and Roman parents, striving for a super-race, used a direct approach. They exposed the weak and handicapped offspring to the elements so that they would perish. In the Middle Ages, the mentally deficient were used as "fools" and "jesters" to entertain the Lords and their Ladies. During the protestant Reformation, handicapped persons were thought to be afflicted because they were "possessed with the Devil," therefore to be cured "the Devil" could be removed only by being beaten out of a person so afflicted.

Prior to 1800, the Church provided the only haven for the weak, retarded and disabled. The teachings of Calvin and Luther were afterward disregarded. During this period the status of the retarded was affected by the philosophy which influenced the thinking of the majority of professional people. Before 1800, the "naturalist" predominated. The trend of thinking concerned the effects of heredity and environment on the growth and development of the child. These men believed that heredity was the first and foremost cause of mental retardation and that it was incurable.

A gradual change of attitude started with the rise of a more modern Christianity. The nineteenth century brought a more scientific approach to the problem of care and training for the mentally retarded. It became apparent that more humane treatment and tolerance would be necessary in caring for them.

Credit has been given to the French physician, Jean Itard, for being responsible for scientific investigation into the problems of mental deficiency, even though his own experiment was a failure. Dr. Itard devoted much time and patience in an effort to educate Victor, the wild boy of Aveyron. Victor, age twelve, was captured in the forests of Aveyron, examined and labelled severely retarded, by the famous physician, Pinel. Dr. Itard taught the boy systematically over a period of five years, emphasizing sense and motor training. Even though this training brought about changes in his behavior, he never learned to talk, nor could he live independently in society.

In dealing with retardation, Dr. Itard discounted the teachings of the naturalists and followed the teachings of John Locke of England and of Jean Jaques Rousseau of France. They believed that anyone could learn if properly taught and trained, because learning came only through the senses.

Edward Seguin, a student of Dr. Itard came to the United States about 1850. He greatly developed and expanded Itard's methods and techniques which later figured prominently in the history of treatment in the United States. The Seguin influence should not be underestimated. Until recently the institutions in the United States were patterned after the one established by Seguin. In this country, Seguin became the first president of the organization which is now the American Association on Mental Deficiency.

About this time, in the early part of the nineteenth century, Horace Mann and Samuel Gridley Howe spoke out in behalf of the retarded child. Schools for the mentally retarded, the blind and the deaf began to appear. Thus, the residential or boarding school came into being, as a significant American institution. The first schools were started largely as experiments to test Seguin's techniques and the theories of the environmentalists. They were not intended to be used as "asylums" but were dedicated to curing retardation. However, the operators of these "schools" did not find a cure. The children placed in these schools were often forgotten. Society had built the institution, placed the children in them for care, and now its obligation had been met. Conscience could easily cease to function.

Today, our residential schools present a contrasting picture. The majority of children admitted are severely retarded and will require life-long care. Youths and adults, who are mildly retarded may be admitted if they present serious social problems.

Day classes for the retarded were first established in Providence, Rhode Island, in 1896. However, it is now common belief that this class and others founded before 1915 were probably filled with "problem children" due to the fact that individual intelligence tests had not been devised. The original Stanford-Binet Test of Intelligence did not appear until 1916. In spite of Stanford-Binet and other fairly reliable intelligence measurement, the special program today still tends to be a panacea for all the ills with which the regular classroom teacher does not desire to cope.

In 1953, it was estimated that almost 5,000 out of the 114,000 retarded pupils in day classes were "trainable" children. Few classes for the "trainable" existed before that date.

Even though the number of special classes have continually increased in the past thirty years, there still is a need for additional classes for the educable retarded.

Today, school services to the retarded are accepted as necessary and valuable. Great improvement is being made in the field. Teachers are receiving professional training. Psychological and supervisory services are being offered. Programs have been extended through the junior and senior high school years. Occupational and work-training programs have been added and parent education groups are constantly being formed. More counseling and guidance services are available. Every state in our great land now provides special education programs for most types of exceptional children.

Professional organizations which function at national, regional, state and local levels have been formed. A teacher may belong to the local affiliate of the Council on Exceptional Children (C.E.C.), Division 22 of the American Psychological Association (A.P.A.), and American Association on Mental Deficiency.

In 1962, at the request of President John F. Kennedy, Congress appointed a national research committee under the direction of the United States Department of Health, Education and Welfare to conduct a survey on mental retardation.

SUMMARY

The public's view of the mentally retarded child has begun to change. There is a tendency to drift away from the precise clinical diagnosis toward a more general appraisal of the child as a person and with more evaluation of his total individual aptitudes.

Doubtless, hundreds of definitions have been proposed to describe mental retardation. No one single definition describes all the mental deficiencies and several will be needed for the different entities. However, this should not retard our efforts in applying current knowledge toward a preventive program. Educators and psychologists appear to be reaching an agreement that mental retardation should be used as a broad generic term including a wide range of psychological and physical syndromes which have one common base—sub-normal intellectual development. There is no universal agreement as to the classification of children who are mentally retarded. Classification, in most respects, seems to be an arbitrary matter.

The greatest percentage of mentally retarded children has an intelligence quotient ranging from 59-70. They have control of bodily functions, can dress themselves, can read and write, will profit from special classroom teaching, with proper training can hold simple jobs, but will require guidance through life.

The problem of mental deficiency has been met and solved according to the prevailing philosophy of the time. The status of the retarded tends to be affected by the current philosophy of a given time which influences the thinking of the majority of professional people. Thus the treatment of today's mentally retarded children presents a contrasting picture to that of the eighteenth century and preceding periods of time.

Progress has been a continual, although slow, process since the first day classes in Providence, Rhode Island during 1896. Presently, school services to the retarded are accepted as necessary and valuable.

SELECTED REFERENCES

Altman, C.: Relationships between maternal attitudes and child personality structure. *American Journal of Orthopsychiatry, 28*:160-169, 1959.

Anderson, G. W.: Current trends in the pathology of human reproductive failure. *American Journal Public Health, 45*:1259-1266, 1955.

Baker, H. J.: *Introduction to Handicapped Children.* Third Edition. New York, Macmillan, 1959.

Barnett, C. D. and Cantor, G. N.: Discrimination set in defectives. *American Journal of Mental Deficiency, 62*:334-337, 1957.

Barr, Martin W.: *Mental Defectives.* Philadelphia, P. Blakiston's Son & Co., 1913.

Basic Considerations in Mental Retardation: A Preliminary Report. New York, Group for the Advancement of Psychiatry Publications Office, Dec. 1959, No. 43.

Beier, E. G., Gorlow, L. and Stacy, C. L.: The fantasy life of the mental defective. *American Journal of Mental Deficiency, 55*:582-589, 1951.

Benda, C. D.: *Developmental Disorders of Mentation and Cerebral Palsies.* New York, Grune and Stratton, 1952.

Bender, L.: *Aggression, Hostility, and Anxiety in Children.* Springfield, Ill., Charles C Thomas, 1953.

Bender, L.: Childhood schizophrenia. *Nervous Children, 1*:138-140, 1942.

Benoit, E. Paul: Relevance of Hebb's theory of the organization of behavior to educational research on the mentally retarded. *American Journal of Mental Deficiency, 61*:497-507, 1957.

Benoit, E. Paul: Toward a definition of mental retardation. *American Journal of Mental Deficiency, 63*:4, 56, 1959.

Blodgett, Harriet E. and Warfield, Grace J.: *Understanding Mentally Retarded Children.* New York, Appleton-Century-Crofts, Inc., 1959.

Book, J. A.: Fertility trends in some types of mental defects. *Eugenics Quarterly, 6*:113-116, 1959.

Brand, H., Benoit, E. P. and Ornstein, G. N.: Rigidity and feeblemindedness: an examination of the Kounin-Lewin Theory. *Journal of Clinical Psychology, 9*:375-378, 1953.

Cassell, R. H.: A rigorous criterion of feeblemindedness: a critique. *Journal Abnormal and Social Psychology, 46*:116-117, 1951.

Clarke, A. B. D. and Clarke, A. M.: Pseudofeeblemindedness, some implications. *American Journal of Mental Deficiency, 59*:507-509, 1955.

Clarke, A. M. and Clarke, A. B. D.: *Mental Deficiency: The Changing Outlook.* London, Methuen and Co., 1958.

Coleman, J. C.: *Abnormal Psychology and Modern Life.* Chicago, Scott Foresman Co., 1950.

Cruickshank, Wm. M. and Johnson, G. Orville: *Education of Exceptional Children and Youth.* Englewood Cliffs, N. J., Prentice-Hall, Inc., 1958, p. 190.

Cruickshank, Wm. M.: *Psychology of Exceptional Children and Youth.* Englewood Cliffs, N. J., Prentice-Hall, 1955.

Dolch, Edward Wm.: *Helping Handicapped Children in School.* Champaign, Ill., The Garrard Press, 1948, pp. 220-221.

Doll, E. A.: Definition of mental deficiency. *Training School Bulletin, 37*:163-164, 1941.

Doll, E. A.: Practical implications of the endogenous-exogenous classification of mental defectives. *American Journal of Mental Deficiency, 50*:503-511, 1946.

Doll, E. A.: The essentials of an inclusive concept of mental deficiency. *American Journal of Mental Deficiency, 46*:214-219, 1941.

Dybwad, Gunnar: In Rothstein, Jerome H.: *Mental Retardation: Readings and Resources.* New York, Holt, Rinehart and Winston, Inc., 1961, p. 5.

Eccles, J. C.: *The Neurophysiological Basis of Mind.* London, Oxford Press, 1953.

Ellis, A. and Beechly, R. M.: A comparison of matched groups of mongoloid and non-mongoloid feebleminded children. *American Journal of Mental Deficiency, 54*:464-468, 1950.

Gibson, R.: A tentative clinical classification of special types in mental deficiency. *American Journal of Mental Deficiency, 54*:382-393, 1950.

Goldstein, K.: Abnormal mental conditions in infancy. *Journal of Nervous and Mental Disorders, 128*:538-557, 1959.

Goldstein, K.: *The Organism.* New York, The American Book Co., 1939.

Goodenough, F. L. and Maurer, K. M.: *Mental Growth of Children Two to Fourteen Years.* Minneapolis, University of Minnesota Press, 1942.

Greene, E. B.: *Measurement of Human Behavior.* New York, Odyssey Press, 1941.

Guertin, W. H.: Differential characteristics of the pseudo-feebleminded. *American Journal of Mental Deficiency, 54*:394-398, 1950.

Guertin, W. H.: Mental growth in pseudo-feeblemindedness. *American Journal of Mental Deficiency, 5*:414-418, 1949.

Guilford, J. P.: The structure of intellect. *Psychological Bulletin, 53*:267-293, 1956.

Heath, S. R.: A mental pattern found in motor deviates. *Journal of Abnormal Social Psychology, 41*:223-225, 1946.

Hebb, D. O.: *The Organization of Behavior.* New York, Wiley, 1949.

Heber, Rick: In Jerome H. Rothstein: *Mental Retardation: Readings and Resources.* New York, Holt, Rinehart, and Winston, Inc., 1961, p. 5.

Heber, Rick: A manual on terminology and classification in mental retardation. *Monograph Supplement, American Journal of Mental Deficiency,* 1959, p. 64.

Hutt, M. and Gibby, R. G.: *The Mentally Retarded Child.* New York, Allyn and Bacon, 1958.

Ingraham, Christine P.: *Education of the Slow Learning Child.* Second Edition. New York, Roland, 1953, p. 4.

Jervis, Geo. A.: Medical aspects of mental deficiency. *American Journal of Mental Deficiency, 57*:175, 1952.

Jordan, Thomas E.: Toward a more effective use of the term, mental retardation. *American Journal of Mental Deficiency, 63*:15-16, 1958.

Jordan, Thomas E.: *The Mentally Retarded.* Columbus, Ohio, Charles E. Merrill Books, Inc., 1961, p. 1.

Jordan, Thomas E.: *The Exceptional Child.* Columbus, Ohio, Charles E. Merrill Books, Inc., 1962.

Kanner, L.: Emotional interference with intellectual functioning. *American Journal of Mental Deficiency, 65*:701-707, 1952.

Kantor, J. R.: Preface to interbehavioral psychology. *Psychological Record, 6*:172-193, 1942.

Kirk, S. A.: *The Early Education of Mentally Retarded Children.* Urbana, University of Illinois Press, 1958.

Kratter, F. E.: The physiognomic, psychometric, behavioral, and neurological aspects of phenylketonuria. *Journal of Mental Science, 105*:421-427, 1959.

Lewis, E. O.: Types of mental deficiency and their social significance. *Journal of Mental Science, 79*:298-304, 1933.

Lightfoot, Georgia: *Characteristics of Bright and Dull Children.* New York, Bureau of Publication, Teachers' College, Columbia University, 1951.

Masland, R. L., Sarason, S. B. and Gladwin, T.: *Mental Subnormality.* New York, Basic Books, 1958.

Maxwell, J.: Intelligence, fertility, and the future. *Eugenics Quarterly, 1*:224-274, 1954.

McCulloch, T. L.: Reformulation of the problem of mental deficiency. *American Journal Mental Deficiency, 52*:130-136, 1947.

McMurray, J. G.: Rigidity in conceptual thinking in exogenous and endogenous mentally retarded children. *Journal Consulting Psychology, 18*:366-370, 1954.

O'Gorman, G.: Psychosis as a cause of mental defect. *Journal of Mental Science, 100*:934-943, 1954.

Oster, J.: Mental deficiency: scientific problems, progress and prospects. *American Journal of Mental Deficiency, 59*:425-433, 1954.

Penrose, L. S.: The supposed threat of declining intelligence. *American Journal of Mental Deficiency, 53*:318-337, 1948.

Perlstein, J. A. and Hood, P. N.: Infantile spastic hemiplegia, intelligence and age of walking and talking. *American Journal of Mental Deficiency, 61*:534-543, 1957.

Perry, S. E.: Some theoretic problems of mental deficiency and their action implications. *Psychiatry, 17*:46, 1954.

Personal correspondence. National Association for Retarded Children, Inc., New York 16, N. Y., Jan. 1958.

Piaget, J. and Inhelder, B.: Diagnosis of mental operations and theory of intelligence. *American Journal of Mental Deficiency, 51*:401-406, 1947.

Porteus, Stanley D. and Corbett, G. R.: Statutory definitions of feebleminded in the U.S.A. *The Journal of Psychology, 35*:103-104, 1953.

Riggs, M. M. and Rain, M. E.: A classification system for the mentally retarded. *Training School Bulletin, 49*:75-84, 1952.

Roulle, E. N.: New horizons for the mentally retarded: when a school looks at the problem as a whole. *American Journal of Mental Deficiency, 59*:359-373, 1955.

Samuels, I.: Reticular mechanisms and behavior. *Psychological Bulletin, 56*:1-25, 1959.

Sarason, Seymour B.: *Psychological Problems in Mental Deficiency.* Third Edition. New York, Harper and Bros., 1959.

Sarason, Seymour B.: In W. W. Cruickshank: *Psychology of Exceptional Children and Youth.* New York, Prentice-Hall, 1955, pp. 440-442.

Strauss, A. A.: The education of the brain injured child. *American Journal of Mental Deficiency, 56*:712-718, 1952.

Strauss, A. A. and Lehtinen, M. A.: *Psychopathology and Education of the Brain Injured Child.* New York, Grune and Stratton, 1947.

The cap that went out of style. A publication of the California Council for Retarded Children, San Diego, Calif.

Town, C. H.: An investigation of the adjustment of the feebleminded in the community. *Psychological Clinic, 20*:42-54, 1931.

Trapp, E. P. and Himelstein, P.: *Readings on the Exceptional Child.* New York, Appleton-Century-Crofts, 1962.

Tredgold, A. F.: *A Textbook of Mental Deficiency.* Baltimore, William Wood and Co., 1937, p. 4.

Tyler, L. E.: *The Psychology of Human Differences.* New York, Appleton-Century-Crofts, 1956, first edition, 1947.

Werner, H.: Abnormal and subnormal rigidity. *Journal of Abnormal Social Psychology, 41*:15-24, 1946.

Yakovlev, P. I., Weinberger, M. and Chipman, C. E.: Heller's syndrome on a pattern of schizophrenic behavior disturbance in early childhood. *American Journal of Mental Deficiency, 53*:318-337, 1948.

Yannet, H.: The problem of mental deficiency in children. *Pediatrics, 10*:223-230, 1952.

Zuk, G.: The mind as an optical system. *Journal of Genetics Psychology, 94*:113-130, 1959.

CHAPTER II

Characteristics of the Mentally Retarded Child

THE DEVELOPMENT OF THE INTELLECT

FOR decades, mental development of children has attracted psychologists in many countries. The term "development" implies that during the process of change from infancy to adulthood, the child is subjected to a continuous process which leads from a less to a more complete state. The mental equipment of a child changes from a lower to a higher state because of inherited potentialities to learn, because biological growth makes it possible to learn, and because opportunity is given for a learning experience. When we speak of levels of mental maturity, we are speaking of central references with ever broadening lower and upper limits.

Alfred Binet, a Frenchman (1857-1911), is called the father of intelligence testing because he devised the first intelligence test of any promise. His test in revised forms is still being given in all parts of the world.

"We may not know what 'intelligence' *really* is, but we know that the word stands for something that is of inestimable value in a competitive world—and we are not offered the choice of living in any other. This competitive world of ours forces us to value 'intelligence' whatever it may be."[1]

In terms of a quality or condition of individual difference, intelligence has been a construct devised to explain the potentialities of the human being for learning, for producing, and for adjusting to the environment. Historically, the differences noted have been speed, accuracy in solving a problem, assembling a device, or devising a plan of action. *The modern emphasis is on process* rather

---

[1] Hardin: *The 61st Yearbook of the National Society for the Study of Education*, Pt. 1, Individualizing Instruction, Chicago, Ill. The Univ. of Chicago Press, 1962, p. 15.

than potential, with a recognition that multiple factors may facilitate or retard the development of the intellect. The intellects of children develop only by what their eyes see, ears hear, noses smell, hands touch, and tongue tastes. The availability and nature of materials and equipment, the access to other children, the degree of health of the senses, all contribute to mental development.

The factors effecting the development of the intellect can be considered under the two categories of heredity and environment. The two are inextricably intertwined with heredity setting the limit within which the organism may develop. "In the case of psychological traits, these limitations for most persons may be so wide as to allow almost unlimited variation. At the same time there seems to be little evidence that a given intellectual trait can be directly dependent upon heredity. The variation in the extent of development of the inherited potentials are a reflection of the stimulation of the environmental conditions."[2]

Hereditary factors include family resemblance, similarities of the biological organism, organic conditions limiting human development, physical deficiencies, and selective breeding. The demands of society or culture may offer specific requirements and stimulation to the development of mental abilities; for example, change of mental abilities occurs as individuals move from impoverished to rich environments.

Intelligence is probably a function of the child's culture. In addition to values and personality traits, each cultural group tends to foster the development of aptitudes. It is quite possible that some intelligence tests are suitable for one culture, but not another.

Evidence from studies of mental maturity indicates that development is continuous from infancy to adulthood unless brain cells are destroyed by disease or injury. (Adulthood varies from C.A. fifteen to twenty-five depending upon test used.)

Rather than intelligence it is more appropriate to speak of intelligences or mental abilities. Each person represents a profile of abilities reflecting the stimulation and opportunity provided by the heredity, culture, education, family, and others. Examples of these abilities are mechanical, social, verbal, abstract, and spatial-

---

[2] Richard Harsh: Intelligence: its nature and measurement. *National Elementary Principal*, 41:23-28, Sept. 1961.

perceptual. Many of our school paper-and-pencil measures of intelligence or mental abilities are really measures of word meaning, manipulation, fluency, attention span, memory, analogies of dissimilar associations or implications, and recognition of rules, principles, or operations, all of which deal with common educational contents of an urban culture. The thing measured by these tests is probably scholastic aptitude; certainly they do not give a comprehensive picture of the intelligence of man. There are also measures of spatial, mechanical, and social abilities which are quite separate from academic abilities. We should, therefore, be as interested in intraindividual differences (trait variability) within an individual as much as we are in differences among individuals.

The theories of J. P. Guilford[3] have had much influence in changing the concept of intelligence as a unitary substance to the concept of intellectual abilities. Intellectual abilities may be classified according to operation (cognition, memory, production, and evaluation); according to content such as figural, symbolic, or semantic; and according to product such as elements, classes, relations, systems, or implications. An emerging factor may be the social or behavioral abilities which have previously been related to personality patterns, but are apparently related to the manner in which the individual receives, focuses, and produces in the various intelligences he possesses.[4]

Notwithstanding the variations in definitions and the theories of intelligence, most people would agree that children differ in maturity at various ages. A detailed description of the characteristics of children with varying ages cannot be made in this volume thus we can use only one age for illustration; *viz* the four-year-old.

The four-year-old is midway in the growth cycle of early childhood (ages 2-6). Early childhood begins when the toddler starts the process of exploring spatial and human relations with complete indifference to the hazards and obstacles. At the end of the sixth year the child is socialized, acculturated, and routinized. Tests of intelligence of early childhood must be sensorimotor in nature. Appraisal must be in terms of the child's neuromuscular

---

[3] J. P. Guilford: Structure of the Intellect. *Psychological Bulletin,* 53:267-293, 1956.

[4] J. P. Guilford: Three Faces of the Intellect. *American Psychologist,* 58:469-479, 1959.

and emotional-social responses. Because there is much fluctuation between tests and retests, their predictive value is small.

"At four, the child comes to nursery school or kindergarten with an already distinct personality and physique. His great developmental task at this time is to gain control over himself. He works hard at developing body balance and grace through the gross motor activities of running, jumping, pulling, pushing, swinging, climbing, and leaping. He is beginning to use his hands and fingers with greater purpose and skill as he pounds with a hammer, cuts with scissors, and works with crayons, brushes, pencils, and other tools. His mind is open and eager for new learning. Language is picturesque and searching. He values his individual rights but is willing to become a member of a group, recognizing that this membership comes through compromise and social concessions."[5]

Nursery school and kindergarten offer the child his earliest opportunity to express himself as an individual, in the midst of others. The manner in which he is accepted, treasured, and guided during the school beginning, and the consistency with which this is practiced in the subsequent years of school, will greatly influence his unity, completeness and strength as a person. It will also become the foundation for the next great developmental threshold —adolescence—when he will face the task of developing a more complex set of personal adjustments, integrations, and controls.

"Some four-year-olds have many characteristics typically found at age three; others closely resemble children of five. Yet, the order, sequence, and progression of human development and maturation make it possible for us to recognize broad attributes characteristic of each age level. A seasoned nursery school teacher can very quickly tell whether she is in the presence of three or four-year-olds. A kindergarten teacher accustomed to working with a group of five-year-olds does not need much time to identify with reasonable accuracy those in her group who are four."[5]

In the continuum of human development, educational guideposts can be found in physical growth, motor skills, emotional and social behavior, intellectual processes, and in expectations of society. These guideposts permit or assist teachers to provide educa-

---

[5] Minnie P. Berson: Individual differences among preschool children: 4 yr. olds. *The 61st Yearbook of the National Society for the Study of Education*, Pt. I, Individualizing Instruction, Chicago, Ill., The Univ. of Chicago Press, 1962, pp. 112-125.

tional opportunities that will cultivate individuality as well as enable them to live and learn in groups.

DEGREES OF RETARDATION

The degrees of mental retardation have traditionally been determined by tests from which an intelligence quotient (IQ) can be calculated. (It is essential therefore, to have an understanding that the IQ is a ratio usually obtained by the formula $\frac{MA}{CA} \times 100 = $.) As an illustration, a pupil's performance on the typical Binet-type tests is stated in terms of the number of years and months of mental age earned by passing certain items. To have a mental age of six years, the number of items passed on the test must be equal to the average number passed by the normative six-year-olds.

It has never been disproved that human abilities tend to be distributed in a normal curve, i.e., with a large number clustering around the center with fewer at either extreme. If the tabulations of scores do not reflect a normal distribution, the cause may usually be traced to sampling irregularities, special environmental conditions, or characteristics of the measuring instrument. The intelligence quotient is merely a numerical representation of how well a given child performs on a particular series of test items in relation to the performance of other children of similar age. Quantitatively, then, test scores can be interpreted only in terms of a norm. The norm must be derived from scores of children who are considered representative of the pupils for whom the test is intended. Norms do not signify what might have been found under other circumstances with different methods, different school and home environment, and educational objectives. The significance of an IQ depends upon its position in a distribution of IQ's.

Historically, the IQ has been used in terms of prediction of academic success. This, essentially, is a deterministic approach with an assumption that the nature of an individual's past will continue into the future. The assumption is hazardous, however, because of the large number of biological, social, cultural, and psychological factors that may affect human beings. Changes in medical treatment and state of health, school environment and method, attitude and training of parents and teachers, and geographical location make prediction based on the IQ inadequate.

How then can the IQ be used as an instrument to identify the mentally retarded child? As a beginning it may be possible to use several intelligence tests. The Goodenough Draw-a-man-test can be used to determine an IQ based upon the graphic motor representation of the human figure which the child draws on a blank sheet of paper.[6] The California test of mental maturity at the primary level requires the child to interpret or imaginably manipulate pictorial material classified according to similarities and differences; to comprehend and manipulate quantitative concepts; and to recognize meaning of words. The IQ can be determined by scores made in reaction to verbal and non-verbal material. Still another IQ may be obtained from responses given to the Otis group intelligence test which asks for comprehension of word meaning, for reasoning and classification, and for numerical reasoning. It should be noted that these tests have only one thing in common; i.e., the comparison of the child's performance with others of his same age. None of these tests nor any other measure of mental ability suggests an IQ to characterize the abilities of a child. Each of the tests present different content and situations which will cause variations in IQ. Inasmuch as they probably measure different abilities, then the variable performance may point up a profile of abilities. Identification and prediction based upon various kinds of intellect is apt to be much more accurate than when based upon one test. It should be noted, however, that because each test calls for the use of different abilities, and has been standardized on different children, thus obtaining different central tendencies and variations, the IQ's should not be averaged. The more use that can be made of separate and discrete measurements to describe the large variety of human abilities the better are we able to identify and predict. Let us never lose sight, however, that potential and prediction should consider current processes of thinking and perception. The qualitative aspects of intelligence reflected in processes of thinking are more significant than the IQ which must be obtained by quantitative means.

For educational purposes, specific and general intelligence can refer to the degree to which a child has potentialities to profit from instruction. The following table suggested by Kirk[7] is most

---

[6] The reliability and validity of this test has recently been questioned. However, experienced psychologists may find it useful to support their judgment or as a quick preliminary procedure to be followed by more refined measures.

[7] Samuel A. Kirk: *Educating Exceptional Children*. Boston, Mass., Houghton Mifflin Co., 1962, p. 90.

beneficial in clarifying terminology and in categorizing according to the type of program provided:

CHILDREN WITH LOW INTELLIGENCE

Nursing Care	Trainable Classes	Educable Classes	Regular Classes
Idiot	Imbecile	Moron	Dull-Normal
Dependent	Semi-dependent	Marginally independent	Independent
Totally dependent	Trainable	Educable	Slow learner
Low grade	Middle grade	High grade	Borderline
IQ—0-25	IQ—25-50	IQ—50-75	IQ—75-90

Kirk[8] continues to describe three general types of degrees of mental retardation as follows:

> "*The totally dependent mentally retarded* child is one who, because of markedly subnormal intelligence, is unable to be trained in self-care, socialization, or economic usefulness, and who needs continuing help in taking care of his personal needs. Such a child requires almost complete supervision throughout his life since he is unable to survive without help.
>
> "*The trainable mentally retarded* child is defined as a child who is so subnormal in intelligence that he is unable to profit from the programs of the classes for educable mentally retarded children, but who has potentialities in three areas: 1) learning self-care in activities such as eating, dressing, undressing, toileting, and sleeping; 2) learning to adjust in the home or neighborhood, though not to the total community, and 3) learning economic usefulness in the home, a sheltered workshop, or an institution.
>
> "*The educable mentally retarded* child is one who, because of slow mental development, is unable to profit to any great degree from the programs of the regular schools, but who has these potentialities for development: 1) minimum educability in reading, writing, spelling, arithmetic, and so forth; 2) capacity for social adjustment to a point where he can get along independently in the community, and 3) minimum occupational adequacy such that he can later support himself partially or totally at a marginal level. The term educability then refers to minimum educability in the academic, social, and occupational areas."[9]

---

[8] Ibid: p. 86.

[9] Samuel A. Kirk: *Educating Exceptional Children.* Boston, Mass., Houghton-Mifflin Co., 1962, p. 86.

Notwithstanding the exceptionality of mentally retarded children, they are more similar to than different from their normal associates. Before discussing differences, therefore, it would be well to consider the theoretical biological and sociological behavioral development of *all* children.

THE PRIMARY BASES OF BEHAVIOR

Living children are active inasmuch as they respond to essentially physiological stimuli caused by the disequilibria demands of food, water, air, temperature maintenance, sex activity, bodily elimination of waste, and several other organic necessities which could be analyzed in minute detail. These necessities of life are known as the basic energetics of activity, or the basic physiological drives. It was Richter[10] who suggested that when the chemical equilibrium of the body is disturbed by a nutritive deficiency, chemical products of the deficiency may directly affect the stomach, setting up hunger contractions which send afferent impulses to the central nervous system to excite activity in the striped muscles. Hunger and thirst are distinctly intraorganic as contrasted to a drive such as the regulatory maintenance of body temperature. External environmental conditions at the skin operate as a stimulus that sets up afferent neural impulses passing into and through the connecting system and out to striped muscles and other effectors, occasioning a change in activity that will be continued until either the organism's production of heat has been readjusted or the environment has been changed to a more equable one.

The primary drives can all be traced to the tissue conditions of the organism. We may generalize that the body is in continuous action to maintain basic equilibria. The dynamic nature of these equilibria and the structure of the body imply a rhythm of activity and rest. A proper balance between activity and rest is essential to optimum physical and mental health.

The first few weeks of a child's life is primarily vegetative. Unfortunately some human beings found in institutions remain that way. The organic wants of the infant, however, must be satisfied through the association of other human beings. As life continues, most of the habits and attitudes of people are acquired in reaction

[10] C. P. Richter: Animal behavior and internal drives. *Quarterly Review of Biology*, 2:307-343, 1927.

to other people. Human behavior that at first resulted from internally generated energies eventually becomes attached to external environmental conditions and especially to other human beings. Essentially, the socialization of human motives is largely the result of approval and disapproval. The effect of this disapproval (or approval) begins at a very young age and continues until the child's entire stock of attitudes and habits bears evidence of social control. By means of social control the individual becomes "socialized" and he develops a set of personal or social needs, one of the strongest being *social approval.*

The understanding of human behavior demands the discovery of behavior symptoms which show satisfaction of needs, partial fulfillment of needs, or frustration because needs are not being satisfied. The word "need" can be used interchangeably with the words "motive" or "drive." It signifies an impulsion to action. When the child needs something, we assume that he is in a certain state of disequilibrium and that this state influences or directs the course of response in an attempt to bring about a state of equilibrium or adjustment. This process of adjusting was described very well by Young[11] several years ago, as a cycle of activity. This cycle of activity may be analyzed into four stages: "1) need, want, drive, or physiological tension resulting from disequilibrium set up by internal or external stimuli; 2) initial seeking of the stimulus or situation which will satisfy this need or striving to avoid a stimulus if it blocks satisfaction; 3) final securing of, or avoidance of the stimulus or situation, and 4) the sense of satisfaction, or release of tension, associated with the state of equilibrium." Perhaps in a more simplified statement we could say that in an "adjustment situation," we have a need, a goal, a barrier, which sets up tension, and finally the reaching of the goal which releases tension.

The rise of needs results from the structure of the organism, the processes of society, and the nature of the child's experiences. A child's behavior is patterned in accordance with what his past experience has taught him to be correct. The task of adults who wish to assist a child to develop is to provide experiences in life which will help the child to feel a state of harmony between the

---

[11] Kimball Young: *Personality and Problems of Adjustment.* New York, Appleton-Century-Crofts, Inc., 1940, p. 65.

needs he feels to be vital and the environment in which he must live. The teacher or parent has solved the most important phase of a task of diagnosis when the answer to this question can be found, what is the child seeking by his present behavior?

WELL-ADJUSTED BEHAVIOR

The term "adjustment" suggests an element of harmony with the world. It is a state of feeling, an ideal probably never reached but possessing various degrees of attainment. It is continuous, and the individual may derive some satisfaction from the struggle toward rather than the attainment of this adjustment. Much joy can be found in working toward the goal of adjustment for it involves a re-estimation of experience and the reformulation of attitudes and values of life. Teachers and parents can aid the adjustment process either by helping to change the environment or by helping to change the pupil's relationship with his environment. One of the most acceptable procedures in the correction of a maladjusted personality is to use the "environmental mass" approach; that is, to make necessary changes in the home, school, or neighborhood.

All needs are linked with pleasant or unpleasant feelings, and these assume an important role in the process of striving to attain the goal, or in failing to secure it. A state of unpleasantness results in tension, the strength of which, depends upon the strength of a need. It is a general characteristic of all needs that when the goal is reached, the tension is discharged, and the need loses its power to impel activity. The mode of behavior in obtaining release of tension may be altered by the presence or acquisition of habits, attitudes, and ideas.

The culture in which a child grows affects practically every personality need he has; thus, in turn, his behavior is also affected. Even the small and large social groups to which he belongs help to determine his attitude and conduct. The determination of the causes of adjustment or maladjustment cannot proceed without first knowing a great deal about the child's home, neighborhood, gang, and associates.

The element of social adjustment requires that personal needs and satisfactions are integrated with the needs and satisfactions of other people in the social milieu. This implies, of course, an acceptance of certain responsibilities.

A CLASSIFICATION OF NEEDS

The numerous classifications of needs by biologists, psychologists, and sociologists make it difficult to make a choice of needs designated for special attention. The classification made by Prescott,[12] however, appears to be satisfactory. This is a threefold classification based on three natural aspects of life: physiological, social, and ego (integrative). Physiological needs most frequently unsatisfied by school children are food, rest, and activity. Social needs include a need of belongingness, a need for affection, a need of recognition, a need for approval. The ego (integrative) needs are intimately concerned with the child's need to believe in himself and have self-respect (self-esteem). These needs grow out of his pattern of values and are achieved to the extent that he measures up to his own level of aspiration. Ego needs cannot be satisfied unless their achievement brings about a unifying point of view, that is, in harmony with fact, and that gives meaning to life. Within this framework of meaning is a feeling of a need to be independent, that is, freedom to make one's own decisions or to hold a personal belief or value. Children also need to feel adequate in capacity and skill to meet a fair degree of success in solving the problems which constantly come before them. Children must also obtain a balance between success and failure in the realization of their desires.

THE BEHAVIOR AND LEARNING OF MENTALLY RETARDED CHILDREN

For educational purposes this textbook will be limited to only two categories of mental retardation: 1) The trainable mentally retarded child, and 2) the educable mentally retarded child.

The Behavior of the Trainable Mentally Retarded Child

Any child's behavior at a given moment overlaps the categories of intelligence, learning, emotion, motor development, social development, and personality. To understand the "trainable mentally retarded child," it is necessary to understand the infant or preschool child in traditional parlance. In every child there occurs a constant process of change and when this change is orderly

---

[12] D. A. Prescott: *The Child in the Education Process.* New York, McGraw-Hill Co., Inc., 1957, p. 25.

and harmonious and enhances the ability of the organism to adjust to its environment, the phenomena may be called development. Even in the mentally deficient there is a constant interplay of the forces of development and decline. Development is *a process* which defies precise measurement and prediction. Each child has its own pattern of sequence in the exact time of sitting before standing, of walking before talking, of gaining control of his bowel movements before the ability to regulate bladder functioning, of walking before running, and so on. Development denotes change. In the mentally deficient, change occurs but at a much slower rate than the normal.

A great variety of change may appear and the factors of environment and heredity which influence and shape the developmental patterns of each individual child are as diverse as there are kinds and types of children. Even in the normal child biological and social forces do not operate evenly in different children. A mentally retarded child whose condition is caused by some organic abnormality such as brain damage, insufficient thyroid during fetal life, or abnormal chromosomes, undoubtedly develops at a different rate than children not so handicapped. Although there are available studies that mentally deficient children develop at a slower rate than normal, the environmental factors of these studies have not been sufficiently controlled to overcome the "error of potentiality." With the advancement of bio-chemistry and pedagogy, it is possible that past and current studies of predictability will be unreliable. It is impossible to estimate precisely the *future of any child* until many external conditions can be assessed.

"Development, we have seen, consists of a continued sequence of individual reactions, chemical and structural. Specific substances are synthesized and properly organized in cells; totipotent cells subdivide, differentiate, and migrate to form their appropriate structures of particular composition. Each new step is based upon the preceding one, and what will happen at any temporal cross section of the developmental process seems to be determined by the past history and the current situation, by the reacting system and the stimuli playing upon it. Having responded, the whole moves on to a new state of being, which will react again in the next step according to its now determined character and the new environmental situation. If the past history of the system be considered its heredity, then, indeed, much environment is woven into this in the course of development.

"The same situation obtains at the behavior level. What one does at any moment depends on what he is and the situation to which he is responding. But what he is at this moment is itself compounded from his previous experiences and his reactions to them as well as from the initial structural endowment received at birth. Or, at the strictly chemical level, the same again holds, for the final products of reactions depend on the initial reagents present but no less on the surrounding temperature, pressure, illumination, and the like; and, of course, the secondary reactions depend on the products of the first ones and, therefore, on the reaction conditions as well as the ingredients of the initial mixture."[13]

Accordingly, the events in a child's life history leaves some sort of residual that will influence his future behavior. The behavior of a child is determined by certain stimulation; the reaction makes a new individual which will now behave differently toward subsequent stimulating conditions.

The Development of Motor Control: Although patience and time are elements in learning to walk, to feed the self, or to talk, maturation and biological development alone are not dependable. Teaching can decrease extraneous, apparent random movement and help the child toward making finer rather than gross movements. For example, what the child gets into his mouth is dependent not only upon head control and how well he can clutch the spoon, but also upon what is placed before him to eat. The beginnings of feelings of adequacy and achievement may be found in the child's experiences with his own body and his efforts, for example, to touch or clutch the thing for which he reaches. Opportunities to handle things along with words of praise and encouragement are significant factors in the development of control and in the beginnings of the child's feelings about himself.

When the child is able to reach for and clutch a spoon when it is placed before him and he has some feeling of satisfaction in doing it, he is developing the first essence of "meaning." The necessary caution, of course, is in knowing that the child has some feeling of accomplishment, when he is able to clutch what he reaches for.

---

[13] R. W. Gerard: *Unresting Cells.* New York, Harper & Bros., 1940, pp. 5, 403.

This we must assume; frequently our assumption is incorrect when observing the trainable mentally retarded child. The child assigns meanings by establishing a relationship between himself and the objects and people in his world.

The Importance of Tactile Experience: One of the most important ways the child explores his environment is through tactile communication. Long ago Montesorri called attention to the importance of the "education of the senses" and that the child between three and seven years of age is in the period when this education can best proceed.

All living things learn through their senses. Civilization of mankind will reach its highest capacity as individuals develop their maximum in hearing, seeing, tasting, smelling, and touching, tempered with knowledge and judgment. Learning should begin through the senses as early as possible in a child's life and should continue as long as possible.

Unfortunately, we have depended too much on the sense of hearing as an avenue of learning in young children. Bright children will fare very well with hearing as the main medium. Normal children will show progress when hearing and seeing are combined. Mentally retarded children, however, must in addition to hearing and seeing, experience also the sense of touch. When possible, tasting and smelling must also be added. This is doubtless the key to success of some teachers who have found the easiest word to recognize as "orange"; when the child peels, smells, tastes, sees, and hears the word. "Banana" would doubtless be the next word to learn.

Tactile experience is necessary in developing memory, imagination, creativity, and ability to plan. Symbolism, for example, develops from images of objects with which the child has had concrete experiences. He can talk about an orange, a spoon, or a ball, without the object being present. He can even pretend he is having breakfast or playing house. Notions of the size of distant objects and their relationship to each other are simple. The distance of an on-coming automobile, or the size of an automobile are, with few exceptions, beyond the comprehension of the trainable mentally retarded child. In other words he probably does not learn how big is big or the fact that the size of an object is constant despite its distance from the viewer. He can, however visualize objects as possessing permanency, can conceptualize simple distance, can orient himself in space.

Perhaps the most difficult concept to develop, simple as it may sound, is *time*. He must learn, however; that it is time for breakfast, time for dinner, time for bed. Concepts of day, week, month, and year, however, will have no meaning except in borderline development between mental deficiency and mental handicap. Ames[14] found that normal five-year-olds knew what day it was and Springer[15] found that four- to six-year-olds are "able to tell the time of activities which occur regularly in their daily schedule. The child is able to tell time by a clock; the hours, then the half and quarter hours."

The child learns that some things are hard, others soft; some large, some small; some move, others remain still. Through tactile communication and increased motor control, the child establishes order and meaning. The appearance of certain objects means increased pleasure and if events occur with regularity, he develops some degree of security. When he learns to walk, he can go to objects rather than wait for them to come to him. As adults guide him in his physical world, the child's concepts of himself are related to his experiences.

Social Development: The child's contacts with people influence the emergence of a "self concept." He learns to perceive others as being distinct from him and will eventually respond to different people in different ways. He learns to trust adults who care for him and to react with distrust to those people who to him are unfamiliar. Exploration of his interpersonal world is rooted in his needs for the familiar and the predictable. In the case of the trainable mentally retarded child, especially, there is ever present the danger of reading adult thoughts into infant minds. The degree of intellectuality present in responses must ever be regarded with conservatism.

In social development, the child orients himself to his environment first with his own body, second with the "constant adults" who surround him, and third, with his physical environment. In

---

[14] L. B. Ames: The development of the sense of time in the young child. *Journal of Genetic Psychology, 68*:97-125, 1946.

[15] D. Springer: Development in young children of an understanding of time and the clock. *Journal of Genetic Psychology, 80*:95, 1952.

normal children both his body and his mother have become fairly stable elements in their perceptual field. In trainable mentally retarded children, such stability develops later—in some cases *very much later*. As the child grows new people are differentiated only in terms of *the old and stable* people; i.e., the self, and mother, or father, and siblings. The mother especially becomes an anchorage point which the child uses to establish himself in his world.

Important in the development of children is the movement from a highly egocentric position toward a position in which he recognizes the individuality of "the other child." In the upper limits of training, the child should know that he is an individual and that all other people are not only separate from him, but that they are individuals, too.

The Development of Language: Language development rests not only upon maturation of the organism but also upon the familiar environment. Language begins with vocalization, cooing, vocalization of discomfort, pleasure, eagerness, satisfaction, and recognition. Further development is detected in response to another's voice, in vocal response to another person, in imitation of sounds, and in imitation of syllables. During the second and third year of life the child understands gestures (e.g., bye-bye); listens with selective interest to familiar words; differentiates words; adjusts to and understands simple commands; understands a demand and gesture; and responds to inhibitory words. More advanced forms of simple language are detected in the child's ability to name objects, ask with words, use simple sentences; point to nose, eye, hair; use first pronoun; and use pronouns past and plural.[16] These last conceptual transactions and self-reference may not occur in some trainable mentally retarded children, even with teaching, until the child is four or five years of age.

As a child develops, he is differentiating a general perception of his world toward more meanings to more events. Although we are not certain, it is probable that the degree of perceptual distortion and inaccurate communication is high. As with normal infants "dog" to the mentally deficient child at first pertains to any animal with four legs and fur. Unlike normal children, a more precise

---

[16] Dorothea McCarthy: Language development in children. In L. Carmichael, editor: *Manual of Child Psychology*. John Wiley, 1954, pp. 499-502 (used in permission).

perception of "dog" develops later—frequently with much more experiential situations with dogs. Much patience is needed to encourage the child to speak; much time must be used in speaking to the child; and even more time must be spent in listening to him. Indifference, neglect, and emotional stress are sure ways to inhibit language development. The mentally deficient child needs to be exposed to spoken language for many months (at least a year) before he can begin to comprehend the meaning of words.

The successes in the child's language must have an emotional impact on the adults who attend him. At first the words he says should be highly satisfying to him; the "feeling tone" is even of more significance than understanding. Later the child will comprehend that language will clarify meanings and expand interpersonal horizons.

Closely related to the development of language is the development of viewing self as like another. "This development of a sense of identity with those around us is the structure upon which all language is built. Even talking birds talk because they have developed a feeling of identity with the human beings around them. Even more crucial than language development, however, is the 'social sense,' the 'human-ness' of man, his need to belong. Society grows out of the development of this sense of identity. Indeed, man would have no awareness of self, no self-system apart from it. He only gains his identity as a man through this process of identification. Some of us so develop this sense that we can perceive all men as being brothers; others restrict themselves to narrower definitions. In either case, the ways in which this was achieved are the same."[17]

The question has been asked, can trainable mentally retarded children think? The answer is yes, but since thinking and perceiving are related to personal meanings, children tend to think *autistically;* that is, their thought processes and perceptions are influenced by their needs, wishes, and self-concepts. Thinking evolves around the child's self-picture. The self, however, includes many differentiations; e.g., self as a boy or girl, a son or daughter, a playmate and friend, and a member of a family or a group.

---

[17] Ira J. Gordon: *Human Development From Birth Through Adolescence.* New York, Harper & Bros. Pub., 1962, p. 79.

The Educable Mentally Retarded Child

The educable mentally retarded child is one with an intelligence quotient between 50 and 75 (or 80). With special instruction these children can acquire sufficient knowledge and ability to enable them to become socially adequate and occupationally or economically self-sufficient as adults. The most accurate information available regarding these children are the data reporting that a substantial majority live in the lower socio-economic, cultural areas of the community.[18] The primary difference between the educable mentally retarded and the normal child is in intellectual development; intellectual growth is significantly retarded.

As a group, these children are somewhat smaller in stature, weigh slightly less, and have a somewhat higher incidence of physical defects.[19] The exceptions are so varied for individuals, however, that the average for the group has little application for practical purposes. As a group, the educable mentally retarded child begins to walk at a later age and talking is significantly delayed.[20] Mental retardation should not be diagnosed on the basis of late walking and talking alone, however, since these skills may be significantly delayed in physically and intellectually normal children.[21]

The Social Behavior of the Educable Mentally Retarded: Everything included in foregoing pages relating to social development of children also applies to the educable mentally retarded. As with any child, the educable mentally retarded child's social behavior will be determined largely by the social environment in which he lives; however, his response to the social environment changes as he matures. Both the teacher and the parent assume a place of great importance. The child watches closely for their

[18] A. B. Finlayson: Social and economic background of retarded children. *Journal of Educational Sociology, 15*:38-45, 1941. W. S. Neff: Socioeconomic status and intelligence: a critical survey. *Psychological Bulletin, 35*:727-757, 1938. H. M. Skeels and E. A. Fillmore: Mental development of children from underprivileged homes. *Journal of Genetic Psychology, 50*:427-439, 1937.

[19] M. P. Honzik and H. E. Jones: Mental-physical relationships during the preschool period. *Journal of Experimental Ed., 6*:139-146, 1937.

[20] N. A. Dayton: The relationship between physical defects and intelligence. *Journal of Psycho-Asthenics, 34*:112-139, 1928-1929.

[21] G. Orville Johnson: The education of mentally handicapped children. In William W. Cruickshank and G. Orville Johnson: *Education of Exceptional Children and Youth.* Englewood Cliffs, N. J., 1959, p. 192.

smiles, their praises, their sarcasm, and their ridicules. Educable mentally retarded children are not born with behavior deviations. Such deviations are caused by the society that places upon the children demands beyond their capacity.

Boys and girls of educable mentally retarded status will play together on equal terms when they begin formal schooling. They will enjoy organized group play, the length of the period depending on group maturity, and if the activities involve skipping, dancing to music, simple games, or elementary dramatic play. Like other children, they like to climb and jump from heights, catch and throw balls, or express themselves through movement. Generally they are interested in the activity rather than result or product: Their attention span is short and they can remain still for a short time only. With maturity, the educable mentally retarded child will outgrow his egocentricity somewhat and want to belong to a group. They are capable of learning how to play fair, dividing spoils, cooperating, and doing one's share in the group. The need to *succeed at something* is strong. They need to excel in at least one thing; if they do not they are capable of seeking prestige through defying authority, acting as a bully, and boasting.

Apparent maladjustment within a particular group may not represent a real maladjustment, but rather that the child is in the wrong group. "When a child does not adjust well to the classroom group in which he happens to be, he should be placed in another group to which he is able to adjust or he should be aided to adjust to his present group if diagnosis indicates it is advisable for him to do so."[22]

Older educable mentally retarded girls beam when grownups notice and admire their new dress, purse, or shoes. Boys like to attract attention by jumping or walking on the edge of a curb or narrow bridge.

Educable mentally retarded children must have the opportunity to participate in worthwhile objectives, to feel that they are valuable, to contribute as members of a group, and to have access in the performance of worthwhile activities. Only continued social experiences and expansion of self-direction will enable these children to grow socially. Achievement in economic dependence as

---

[22] R. DeVerl Willey: *Guidance in Elementary Education.* New York, Harper & Bros., 1952, p. 592.

an adult is largely a matter of personal and social adjustment.

Acquiring Academic Skills: The area of greatest disability for educable mentally retarded children is academic. It is especially important, therefore, that the learning environment must be carefully planned and provided. Objectives of the curriculum should be: 1) personal or emotional adjustment; 2) social adjustment, and 3) economic adjustment. The total impact and value of any one experience, for example, acquiring a skill in reading or arithmetic, should result in achievement of all these objectives. The higher incidence of physical and sensory disabilities among the educable mentally retarded accentuates the need to emphasize the acquisition of habits of health, cleanliness, and safety. Visual and auditory examinations, immunization, wearing suitable clothing, habits of washing, brushing teeth, personal grooming, are all significant items to be included in the child's educational program.

Learning must be characterized by a step-by-step procedure in instruction with a simple-to-more-difficult sequence of activities distributed over a much longer time than is used for normal children. The things to be learned should be presented in a large variety of situations rather than in repetition of the same.

Motor Abilities: Educable mentally handicapped youngsters go through the same developmental sequence as normal children, yet at a much slower rate. During their first year in school, they learn to skip with both feet, march to music, and hop. More difficult skills are required in playing jump-the-rope, distance jumping, or walking downstairs by alternating forward foot. Motor skills are acquired by drawing, coloring, cutting, pasting, writing, modeling clay, and so on.

Language Development: The educable mentally retarded child acquires speech and language skills by imitating other human beings with whom he associates. The emphasis should be on meaningful speaking and listening. It should be expected that functionally complete but structurally incomplete sentences decrease with maturity. Incomplete sentences comprise as much as one-third of the speech of normal 9½ year-old children.[23]

Because the largest number of educable mentally retarded chil-

---

[23] D. McCarthy: Language development in children. In Carmichael, L., ed.: *Manual of Child Psychology*, 2nd Ed. New York, John Wiley & Sons, Inc., 1954, chapter 9.

dren are found in the lower socio-economic strata, these children often must learn two languages, i.e., the middle-class standard of school and the lower-class standard of home and neighborhood. Care must be used not to create feelings of inferiority and inhibition of spontaneity in children of the lower classes by punishing and otherwise humiliating them when they persist in using the language they hear at home. Oral language will be used mostly by educable mentally retarded children in their vocational pursuits. The emphasis in instruction, therefore, should be in good conversation, giving directions, explanation, and effective listening.

Reading: Skills in reading are acquired very slowly by educable mentally retarded children. Most of these children will rarely achieve beyond fourth-grade ability. Reading skills are so closely integrated with all learning that they defy isolation in instruction. Visual and auditory senses must receive special attention. Speech, visual memory and discrimination, and above all, *thinking,* are involved in the acquisition of reading skills. There is no one approach suitable to teach all children to read. One approach that has been relatively successful throughout the years, however, is that known as "The Kinaesthetic Approach." Described by Maria Montessori in 1912[24] and later made popular by Helen B. Keller and Grace M. Fernald[25] the method is still being used successfully.[26] Through emphasizing a combination of training, writing, and spelling, the Kinaesthetic approach is organized in terms of steps and stages. No commercial material is used in the initial phases of instruction. The child is asked to tell the teacher a few words he would like to learn, and each word is considered individually until he can master a small list. As soon as he learns a few words, he is encouraged to compose a little story and is taught any words in the story that he doesn't already know. At first the compositions are dictated by the teacher and later are written by the child. The child then reads his own story in written form. The next day he is presented his story in typed form. These stories,

[24] Maria Montessori: *The Montessori Method.* London, England, William Heinemann, 1912, Chapter XVI.

[25] Grace M. Fernald: *Remedial Techniques in Basic School Subjects.* New York, McGraw-Hill Book Co., 1943.

[26] R. DeVerl Willey: *The Kinaesthetic Approach to Teaching Reading.* Reno, Nev., Touch, Inc., 1962.

comprising the child's own compositions, are the only materials used until a fairly large sight vocabulary is learned. The methods of teaching words change as the child's ability to learn words improve.[27]

Arithmetic and Numbers: At least some quantitative concepts are necessary if the child is to make an adjustment to his social and economic world. The educable mentally retarded child can be expected to learn only the most elementary forms of the addition, subtraction, multiplication, and division processes; i.e., the curriculum usually taught to children in the first four grades. Essential are basic concepts of amount, counting, language used in dealing with quantities, and recognition and association of the written number with the quantity and process involved.

Functional, real-life situations should be used whenever possible. It may be necessary for the teacher to arrange purposely for an arithmetical situation to arise. Usually the experience units and normal daily activities of the children provide ideal material for the need of quantitative thinking. Only after the child has initially learned a concept and understands its application should he receive further practice. So-called drill and repetition exercises are used to insure retention; they are not teaching devices. The application of arithmetic skills should be integrated with skill development from the beginning. The development of skills in the primary grades with postponement of application until junior or senior high school cannot be justified.

Conclusion

Two categories of children with low intelligence have been given attention in this chapter: 1) the trainable mentally retarded, and 2) the educable mentally retarded. Trainable mentally retarded children have been described as being able: to achieve competence in self-care skills, to develop proper self-concept, to adjust to home and neighborhood, and to become economically useful in the home or other sheltered environment.

The educable mentally retarded child has been described as one who is able to: receive and profit by a minimum academic school program, make social adjustment in the home and community,

---

[27] The reader should refer to subsequent chapters to find practical application of this approach.

and to find occupational usefulness at unskilled or semi-skilled levels. As a group their rate of growth in the physical traits of height, weight, and motor coordination is a little slower than normal. The exceptions for individuals are so numerous, however, that group norms should not be used for individual diagnostic or prognostic purposes. Their rate of development in mental, social, and academic areas in only about half (in many cases only three-fourths) as great as normal.

The bases of behavior as related to physical and personal needs of these children are the same as normal children. In other words, all children have more similarities than differences—probably because they are human beings.

Only the minimum elements in the education of these children were considered in this chapter. More detailed discussion of curriculum will be discussed in Chapters IV, V, VI, and VII.

SELECTED REFERENCES

Allen, R. M.: Intellectual evaluation in cerebral palsy. *Exceptional Children,* 27:202-204, Dec. 1960.

Ames, L. B.: The development of the sense of time in the young child. *Journal of Genetic Psychology,* 68:97-125, 1946.

Anastasi, A.: Psychological tests; uses and abuses. *Teachers College Record,* 62:389-393, Feb. 1961.

Barmack, F.: Intelligence: fiction, faculty, or function? *High Points, 43:*51-53, Oct. 1961.

Beck, H. S.: Detecting psychological symptoms of brain injury. *Exceptional Children, 28:*57-62, Sept. 1961.

Bensberg, G. T.: Concept learning in mental defectives as a function of appropriate and inappropriate attention sets. *Journal of Educational Psychology, 49:*137-143, June 1958.

Berson, Minnie P.: Individual differences among preschool children: 4 year olds. *The 61st Yearbook of the National Society for the Study of Education,* Pt. 1, Individualizing Instruction, Chicago, Ill., The University of Chicago Press, 1962, pp. 112-125.

Bialer, I.: Conceptualization of success and failure in mentally retarded and normal children. *Journal of Personality, 29:*303-320, Sept. 1961.

Bobroff, A.: Stages of maturation in socialized thinking and in the ego development of two groups of children. *Child Development, 31:*321-338, June 1960.

Bolduc, E. T.: Social value—need patterns in mental retardates. *Journal of Consulting Psychology, 24:*472-479, Dec. 1960.

Bradway, K. P. and Robinson, N. M.: Significant IQ changes in twenty-five years: a follow up. *Journal of Educational Psychology, 52:*74-79, April 1961.

Braen, B. A. and Masling, J. M.: Intelligence tests used with special groups of children. *Exceptional Children, 26*:42-45, Sept. 1959.

Burt, C. L.: Interaction of heredity and environment in regard to measured intelligence: reply with rejoinder. *British Journal of Educational Psychology, 30*:273-276, Nov. 1960.

Carriker, W. R.: Research related to the education of mentally retarded children. *School Life, 42*:26-28, Jan. 1960.

Cashdan, A.: Intellectual powers of subnormal children. *Educational Research, 4*:84-99, Feb. 1962.

Cassel, R. N.: Interpreting the IQ to pupil and parent. *Journal of Secondary Education, 37*:201-205, April 1962.

Cautela, J. R.: Meaningless questions concerning intelligence. *Education, 80*:33-36, Sept. 1959.

Cromwell, R. L.: Selected aspects of personality development in mentally retarded children. *Exceptional Children, 28*:44-51, Sept. 1961.

Culbertson, E.: Patterns of hostility among the retarded. *American Journal of Mental Deficiency, 66*:421-427, Nov. 1961.

Doll, E. A.: Mentally retarded. *Exceptional Children, 27*:487-493, May 1961.

Escalona, S. K. and Moriarty, A.: Prediction of schoolage intelligence from instant tests. *Child Development, 32*:597-605, Sept. 1961.

Finlayson, A. B.: Social and economic background of retarded children. *Journal of Educational Sociology, 15*:38-45, 1941.

Freeman, G. G. and Lukens, J.: Speech and language program for educable mentally handicapped children. *Journal of Speech and Hearing Disorders. 27*:285-287, Aug. 1962.

Gerard, R. W.: *Unresting Cells.* New York, Harper & Bros. Pub., 1940.

Goldstein, H. and Kass, C.: Incidental learning of educable mentally retarded and gifted children. *American Journal of Mental Deficiency, 66*:245-249, Sept. 1961.

Gordon, Ira J.: *Human Development From Birth Through Adolescence.* New York, Harper & Bros. Pub., 1962, p. 79.

Guilford, J. P.: The structure of the intellect. *Psychological Bulletin, 53*:267-293, 1956.

Hardin, G.: Biology and individual differences. *The 61st Yearbook of the National Society for the Study of Education,* Pt. 1, Individualizing Instruction, Chicago, Ill., The Univ. of Chicago Press, 1962, p. 15.

Harsh, Richard: Intelligence: its nature and measurement. *National Elementry Principal, 41*:23-28, Sept. 1961.

Holowinsky, I.: IQ constancy in a group of institutionalized mental defectives over a period of three decades. *Training School Bulletin, 59*:15-17, May 1962.

Honzik, M. P. and Jones, H. E.: Mental-physical relationships during the preschool period. *Journal of Experimental Education, 6*:139-146, 1937.

Harley, J. R.: Maternal attitudes and children's intelligence. *Journal of Clinical Psychology, 15*:291-292, July 1959.

Johnson, C. D. and Barnett, C. D.: Relationship of physical stigmata to intellectual status in mongoloids. *American Journal of Mental Deficiency,* 66:435-437, Nov. 1961.

Johnson, G. O. and Capobianco, R. J.: Physical condition and its effect upon learning in trainable mentally deficient children. *Exceptional Children,* 26:3-5, Sept. 1959.

Johnson, G. O. and Blake, K. A.: Learning performance of retarded and normal children. New York, Syracuse University Press, 1960.

Johnson, G. Orville: The education of mentally handicapped children. In William M. Cruickshank and G. Orville Johnson: *Education of Exceptional Children and Youth.* Englewood Cliffs, N. J., 1959, p. 192.

Kaariainen, R. and Dingman, H. F.: Relation of the degree of mongolism to the degree of subnormality. *American Journal of Mental Deficiency,* 66:438-443, Nov. 1961.

Kirk, Samuel A.: *Educating Exceptional Children.* Boston, Mass., Houghton Mifflin Co., 1962, p. 86.

Kvaraceus, W. C.: Selected references from the literature on exceptional children: mentally and physically handicapped. *Elementary School Journal,* 60:347-348, March 1960; 61:341-442, March 1961.

Kubala, A. L. and Katz, M. M.: Nutritional factors in psychological test behavior. *Journal of Genetic Psychology, 96:*343-352, June 1960.

Liverant, S.: Intelligence: a concept in need of re-examination. *Journal of Consulting Psychology, 24:*101-110, April 1960.

Little, C. E.: Can intelligence be taught? *Education, 81:*235-238, Dec. 1960.

Levinson, Abraham: *The Mentally Retarded Child.* New York, The John Day Co., 1952.

Masland, R. L., Sarason, S. B. and Gladwin, T.: *Mental Subnormality.* New York, Basic Books, Inc., 1958.

McCarthy, D.: Language development in children. In Carmichael, L., ed.: *Manual of Child Psychology.* Sec. Ed. New York, John Wiley and Sons, Inc., 1954, Chapter 9.

Malpass, L. F.: Responses of retarded children to the children's manifest anxiety scale. *Journal of Educational Psychology, 51:*305-308, Oct. 1960.

Meyerowitz, J. H.: Self-derogations in young retardates and special class placement. *Child Development, 33:*443-451, June 1962.

Montessori, Maria: *The Montessori Method.* London, England, William Heinemann, 1912, Chapter XVI. Fernald, Grace M.: *Remedial Techniques in Basic School Subjects.* New York, McGraw-Hill Book Co., 1943.

Neff, W. S.: Socioeconomic status and intelligence: a critical survey. *Psychological Bulletin, 35:*727-757, 1938.

Pidgeon, A.: Design, construction and use of standardized tests; the interpretation of test scores. *Educational Research, 4:*33-43, Nov. 1961.

Pritchett, A. A.: Aliveness then retention. *Elementary English, 38:*581-583, Dec. 1961.

Richter, C. P.: Animal behavior and internal drives. *Quarterly Review of Biology, 2:*307-343, 1927.

Ringness, T. A.: Emotional reactions to learning situations as related to the learning deficiency of mentally retarded children. Madison, Wisc., University of Wisconsin, 1959.

Rosinski, E. F.: Must all tests be multi-factor batteries? *Journal of Experimental Education, 28*:235-240, March 1960.

Rosenzweig, Louis F. and Long, Julia: *Understanding and Teaching the Dependent Retarded Child.* Darien, Conn., Educational Pub. Corp., 1960.

Sarason, S. B.: *Psychological Problems in Mental Deficiency.* 3rd Ed. New York, Harper & Bros. Pub., 1959.

Scott, D. H.: Interaction of heredity and environment in regard to measured intelligence. *British Journal of Educational Psychology, 30*:95-102, June 1960.

Skeels, H. M. and Fillmore, E. A.: Mental development of children from underprivileged homes. *Journal of Genetic Psychology, 50*:427-439, 1937.

Springer, D.: Development in young children of an understanding of time and the clock. *Journal of Genetic Psychology, 80*:83-96, 1952.

Stevenson, H. W. and Snyder, L. C.: Performance as a function of the interaction of incentive conditions. *Journal of Personality, 28*:1-11, March 1960.

Start, K. B.: Relationship between intelligence and the effect of mental practice on the performance of a motor skill. *Research Quarterly, 31*:644-649, Dec. 1960.

Suchman, J. R. and Aschner, M. J. M.: Perceptual and cognitive development; development of intelligence. *Review of Educational Research, 31*:455-456, Dec. 1961.

Suinn, R. M.: Shipley-Hartford retreat scale as a screening test of intelligence. *Journal of Clinical Psychology, 16*:419, Oct. 1960.

Thompson, J. M. and Finley, C. J.: Further comparison of the intellectual patterns of gifted and mentally retarded children. *Exceptional Children, 28*:379-381, March 1962.

Thorp, T. R. and Mahrer, A. R.: Predicting potential intelligence. *Journal of Clinical Psychology, 15*:286-288, July 1959.

Tong, J. E. and Murphy, L. C.: Rorschach Indices and automatic stress reactivity. *Journal of Clinical Psychology, 16*:324-328, July 1960.

Tredgold, A. F. and Tredgold, R. F.: *A Textbook of Mental Deficiency.* 8th Ed. Baltimore, Md., Williams and Wilkins Co., 1952.

Tyler, F. T.: Search for evidence about individual differences. *The 61st Yearbook of the National Society of the Study of Education.* Pt. 1, pp. 95-111.

Tyler, F. T.: Intraindividual variability. *The 61st Yearbook of the National Society of the Study of Education.* Pt. 1, pp. 164-174.

Wallin, J. E. Wallace: *Children with Mental and Physical Handicaps.* New York, Prentice-Hall, Inc., 1949.

Wallin, N. E.: Development and application of tests of general mental ability. *Review of Educational Research, 32*:15-24, Feb. 1962.

Warren, B. F.: Intelligence testing: what is your IQ? *Clearing House, 36*:486, April 1962.

Warren, S. A. and Kraus, M. J.: WAIS verbal minus performance IQ comparisons in mental retardates. *Journal of Clinical Psychology, 17*:57-59, Jan. 1961.

Wendland, L. V., *et al.*: Intellectual functioning of postpoliomyetic patients. *Journal of Clinical Psychology, 16*:179-181, April 1960.

Willey, R. DeVerl: *Guidance in Elementary Education.* New York: Harper & Bros., 1952, p. 592.

Willey, R. DeVerl: *The Kinaesthetic Approach to Teaching Reading.* Reno, Nev., Touch Inc., 1962.

Wolkinsky, G. F.: Piaget and the psychology of thought: some implications for teaching the retarded. *American Journal of Mental Deficiency, 67*:250-256, Sept. 1962.

Wolf, W. and Stroud, J. B.: Contribution of response in mental measurement. *Journal of Educational Psychology, 52*:249-253, Oct. 1961.

Young, Kimball: *Personality and Problems of Adjustment.* New York, Appleton-Century-Crofts, Inc., 1940.

Zigler, E.: Overview of research in learning, motivation, and perception. *Exceptional Children, 28*:455-458, May 1962.

Zuk, G. H.: Psychodynamic implications of self-injury in defective children and adults. *Journal of Clinical Psychology, 16*:58-60, Jan. 1960.

CHAPTER III

Etiology of Mental Deficiency

THERE are numerous sources of mental retardation and it manifests itself in various forms. The way a mentally retarded child grows depends mainly on the basis of his intellectual inadequacy. There are many sources of intellectual inadequacy; therefore, many patterns of growth may result. Some consistent patterns and inconsistencies both will result from each syndrome. Patterns of mental deficiency cannot be stereotyped.

Symptoms in mental retardation have been schematically presented by several authors as follows:

Malamud:[1]
1. Malformation.
2. Destructive processes.
3. Metabolic disorders.

Clarke and Clarke:[2]
1. Subcultural defect.
2. Genetic defects—dominant.
3. Genetic defects—recessive.
4. Defects of obscure origin.

Hilliard and Kirman:[3]
1. Mongolism.
2. Metabolic syndromes.
3. Morphological syndromes.

Kugelmass:[4]
1. Development varieties.
2. Metabolic varieties.

---

[1] N. Malamud: Recent trends in classification of neuropathological findings in mental deficiency. *American Journal of Mental Deficiency,* *58*:438-447, 1954.

[2] Ann M. Clarke and A. B. D. Clarke: *Mental Deficiency—The Changing Outlook.* London, Methuen and Company, Ltd., 1958.

[3] L. T. Hilliard and B. H. Kirkman: *Mental Deficiency.* Boston, Little, Brown & Co., 1957.

[4] I. N. Kugelmass: *The Management of Mental Deficiency in Children.* New York, Grune and Stratton, 1954.

3. Neuromotor varieties.
4. Psychological varieties.

Benda:[5]
1. Antenatal disorders.
2. Metabolic disorders and degenerative disease.
3. Total personality disorders.

CAUSES OF MENTAL RETARDATION AND DEFICIENCY

The causes of mental deficiency and retardation may be listed in four main groups for simple classification:

1. Antenatal—retardation established before birth, including all familial and congenital types.
2. Prenatal—retardation due to complications arising during the pregnancy.
3. Paranatal—due to injuries at birth.
4. Postnatal—due to injuries, disease, toxic agents, and infection occurring after birth but before completion of mental development.

Some causes acting before birth:

1. Antenatal

It has been variously estimated that from 5 to 75 per cent of deficiencies arise from causes existing prior to birth. This includes both familial and genetic causes.

"Familial" or "sub-cultural" retardation, due to factors inherent in the genes; one or both parents are in the low-normal range of intelligence and this inferiority is transmitted to their offspring in different degrees. Some of their children may be normal, some abnormal, or some low-normal like the parents or parent. This is a hereditary condition of familial characteristics; e.g., the same as the color of the hair and eyes. Less than 10 per cent of retardation is due to this familial cause.

The second group in the hereditary classification is entirely different from the above. The genetic factors involved in this category are considered pathological because they determine structural, cerebral, and metabolic disorders. These result from dis-

---

[5] C. E. Benda: *Developmental Disorders of Mentation and Cerebral Palsies.* New York, Grune and Stratton, 1952.

turbance in the enzyme system and are often referred to as "inborn errors of metabolism." They are represented in the metabolic processes associated with lipids, carbohydrates, and proteins. Some of the more important conditions represented in this group are:

Tay-Sach's Group of Cerebral Lipoidoses, intracellular lipid metabolism of the brain cells is abnormal. This condition involves degeneration of the retina and is sometimes called cerebromacular degeneration. Death often follows tetraplegia, blindness, and seizures.

Phenylketonuria (Folling's Disease) often referred to as PKU, defect in protein metabolism, symptoms of the condition apart from urinalysis are seizures in some cases, brisk reflexes, increased muscle tone, epileptic fits, short stepped gait, distractability, and hyperkinetic movements.

Galactosemia, defect in carbohydrate metabolism affecting the metabolism of galactose. Liver becomes progressively larger after birth, albumin appears in the urine, both jaundice and cataracts may be found early. Mental retardation of some degree has been found in most all cases.

Glycogenosis, involving carbohydrates, and affecting the metabolism of glycogen (animal starch); this enzyme defect converts glycogen to glucose in the liver. The liver becomes firm and enlarged. Convulsion may occur because of low blood sugar. Mental retardation resulting from this disease is not severe.

Cerebral Sclerosis, a degenerative disease due to the disturbance of the lipid metabolism of the brain. Child appears normal at birth; at four to six months of age, convulsions and spasticity develop, head becomes retracted, arms flexed, legs extended, blindness and deafness occur and death follows.

Gargoylism (Hurler's Disease), a rare disease complex in nature, involving more than one metabolic system. Mental retardation is but a part of the over-all disturbance of the body. Physical signs are skeletal. These people are dwarfs who have heads of normal size. Most all have masculine characteristics, protruding abdomen, depressed nose, large mouth, and often the spine is abnormal. Its origin is mainly hereditary.

This group of genetically determined conditions displays maldevelopment of the skull in addition to the cerebral defect. These include:

Microcephaly: Subject has extremely small head which may have resulted from some intrauterine cause such as cytomegalic inclusion or toxoplasmosis, irradiation of the pelvis during pregnancy, or it could be a hereditary defect.

Craniostenosis (Premature Cranial Suture Closure): This is a condition in which the bones of the skull fuse permanently into various shapes which deviate from the normal. Comparable disorders are oxycephaly (very high head), brachycephaly (unusually broad head), scaphocephaly (long head). In craniostenosis, mental retardation is second to skull deformity. Treatment of the physical disorder may prevent mental retardation.

Hypertelorism: Widely separated eyes give an animal like appearance to the subject. In addition to eye placement, the bridge of the nose is broad and flattened, high palate, and there may also be congenital malformation of the heart and anomalies of the fingers.

This group of genetically determined conditions have in common a cellular dysplasia which may include other organs of the body along with the brain. These conditions present many similarities and overlapping of clinical features and familial genetic manifestations which suggests a unitary genetic mechanism. They are commonly called the congenital ectodermoses. They include:

Tuberous Sclerosis: A neurologic disorder with protean expressions involving the brain, skin, and other organs. Adenoma sebeceum (a facial rash) appears on either cheek in a butterfly shaped area. Epilepsy occurs in many cases and the degree of mental defect may range from idiocy to normal intelligence. Mental defect and epilepsy are caused by the hard white or yellowish-gray nodules scattered throughout the brain tissue and central nervous system. Tumor formations have been found in the heart, liver, kidney, and thyroid.

Neurofibromatosis (Von Recklinghausen's Disease): This condition is characterized by multiple tumors of the nerves. In most cases the skin has single or multiple coffee colored areas. Depending on the nerves affected, blindness, deafness, or elephantiasis of an arm or leg may occur. There may also be physical giantism, as reported by Jordan.[6]

---

[6] T. E. Jordan: Psychological findings in a case of Von Recklinghausen's Disease and hyperpituitarism. *Journal of Clinical Psychology, 12:*389-391, 1956.

Cerebral Angiomatosis (Sturge-Weber Syndrome): This is characterized by a unilateral port wine discoloration on the face, convulsions, intracranial calcification, cerebral angiomatous lesions, mental retardation, and hemiplegia.

2. Prenatal: Prenatal Infections

Congenital Toxoplasmosis: This is a disease caused by a protozoan. The subjects may develop jaundice, convulsions, hypertonia, lethargy, or paralysis. The liver and spleen may be enlarged and usually hydrocephalus or microcephaly of some degree will develop. Microcephaly patients should be checked for toxoplasmosis infection.

Maternal Rubella (German Measles): May cause blindness, deafness, and mental retardation in a child if the mother is affected with this disease during the first three months of pregnancy.

Congenital Syphilis: The two forms encountered in mental deficiency are diffuse syphilitic encephalitis (general paralysis) and meningovascular syphilis. Congenital syphilis is on the decrease. About 6 per cent of those institutionalized show a positive Wasserman reaction.

Kernicterus: A disease resulting from high levels of bilirubin in the infant's blood. It is debatable whether or not this should be classed as belonging in the prenatal category. But it is placed here because the most common cause of its development is erythroblastosis due to the Rh blood factor, ABO and rare blood factors such as Kell and MNS.

Endocrine disorders are common among the mentally retarded but the only hormone for which a cause-and-effect can be established is the thyroid.

Congenital Athyroidism (Common Cretinism): At the age of six months, most of the symptoms are present. These are: slow to gain weight, feeding problems, hoarse voice, constipation, decreased activity, and respiratory symptoms. Physical indications are retarded growth (short arms and legs and long trunk), depressed bridge of the nose, square hands, large abdomen, dry skin, large protruding tongue. In this type of cretin, the thyroid gland is not palpable.

Goitrous Cretinism: In addition to all the above characteristic symptoms and physical findings, the thyroid gland may be palpable at birth or will enlarge in the first few months.

Acquired Hypothyroidism: This condition will no doubt be found listed under endocrine disorders, but, according to this classification (prenatal) it definitely does not belong in this category since it is acquired after birth. Often this occurs in the second year of life.

Mongolism: No definite clue as to the cause of this condition has yet been established. Much of the work on this subject has been only speculation. Levinson and Bigler[7] has listed the following theories:

1. The germ cell theory which assumes that the same defect is present in the individual gametes, maternal or paternal, before fertilization.
2. The environmental theory, which assumes that the defect occurred after fertilization, some time up to the eighth week.
3. Hormonal deviation in the mother or infant.
4. Metabolic or chemical errors present in the mongol.
5. Hereditary defect that operates as a recessive, influenced by all the aforementioned factors.

Mongolism is a common condition. It has been found that there is a greater tendency for the child to have a palm line resemblance to that of the mother than to that of the father. Even though mongoloids are born to all age groups, the largest percentage are born to the very young and the older mothers. There are almost twice as many mongoloid boys as girls.

These children are short, head is smaller than normal, short fat neck, the slanted eyes have small orbits, high palate, teeth misshapen and incomplete, scrotal tongue, mouth often open; the nostrils of the small nose are tilted forward, nasal discharge the year around, dry, rough, abnormal skin, lacks elasticity. Both fingers and palms are short, little finger is often curved, the toes are short and stubby with a wide separation between the big and second toe.

Miscellaneous causes, which may have an adverse effect on the fetus and from which retardation may occur are:

1. Trauma during pregnancy caused when the mother suffered a blow or a fall.

---

[7] Abraham Levinson and John A. Bigler: *Mental Retardation in Infants and Children.* Chicago, The Year Book Publishers, 1960, p. 215.

2. Attempted abortion (induced or accidental).
3. Quinine consumed by the mother.
4. Irradiation of the pelvis.
5. Uterine hemorrhages from any cause.
6. Toxemia of pregnancy, the presence of toxicants in the mother, lowers the blood oxygen of the baby and causes retardation.
7. Premature birth.

3. Paranatal

This group is comprised of cerebral injuries due to factors connected with the birth process. Authorities have postulated that not more than 1 to 2 per cent of mental retardation is caused by birth injury. These include: instrument delivery, prolonged or difficult labor, compression of the umbilical cord, premature separation of the placenta, anoxia due to inhalation of fluid, effect of drugs used during labor or delivery, caesarean section, breech or transverse presentation.

4. Postnatal

Diseases which produce inflammation of the central nervous system. Encephalitis may be caused by either bacteria or virus and sometimes follows other diseases, such as measles, whooping cough, mumps, and chicken pox. Viral encephalitis is highly contagious and results in epidemic form. It may be diagnosed from fever, convulsions, lethargy, coma or paralysis and in some cases there will be cerebrospinal fluid changes. Encephalitis is an inflammation of the brain substance.

Meningitis is an inflammation of the meninges, the three membranes (the dura mater, arachnoid, and pia mater) which envelop the brain and spinal cord. This illness is accompanied by a rise in temperature, vomiting, restless delirium, coma or stupor; often there is a headache, some kind of paralysis, rigidity of the neck, and convulsions. Until recently meningitis was invariably fatal so that it was not a cause of mental retardation. Now, with modern medicine and antibiotics, this picture has changed. Consequently about 1 per cent of mental deficiency in the institutional population is caused by this disease.

Cerebral trauma caused by: 1) various accidents during infancy, such as a fall, accidental blow on the head, and auto accidents; 2) subdural hematoma, an accumulation of blood under the sub-dural layer of the meninges of the brain. This can result from several causes, such as a subdural abscess or syphilis, but direct intracerebral bleeding is more common. If the hemorrhage area is small it may be entirely absorbed. If the blood accumulates instead, the result is subdural hematoma. Some symptoms are convulsions, lethargy, coma, retinal hemorrhage and paralysis.

Foreign agents can cause poisoning, such as lead, carbon mon-oxide, coal tar derivatives, and certain types of vaccines; the latter is very rare indeed.

Mental retardation should be considered, not so much as a basic problem, but as a symptom of another problem, producing the physical disorder which projects a set of behavioral and social problems. The attempt to classify children according to cause of mental retardation is very baffling. The main problem in the causes of mental retardation is the matter of evidence and its interpretation. In a special education program the cause is not the important factor. Regardless of why retardation developed, the school must devise ways and methods of giving these children an opportunity to develop to the maximum of their potential.

Therefore, the foregoing classifications and causes of mental retardation are offered solely as basic information for the teacher new to the field. For the same reason the actual case histories of children with whom one of the writers has worked is given below. Names and dates have been changed to protect the identity of these children.

CASES OF MENTAL RETARDATION

The following are actual cases of retardation which demonstrate some of the causes discussed in the beginning of this chapter.

Boys

1. B. C., age 18, IQ 75, clean and neat in appearance, very polite and well-mannered, works part time in a service station, well-liked by manager of station, resides with grandmother, age seventy-two years. The two live alone in a trailer, his level of reading, spelling and arithmetic is fair, fifth grade. His alco-holic mother died at age of forty-five when he was thirteen years old. His father was twenty-two years older than the mother. He deserted the family when the son was four years of age because

of mother's drinking. There were two children born to the couple. His normal sister is two years older than he.

2. F. M., age 13 years, 9 months, IQ 62, handsome, well-built lad, slightly crippled, right leg shorter than left due to birth injury which caused mild cerebral palsy and mental retardation. Father's present age is forty-one, mother's age is thirty-four; boy has three brothers, one older and two younger, all three are considered normal, however, all three boys display temper tantrums, while F. M. does not have this tendency even though he is argumentative. For the most part he is pleasant and has a good disposition. His academic ability is practically non-existent, his muscular coordination is poor which presents problems in his attempt to write. Boy's father has a terrible temper and mother's IQ is probably not over 100. She had a great deal of difficulty with school and quit during her freshman year in high school and married. The father works at a service station and the mother stays at home.

3. H. A., age 13 years, 3 months, IQ has varied—first test showed 106, second 86 and most recent test 81. Tall, well-built boy, who is never without dark circles under his eyes, frequent temper tantrums, always neat, clean and well dressed. He functions in reasoning ability in low, low third grade level, problem solving, low fourth, mechanics of English is nil, refuses to use capital letters and simple punctuation such as period or question mark at the end of a sentence. Handwriting very small, cramped, and illegible even though his coordination seems to be all right. Word calls (reading) on sixth grade level but apparently comprehends little of what he reads. He is next to the youngest of five children. Sister age twenty-seven is oldest of the family. She started nurse training after high school but dropped out. Brother number one who is twenty-three, attended college but left to play baseball with Chicago Cubs, pitched for about one season, then returned home. Now works for a trucking firm. Brother number two attended college for about two years, dropped out, went to work as a produce clerk in a grocery store. The father is a truck driver and mother is a telephone operator. Youngest member of the family, sister age eight years, attends regular third grade class.

L. O., age 13 years, 3 months, IQ has varied from 81-88 on recent tests. It is felt that neither test score presents a true picture, that the boy is pseudo-retarded due to emotional problems. He is achieving academically, middle seventh grade level. His home life leaves much to be desired. He and two brothers, one younger and one older, live with an alcoholic-prostitute mother. She is seldom sober, never cooks a meal, nor cleans the house, nor washes or irons clothes. Consequently, the boys go to school in filthy, smelly, tattered clothing; they are very unkempt, dirty bodies, faces and grimy hands because they do not wash or bathe. Whatever meal preparation, house-cleaning or washing of clothes that takes place is done by the two older boys. Naturally this is very little. The father divorced the mother who was nine years his senior, when L. O. was six years old. Since that time the monthly support money from the father for the children, plus the monthly welfare check has been used by the mother for the purpose of quenching her thirst and treating various and sundry men (bums) picked up in dives. Many of them are taken to her home to live until they wish to move on. The brothers have not developed emotional problems to the extent of L. O.'s and therefore have not required special class services.

5. N. T., age 15 years, IQ 70, tall and thin cretin type, hyperactive, shows very poor judgment. When aroused to anger (seldom occurs) feelings are so intense that he becomes ill. He works diligently, trying to succeed with school subjects. He reads fair at the fourth grade level. Mechanics of fourth grade level English are fair. Spelling is poor, does exceptionally well with straight problem solving on fifth grade level but has extreme difficulty with reasoning problems. Coordination is poor and writing presents a problem. Mother married his soldier father at the end of World War II. When boy was an infant the father was confined to a veteran's hospital as a mental patient where he remained until he died a few years later. The mother re-married a carnival worker and the three traveled for some time, then left the carnival and opened a bar. This was operated by the mother and step-father. The boy spent a great deal of time in the bar. When the boy was eleven years old, the mother divorced husband No. 2 and married one of her bar customers. This marriage ended recently even though they have a two year old daughter. The boy is very fond of this step-father (he cannot remember his own father since he was hospitalized before the boy was one year old). He shows much affection for the sister and he has good rapport with the mother.

6. P. C., age 13 years, 8 months, IQ 80, normal in appearance, coordination is good, slow moving, mild-mannered and docile,

can be aroused to anger if continually pressed. When this occurs, he bites, kicks and slugs. He is a typical example of familial retardation. A very poor reader, good in problem solving at fifth grade level. Also does well with written problems which require reasoning if the teacher assists with the reading. Has much difficulty with spelling at fourth grade level. He is the seventh child in a family of eight children. The two oldest brothers finished high school. One is a postman and the other is a lineman for a power company. Older sister No. 1 attended high school for one year and dropped out—she is a nurse's aid. Sister No. 2 attended seventh grade for a period of two weeks and quit completely because she objected to having P.E. classes. She has never worked. The father, who isn't as intelligent as P. C., forbade the girl to undress and wear P.E. shorts because it was indecent, created such a furor at school and at the general administration office of the school system that no one opposed him when the girl was removed from school. Sister No. 3 was killed in an auto accident at the age of six months, and No. 4 was born dead. The youngest member of the family, a girl age eleven, is attending a regular third grade class. The father is a retired railroad switchman and the mother has always remained in the home.

7. R. T., age 14 years, IQ 88, nice looking, well developed physically, good disposition, has difficulty with reading but does well on third grade level, fourth grade level arithmetic good, mechanics of remedial English fair, third grade level spelling good. Comprehension very good. Present indications point to emotional involvement which simulates mental retardation, pseudo-retardation in this case could be due to the home situation. This boy is the youngest of three children. A sister is sixteen years old and a brother is fifteen years old. He is very fond of both his father and mother and has attachment to siblings. The mother divorced the building engineer father and married a bartender when the boy was nine or ten years of age. All three children remained with the mother. This marriage lasted less than two years. The mother obtained a divorce and remarried the children's father. This remarriage lasted about two years and ended in divorce. R. T. and the mother now live alone and the two older children live with the father.

Girls

1. B. C., age 14 years, 4 months, IQ 67. This girl has a good attitude toward others, nice disposition, children like her, espe-

cially boys, neat and clean, hair well kept, applies herself to classroom tasks which she does well on third grade level, works in school cafeteria at noon time. She lives with her married sister, aged thirty-five years. At the age of fifty-nine, the mother died of cancer. B. C. was thirteen years old at the time. The father, who was sixty-two years of age at that time, sent this girl and her thirteen year old brother to another state to live with the married daughter. The father now resides with his aged mother. In addition to the sister and brother mentioned above, there are eleven more brothers older than B. C. making a total of fourteen children in the family. None of these brothers and sisters attended high school. One brother is a carpenter, one is a service station attendant, one works at an animal shelter, and two are serving with the U. S. Army; the married sister is a cleaning woman; the occupations of the others are unknown to the writer. The father is a retired odd job man and the deceased mother was a cleaning woman. This girl is an ideal example of "familial" or "sub-cultural" retardation.

2. C. F., age 15 years, 10 months, IQ 56 (this rating is several points too high). This girl is not educable and little accomplishment has been made in performing the simple tasks usually mastered by some trainable children. She has a sweet disposition as long as she is allowed to do as she wishes. When crossed, she yells, screams, and stamps her feet. The majority of these outbursts occur at home. This girl is overweight, has a speech impediment, but is clean and neatly dressed. She is very affectionate toward people she likes. Her retardation is due to premature birth. She and her identical twin were born at six and one-half months. The twin died a few hours after birth. The mother had one normal girl who is now in the mid-thirties by her first marriage. The husband died, and at the age of forty, she married a man several years her senior. Within a year, a daughter was born. This girl has low-normal intelligence and has never achieved very highly academically. When she was eleven months of age the mother gave birth prematurely to C. F. and her twin. Even if the children had been full term babies, there is a possibility, but no positive assurance, that their intelligence range would have been low-normal like that of the sister. The father had no children by his previous marriage.

3. H. V., age 14 years, 9 months, IQ 71, was placed in special class for the first time at the age of fourteen years and three months. She was removed from a regular seventh grade class where she had developed many unsuitable habits—lying, mani-

festations of overt behavior, and an inferiority complex. In addition to this, she was "boy crazy," and she did not want to do any school work. During the six months period here, much improvement has taken place in her manner of dress (skirts no longer four to six inches above the knee), in her attitude toward others, fabrications have been reduced, and she does all school assignments (working at third grade level in most subjects). She is happy with her academic success, and her "boy craze" is fading some. She lives with her non-working mother and heavy equipment operator father. She has a ten year old sister. The family lives in a trailer. H. V. doesn't get along well with sister, mother, or father. The mother and father quarrel frequently because of this girl's escapades. The father blames the mother for the girl's conduct. In this he is correct; the mother exercises no discipline at all during the father's absence from home. The sister attends a regular sixth grade class and is considered normal.

4. M. N., age 13 years, 7 months, IQ 70, small for her age, very well mannered and polite; quiet, pleasant child who craves love and attention, strongly; she is a good student in most academic subjects and is achieving on high third grade and low fourth grade levels. She applies herself diligently to tasks. Her most serious fault is lying about various situations and circumstances when they arise, such as what happened to her lunch money, etc. In consideration of her family history, the child is fortunate to be as she is. The father and mother are unknown. They abandoned her as a baby, along with a brother, who was about two years of age at the time. Both children became wards of the state and were placed in foster homes by the Welfare Department. The girl has been in many foster homes as well as the state orphanage during her few years of life. The brother is severely retarded and attends school for the trainable.

5. S. K., age 14 years, 11 months, IQ 68, neat, clean child, seeks attention in a quiet manner; very slow moving; resists doing anything academic, even at her level of accomplishment. It is felt that she could do simple second grade level work if only she would try. She has a violent temper. When aroused screams, swears, uses foul language and strikes. It is difficult to understand her during a conversation, even though there is no speech defect. She uses a low whining tone. All words seem to run together and sounds are produced deep within the throat. However, she can speak more clearly and concise if she is asked. The characteristics of this child point to "familial" retardation.

The father is a truck driver, unemployed much of the time. The mother is a waitress. There are three other children in the family. A brother, seventeen years old, causes much dissention in the home because he beats the other children severely when he becomes angry. The mother and father quarrel a great deal over this situation and over finances. Two sisters, one seven years of age and one ten years of age, complete the family.

6. F. G., 14 years of age, IQ 72, is a pretty girl, neat, clean, nicely dressed, very cooperative with the teacher. However, she quarrels with some of the other children from time to time. She seems to enjoy an occasional quarrel. She will impulsively reach out and strike or kick a child as he passes by her desk, that is, if she happens to be angry with the child or has quarreled with him. Often she plays games with herself, by making her hand into a fist, then slightly opening the fist and peeking into the palm gradually as the fingers open. While this takes place she talks and laughs. Some words are loud enough to be heard by others. Once she said, "I see a movie star; it is. . . ." Other times she has said, "I see a little baby," and many other statements of things she sees. She does all her class assignments, but rushes very rapidly through them. This results from trying to compete in the regular class. It is very difficult to read her writing. This could be improved if she would slow down and not proceed at such break-neck speed. At present she is reading from a sixth grade level book but comprehension is very poor. She cannot comprehend third grade level written problems, regardless of their simplicity. She is the youngest of four children. The two oldest, a brother and sister, graduated from high school. Both are married. The brother is a carpenter. The sister is a housewife. The third child (girl) is a senior in high school and plans to attend college next year. The father is employed by a railroad. The mother is a nurse's aide. F. G. had meningitis when she was a very small child, which left her mentally retarded.

SUMMARY

There are many forms of mental retardation and it manifests itself in various forms. The way a mentally retarded child grows depends mainly on the basis of his intellectual inadequacy, therefore, many patterns of growth may result. Some consistent patterns will be present in individuals who share a common pathology. Both consistencies and inconsistencies will result from each syndrome. Patterns of mental deficiency cannot be stereotyped.

For simple classification the causes of mental deficiency and retardation may be listed in the four main groups which follows:

1. Antenatal—retardation established before birth, including all familial and congenital types.
2. Prenatal—retardation due to complications arising during the pregnancy.
3. Paranatal—due to injuries at birth.
4. Postnatal—due to injuries, disease, toxic agents, and infection occurring after birth but before completion of mental development.

Various causes which make up the main groups have been discussed in the beginning of this chapter along with actual cases of mental retardation which illustrate some of the causes. Mental retardation should be considered, not so much as a basic problem, but as a symptom of another problem, producing the physical disorder which projects a set of behavioral and social problems.

The main problem in the cause of mental retardation is the matter of evidence and its interpretation. In a special education program the cause is not the important factor. Regardless of why retardation developed, the school must devise ways and methods of giving the children an opportunity to develop to the maximum of their potential.

SELECTED REFERENCES

Albright, F., et al.: Pseudo-hypoparathyroidism. *Endocrinology, 30*:922, 1942.

Baron, D. M., Dent, C. H., Harris, H., Hart, E. W. and Jepson, J. B.: Heredity pellagra-like skin rash with temporary ataxia, aminoaciduria and other bizarre biochemical features. *Lancet, 2*:421, 1956.

Barr, M. W.: *Mental Defectives: Their History, Treatment and Training.* Philadelphia, P. Blakiston's Son and Company, 1913.

Bearn, A. G.: Wilson's disease. *American Journal of Medicine, 22*:747, 1957.

Beidleman, B.: Mongolism: a selective review. *American Journal of Mental Deficiency, 50*:35, 1950.

Benda, C. E.: *Developmental Disorders of Mentation and Cerebral Palsies.* New York, Grune and Stratton, 1952.

Benda, C. E.: *Mongolism and Cretinism.* New York, Grune and Stratton, 1949.

Boldt, W. H.: Postnatal cerebral trauma as an etiological factor in mental deficiency. *American Journal of Mental Deficiency, 55*:345-365, 1951.

Book, J. A.: Fertility trends in some types of mental defects. *Eugenics Quarterly, 6*:113-116, 1959.

Bourne, H.: Does virus encephalitis cause mental defect? *American Journal of Mental Deficiency, 61*:198-203, 1956.

Bower, Eli M. and Rothstein, Jerome H.: Diagnostic problems in mental retardation. *California State Department of Education,* Bull. No. 7, Vol. XXVII, Sacramento, August 1958.

Burt, C.: Inheritance of mental abilities. *Nature, 179*:1325, 1957.

Carter, C. H.: Ten most common types of mental retardation. *Current Medical Digest, 27:10*:61-72, 1960.

Clarke, Ann M. and Clarke, A. D. B.: *Mental Deficiency: The Changing Outlook.* London, Methuen, 1958.

Cook, R. C.: The Rh gene as a cause of mental deficiency. *Journal of Heredity, 35*:133-134, 1944.

Cowie, V. and Coppen, A.: Protein-bound iodine in phenylketonuria. *Journal of Mental Deficiency Research, 3*:94-95, 1959.

Davis, M. E. and Potter, E. L.: Congenital malformation and obstetrics. *Pediatrics, 19*:719-724, 1957.

Day, R. and Haines, M. S.: Intelligence quotients of children recovered from erythroblastosis fetalis since the introduction of exchange transfusion. *Pediatrics, 13*:333-338, 1954.

DeKaban, A., O'Rourke, J. and Cornman, T.: Abnormalities in offspring related to maternal rubella during pregnancy. *Neurology, 8*:387-395, 1958.

Doll, E. A., Phelps, W. M. and Melcher, R. T.: *Mental Deficiency Due to Birth Injuries.* New York, The Macmillan Company, 1932.

Flippen, J. H., Jr.: Cranio-facial dysostosis of crouzon. *Pediatrics, 5*:90, 1950.

Ford, F. R.: *Diseases of the Nervous System in Infancy, Childhood and Adolescence.* Springfield, Illinois, Charles C Thomas, 1944.

Frazier, R. L.: Phenylpruvic amentia. *American Journal of Mental Deficiency, 51*:577-586, 1947.

Gibson, R.: Familial idiopathic methaemoglobinaemia associated with oligophrenia. *American Journal of Mental Deficiency, 61*:207-209, 1956.

Gilmour, D.: The Rh factor: its role in human disease with particular reference to mental deficiency. *Journal of Mental Science, 96*:359, 392, 1950.

Gunther, M. and Penrose, L. S.: The genetics of epiloria. *Journal of Genetics, 31*:413, 1935.

Halperin, S. L.: A clinico-genetical study of mental defect. *American Journal of Mental Deficiency, 50*:8, 1945.

Hilliard, L. T. and Kirman, B. H.: *Mental Deficiency.* Boston, Little, Brown and Company, 1957.

Holt, L. E.: Maple sugar urine disease. *Pennsylvania Medical Journal, 60*:496, 1957.

Hsia-yi-y, D.: Recent developments in inborn errors of metabolism. *American Journal of Public Health, 50*:1653-1661, 1960.

Ingalls, T. H.: Etiology of mongolism: epidemiologic and teratologic implications. *American Journal of Disturbed Children, 74*:147, 1947.

Ingraham, F. D. and Matson, D. M.: *Neurosurgery of Infancy and Childhood.* Springfield, Illinois, Charles C Thomas, 1954.

Jordan, T. E.: Psychological findings in a case of Von Recklinghausen's disease and hyperpituitarism. *Journal of Clinical Psychology, 12*:389-391, 1956.

Kanner, L.: A miniature textbook on feeblemindedness. *Child Care Monthly*, *1*, 1949.

Knehr, C. and Sobol, A.: Mental abilities of prematurely born children at early school age. *Journal of Psychology, 27*:355-361, 1949.

Knoblock, H. and Pasamanick, B.: Syndrome of minimal cerebral damage in infancy. *Journal of American Medical Association, 170*:1384-1387, 1959.

Knoblock, H. and Pasamanick, B.: Seasonal variations in the birth of the mentally deficient. *American Journal of Public Health, 48*:1201-1208, 1958.

Kratter, F. E.: Mental deficiency and its causations. *Disorders of the Nervous System, 21*:163-164, 1960.

Kugelmass, I. N.: *The Management of Mental Deficiency in Children.* New York, Grune and Stratton, 1956.

Lemkau, P., Tietze, C. and Cooper, M.: Mental-hygiene problems in an urban district. *Mental Hygiene, 25*:624, 1941.

Levinson, Abraham and Bigler, John A.: *Mental Retardation in Infants and Children.* Chicago, The Year Book Publishers, Inc., 1960.

Levinson, A.: Medical aspects of mental deficiency. *American Journal of Mental Deficiency, 54*:476-483, 1950.

Levy, S. and Perry, H. A.: Pertussis as a cause of mental deficiency. *American Journal of Mental Deficiency, 52*:217-226, 1948.

Malamud, N.: Recent trends in classification of neuropathological findings in mental deficiency. *American Journal of Mental Deficiency, 58*:438-447, 1954.

Malzberg, B.: Statistical aspects of mental deficiency due to birth traumas. *American Journal of Mental Deficiency, 54*:427-433, 1950.

Maxwell, J.: Intelligence, fertility and the future. *Eugenics Quarterly, 1*:244-274, 1954.

Mohr, O. L.: Dominant acrocephalosyndactyly. *Heredity, 25*:193, 1939.

Morch, E. T.: Inheritance of achondroplasia. *Heredity, 31*:439, 1940.

Neel, J. V.: Genetics and human congenital malformations. *Pediatrics, 19*:749-754, 1957.

Nelson, M. M.: Production of congenital anomalies in mammals by maternal dietary insufficiencies. *Pediatrics, 19*:764-776, 1957.

Norman, R. M.: Primary degeneration of the granular layer of the cerebellum. *Brain, 63*:365, 1940.

Pauling, L.: The molecular basis of genetics. From a paper presented at the meeting of the American Psychiatric Association, Chicago, May 2, 1956.

Pasamanick, B. and Lillienfeld, A. M.: The association of maternal and fetal factors with the development of mental deficiency. *American Journal of Mental Deficiency, 60*:557-569, 1956.

Pasamanick, B. and Lillienfeld, A. M.: The association of mental deficiency: I. Abnormalities in the prenatal and paranatal periods. *Journal of American Medical Association, 159*:155-160, 1955.

Pentschew, A.: The genesis of encephalopathia posterica infantum (kernicterus). *American Journal of Mental Deficiency, 53*:145-152, 1948.

Reed, S. C., Reed, E. W. and Palm, J. D.: Fertility and intelligence among families of the mentally deficient. *Eugenics Quarterly, 1*:44-52, 1954.

Richards, B. W.: Kernicterus. *American Journal of Mental Deficiency, 55*:529-534, 1951.

Richards, B. W. and Rundle, A. T.: A familial hormonal disorder associated with mental deficiency, deaf mutism and ataxia. *Journal of Mental Deficiency Research, 3*:33-55, 1959.

Rollin, H. R.: Personality in mongolism with special reference to the incidence of catatonic psychosis. *American Journal of Mental Deficiency, 51*:219-237, 1946.

Sarason, Seymour B.: *Psychological Problems in Mental Deficiency*. Third edition. New York, Harper and Brother Company, 1959.

Schmid, Werner, Lee, Chi Hao and Smith, Priscilla M.: At the borderline of mongolism: report of a case with chromosome analysis. *American Journal of Mental Deficiency, 66*:3, 1961.

Trapp, E. P. and Himelstein, P.: *Readings on the Exceptional Child*. New York, Appleton-Century-Crofts, Inc., 1962.

Tredgold, R. F. and Soddy, K.: *A Textbook of Mental Deficiency*. Baltimore, The Williams and Wilkins Company, 1956.

Werner, H.: Abnormal and subnormal rigidity. *Journal of Abnormal Social Psychology, 41*:15-24, 1946.

Whitney, E. A.: A pathetic type—the borderline defective. *Journal of Child Psychiatry, 2*:176-186, 1951.

Wildenskov, H. O.: *Investigations Into the Causes of Mental Deficiency*. London, Oxford Press, 1934.

Yacorzynski, G. K. and Tucker, B. E.: What price intelligence? *American Psychology, 15*:201-203, 1960.

Yakovlev, P. I., Weinberger, M. and Chipman, C. E.: Heller's syndrome of a pattern of schizophrenic behavior disturbance in early childhood. *American Journal of Mental Deficiency, 53*:318-337, 1948.

Yannet, H.: The etiology of congenital cerebral palsy; statistical and clinical study. *Pediatrics, 24*:38, 1944.

Yannet, H.: The problem of mental deficiency in children. *Pediatrics, 10*:223-230, 1952.

Section Two

EDUCATION AND TRAINING OF
THE MENTALLY RETARDED

Section two contains four chapters devoted to the education and training of retarded children. Chapter Four deals with provision of special education, assignment to special class, approaches to overcoming instructional problems and guiding principles for teaching retarded children. Chapter Five is concerned with curriculum based on chronological and mental age. Chapter Six deals with social studies, health, and the fine arts. Chapter Seven considers procedures and routines for training the severely retarded.

CHAPTER IV

Education of the Mentally Retarded

BASIS FOR PROVISION OF SPECIAL EDUCATION

WHEN one considers American public education at the present stage of its evolution, one is immediately impressed by influence and impact of democratic personnel administration and supervision on the public schools. Industry has concerned itself with democratic personnel policies and practices to meet the demands of our present-day mobile industrialized and astronaut-conscious society. Consequently, our educational administration at local, intermediate and state levels has undergone many distinct changes to provide special educational services for our children and youth.

Parents should be acquainted with the many types of educational services that can be enjoyed by today's children for the asking. With this in mind we must recognize the importance of placing each child in the educational program that will best fit his own particular needs. Control of public education rests at the State level and each State provides educational services for children according to their classification:

1. Normal.	4. Physically handicapped.
2. Emotionally disturbed.	5. Gifted.
3. Mentally retarded.	6. Educationally handicapped.

With these educational services in focus we may examine further the above classifications.

1. Normal: What is normal in thought, speech or overt behavior depends on three factors: 1) the cultural standards of acceptable thought and conduct as usually defended and maintained by the dominant elements in a given community or society; 2) the nature of the social interaction which furnished the genesis and constant support of the personality. Here, of course, the culturally determined definitions of conduct come into play but many variations are possible in concrete interactions, so that the applied norm tends, with few exceptions, to be at best an approximation of the

73

ideal norm; 3) the manner in which the individual recognizes his own experience, i.e., how his values or frames of reference are set up, that is how he accepts, rejects or modifies this or that cultural definition.[1]

Normal children—in physical traits they are neither near-sighted nor far-sighted, they are neither hard-of-hearing nor with over-sensitive hearing, have no particular speech defect, are of average intelligence, have normal hearts, good teeth, no tendency toward tuberculosis, are free from epilepsy, are not afflicted with encephalitis, have no problems of behavior and no educational disabilities.[2]

2. Emotionally Disturbed Children: Children showing hyper-activity, distracting, attention-getting behavior; or withdrawn, un-cooperative behavior, or those showing both of these tendencies, may be the general definition or description commonly expressed by most teachers. However, Eli M. Bower, research coordinator in the area of emotionally disturbed children for California State Department of Education, Sacramento, California, describes them in terms of their recognition in school. Children who demonstrate one or more of the following characteristics to a marked extent and over a period of time:

1. An inability to learn which cannot be explained by intellectual, sensory or health factors.
2. The inability to build or maintain satisfactory interpersonal relationships with peers or teachers.
3. Inappropriate types of behavior or feelings under normal conditions.
4. A general pensive mood of unhappiness or depression.
5. A tendency to develop illness, pains or fears associated with personal or school problems.[3]

3. Mentally Retarded: For legal reasons, each state has its own definition of mental retardation. For example, the state of Illinois defines the mentally retarded as, any person whose mental abilities have been arrested from birth, or whose mental development

---

[1] Kimball Young: *Personality and Problems of Adjustment.* New York, Appleton-Century-Crofts, Inc., 1952.

[2] Harry J. Baker: *Introduction to Exceptional Children.* New York, Macmillan Co., 1953.

[3] Eli M. Bower: The emotionally handicapped child and the school. *Exceptional Children,* 26:6-11, September 1959.

has been arrested by disease or physical injury occurring at an early age, who requires care, treatment, detention or training in a hospital or under guardian or conservator, for his own welfare or the welfare of others, or the community. Some acceptable definitions of mental retardation proposed by authorities in the field are given in Chapter One.

4. Physically Handicapped Children: These are children who are blind, or partially seeing, deaf, or hard of hearing, speech handicapped, neuromuscular disabilities, cerebral palsy, with convulsive seizures, delicate children (asthmatic, heart disease, tubercular) and multiple handicapped with more than one of these above mentioned disabilities.

5. Gifted Children: When we speak of the gifted, we mean pupils whose potentialities may be greater than those of the bright, but we do not separate the bright from the gifted in any hard and fast manner.[4]

6. Educationally Retarded: These children are backward in one or more of their school subjects but appear to be normal mentally. Their failure is particularly puzzling to parents who recognize them as normal in all respects. These children we must consider as educationally retarded.[5]

WHO ARE THOSE ENTITLED TO AN EDUCATION?

Each boy and girl as a person is worthy. As a pupil, each has an equal educational opportunity. Education is society's way of making the future better than the past and of aspiring for personal and social values that can be realized only in the fruition of the potentialities of all its members. Waste of human resources by default of education must be deplored, but most tragic of all wastes is that which results when education is not provided. These observations are applicable to any segment of the school population and especially to those who are handicapped.[6]

Normal Children: It has been estimated that approximately 80 per cent of all children are normal and attend regular classes

---

[4] Norma Cutts and Nicholas Moseley: *Teaching the Bright and Gifted.* Englewood Cliffs, N. J., Prentice-Hall, Inc., 1957.

[5] Harry J. Baker: *Introduction to Exceptional Children.* New York, Macmillan Co., 1953.

[6] Roy E. Simpson: *Education of Mentally Retarded Minors in Public Schools in California.* Volume XXVIII, No. 8, October 1959.

in our public and private schools. With this in view one can easily understand why the public school systems in our country have until recently been concerned only with providing educational services for normal children. Most everyone is familiar with or at least aware of educational objectives and curriculum content in the field of general education. Parents and the community are interested in the public school's regular program. The "regular program" is a familiar term to the parents and their children are a part of it because they are "normal."

In more recent years modern education has found itself faced with many new and important problems. Most of these have special meaning with respect to exceptional children, and some of them had their origins in the exceptional.

Emotionally Disturbed Children: Efforts to develop special classes in the regular school settings for emotionally disturbed children have been few to date. All schools must somehow cope with the emotionally disturbed children, whether they promote them, demote them, permit them to flounder, exclude them from school or set up special classes for them. Somehow the schools must assume the obligation of developing ways to help them educationally and to cope with their behavior. Most of the states that provide services to emotionally disturbed children do so through legal exclusion and provision for visiting or home teachers.

Some states are offering special classes in the schools to provide for the emotionally disturbed, set up in a comparable way to programs for the mentally retarded. At present, California is conducting a research project to find out how emotionally disturbed children can be identified early and what kinds of programs would be most effective in helping them.

Among other states offering some type of educational services to this class of children are: New York, New Jersey, Massachusetts, Pennsylvania, Illinois and Maryland.

Mentally Retarded: It has been estimated that perhaps one-fifth of all school children are slow learners, but only approximately 3 per cent of all people are mentally retarded. If this proportion is correct for the population as a whole, one can readily see that mentally handicapped school children are very few in contrast to slow learners.

The main objectives of education are self-realization, human relationships, economic security, and civic responsibility. In the education of exceptional children it is an immediate challenge to meet and realize these objectives. This challenge readily becomes clear that all remediable defects must be corrected, that the un-correctable ones be treated intelligently and effectively, and others be substituted and utilized in maximum ways.

The problem of curriculum for the mentally retarded, or any type of the exceptional, offers as great a challenge as the develop-ment of general curriculum for all children. It is the accepted opinion of people in the field of special education that more has been done and continues to be done to educate and train the men-tally retarded child than for any other type of exceptional child. In view of this it is logical to assume that more states have made provision for educational services to the mentally retarded than for children with other handicaps.

Educational programs for mentally retarded children emphasize social and emotional growth, the improved use of motor coordina-tion, visual, auditory and kinesthetic discrimination, as well as the development of language and number concepts and accept-able behavior.

School administrators should bear in mind that, regardless of a child's intellectual level, he must meet certain fundamental re-quirements which are demanded by society if he is to become a part of the community. Therefore, the whole program of educa-tion of the mentally retarded child should be based on the premise that the prime consideration in his education is to make him ac-ceptable to his fellows.

Physically Handicapped: Of the three reasons for educating children who have any type of handicap, the practical one is to keep them out of the state supported institutions, the sentimental one of being sorry for them, and the democratic reason of giving each child a fair chance, the last is the one that should be empha-sized at all times.

The contrast of today's educational programs for the physically handicapped children versus the first special classes for crippled children organized in Chicago at the turn of the century shows some major changes in this area. Formerly, children with crip-pling conditions, special health problems, illness, and orthopedic handicaps would undergo long term treatment and care away from home. Therefore, the instructional programs were instituted in hospitals and convalescent homes. Other programs were started in sanatoriums for tuberculosis patients. Thus the public schools did not begin special classes for physically handicapped children until 1899.

Due to progress made in science, medicine, education and re-habilitation, a tremendous change has been wrought in the picture of crippling conditions and special health problems of children. Various new educational practices and programs have been developed to meet the special health needs of these children. Today, efforts are being made to educate physically limited children in regular classes whenever possible. However, the educational needs of many of these children are so complex that it would be folly to expect them to make progress without the special adaptations that are possible through a special class program. Special classes should be and are, to a greater extent, located in the regular school building. The "team" teaching approach has become a standard operational procedural goal in almost all instances. The teacher, speech correctionist, physician, physical therapist, occupational therapist, school psychologist, social worker and vocational rehabilitation counselor are uniting their efforts in behalf of the "whole" child.

Aiding physically handicapped children to make adjustments in regular class programs is exemplified by New York and other States. They reimburse local school systems for the cost of salaries for special teachers who assist regular classroom teachers in providing educational services for physically handicapped children in regular classes.

The recent survey of handicapped children made by the Western Interstate Commission on Higher Education is a step toward a comprehensive look at the staffing needs for special education in the thirteen states of the Western Compact. This forward look to present and future goals will undoubtedly bring further changes in education for the handicapped.

The Gifted: During the past few years, not only has interest and attention to the educational needs of gifted pupils increased but the concern about quality in programs for such pupils has increased. In the year 1960, a survey was conducted to find out the extent to which states are aiding programs for gifted children. Forty states responded to questions asked during the survey to determine the manner of financial support, curriculum specifications, teacher certification requirements, and leadership functions and services rendered to provide for the gifted.

In 1957, Oregon identified giftedness by an IQ of 135 or higher, and financial aid of $25,000 per year appropriation was made. Again in 1959 new provision was made, setting the IQ at 120 and appropriating $250,000 per year in support.

In 1959, Rhode Island passed a bill to permit the state to reimburse each city and town in an amount not to exceed one-half of the sum of instructional salaries, textbooks, and supplies expended for each approved program for gifted pupils. The General Assembly appropriated for the year ending June 30, 1959, a sum of $60,000 for this purpose.

In 1958, New York State passed a bill providing funds of $200,-000 for the 1958-59 school year to encourage experimental programs in the schools of that state for gifted children. This bill was renewed in January of 1959 for the school year '59-'60.

In June 1959, Illinois passed a bill approving pilot studies by school boards that wished to participate and the sum of $150,000 was allocated for reimbursement to local school districts. On July 17, 1959, Ohio enacted a bill granting the State Department of Education $250,000 for two years to encourage the development of programs for the gifted of that State.

Delaware has a bill under the heading of "exceptional children," which provides for the gifted. West Virginia has passed similar legislation. North Dakota includes the gifted in their law as it now stands. Several states have been working toward definite legislation but have failed to pass the bills. New Mexico, Iowa, and Connecticut have had proposals unacceptable to the voters. California, Michigan, North Carolina and Minnesota are at present conducting studies of programs for the gifted. The State of Washington is among those in which state-level leadership is being provided, both through legislation and through various in-service activities.

Over half of the states have indicated that there are plans for expanding state-level services to the gifted. Other states plan more intensive work in curriculum study so that school district personnel will have further specific guidance in ways to adapt their offerings for the gifted.

We are deeply gratified that the present trend in American Education is concerned for a more adequate education for children variously designated as gifted or talented.

Educationally Handicapped: The educationally handicapped make up a large group of children in our schools. This group does not include educational handicaps caused by physical or mental illness or mental slowness. Reference is being made only to those children whose handicaps are migrant parents, antagonism against school, poor teaching materials and indifferent methods.

Educational retardation occurs in all fields of instruction. Most of the experimental work has been done in the four fundamental subjects of handwriting, arithmetic, spelling, and reading with emphasis upon reading as the most important tool subject.

Most all school systems in our country make provision for the educationally retarded. Some may not have special programs for the other five types of handicaps discussed above, but they will have special instructors referred to as remedial teachers. They will teach remedial reading, arithmetic and language arts. In small cities or districts a teacher may travel between several buildings or he may devote part of his time to regular classes. In the larger systems it is more economical to have the remedial teachers arrange the programs similar to those of the speech correctionist.

This text is limited to educational procedures for the mentally retarded and will not attempt to discuss educational services for the other five above-mentioned classifications.

SELECTION FOR ASSIGNMENT TO A SPECIAL CLASS

The modern public school needs to provide each child with an equal opportunity to develop his abilities for successful and happy living, both for self-realization and as a member of the group. Programs should be planned for those of limited intellectual ability as well as for those with average and superior ability.

If education is for *all*, then schools must take into account the variability of interests, abilities, socio-economic background and physical condition of every pupil. It is essential that the curriculum be modified to serve individual children rather than groups of children. If one subscribes to such a philosophy, particularly if he is acquainted with the difference in capacities that develop among a group of pupils, he can readily understand that to offer the same educational program to all pupils does not give the same opportunities to each one. During the past few years new techniques have been developed for determining individual differences among pupils. Special schools and classes are being developed nation-wide to provide educational opportunities for pupils whose mental capacities make it impossible for them to profit from the regular educational program.

Mentally retarded children have the same physical, emotional and psychological needs as all children. They desire friends and the approval of others. The educator's responsibility to the mentally retarded child is to provide a special program of instruction which offers educational experiences that are worthwhile to each child and are within his limitations of accomplishment. The ideal class for the mentally retarded child must offer a varied curriculum adjusted to the limitations, needs, and abilities of each individual pupil.

The development of effective educational experiences for the retarded requires a thorough understanding of the child and his community. Much of the progress made in the education of these children has resulted from a change in attitude in the community. The public schools, in accepting their responsibility and providing learning activities at the child's level, are giving the mentally retarded child an opportunity to become a self-supporting, contributing member of the community.

Children having IQ's of between 50-75 present an educational problem with which the "average" teacher cannot cope adequately in a class of thirty or more children. The extreme range of behavior, interests and abilities of these children make severe demands upon the teacher's time and energy. She will find it necessary to neglect either the retarded children or the larger group of average children in her class. Therefore, it seems sound practice to place the child with retarded intellectual development under a special teacher for the academic phase of his school life.

Some advantages of the special class are:

1. The class can have fewer enrolled members than average classes, thereby making for greater individualization of instruction.

2. The teacher can be one who is specially trained in teaching the mentally retarded.

3. The curriculum can be planned to provide an educational program more suitable for mentally retarded children.

Adequate diagnosis of these children should be made before they are referred to a special class. Prior knowledge of each child's assets and liabilities is desirable in order to proceed with developing a program in the special class. Care must be taken not to assign pupils educationally retarded because of physical handicaps, emotional disturbances, or lack of school experience to classes for the mentally retarded pupils. A child who is educationally retarded does not have educational problems similar to the child who is mentally retarded.

The parents' cooperation should be obtained prior to assignment to a special class. The parents' acceptance and understanding of their child's retardation and need for special facilities largely determines the success of the special class placement. Promotion and sponsorship of these special classes through local Parent-Teacher Associations are desirable methods to develop acceptance and understanding on the part of the school staff, parents and community.

Making the decision regarding the selection of a child for assignment to a special class for the educable mentally retarded requires more information than an IQ rating supplied by psychological testing. Data of physical condition, combined with the results of psychometric examinations, educational achievement tests, social maturity ratings, and a careful study of developmental, social, and family history provide a basis for judging the suitability of a child for the special class. Decisions based upon thorough analysis of this data could change the entire pattern of life for a child. Therefore, it is of the utmost importance that a capable, competent person deals with pertinent information. We cannot stress this point too strongly.

Factors that are considered in selecting pupils for assignment to special classes for educable mentally retarded minors in the State of California may be found in the following quotation: "Care must be taken that assignment of pupils to special classes for the educable mentally retarded is made on the basis of retarded intellectual development rather than academic retardation. Pupils who are academically retarded because of physical handicaps, emotional disturbances, bilingual difficulties, or inadequate school backgrounds have educational needs that are unlike those of educable retarded pupils. The program for educable mentally retarded pupils is not designed to meet these needs, and therefore academically retarded pupils are not eligible for enrollment in special classes for the educable mentally retarded.

"While the school psychologist has responsibility for identifying mentally retarded pupils and certifying their eligibility for special class placement, assignment of pupils to the special class is the responsibility of the administrative head of the school-district or an employee of the district designated by him."[7]

"The assignment can be made only after a group conference of the psychologist, the school principal, the child's teacher, the school physician or nurse, if any, and other person designated by the administrator."[8]

General procedures used by some Eastern States for selecting pupils for assignment to a special class are:

1. The classroom teacher frequently has the first professional responsibility for locating and identifying the mentally retarded child and for initiating further action. The teacher's referral is usually based on the child's failure to make normal school progress, low test performance on group intelligence tests and low test scores on group achievement tests. Any of these may be combined with an unusual behavior pattern, including social and emotional immaturity and over-age for his group.

2. The next step is the screening of these children by a qualified psychologist. He is likely to administer an individual test of intellectual capacity, a test of school achievement and a test of social maturity. He may also study the personality characteristics of the child.

3. A complete medical examination is also desirable but not always essential.

4. A study of the child's cumulative record proves helpful.

5. The child should be checked for vision or hearing loss.

6. A group conference is desirable. This may include some of the following: the parents, school principal, regular classroom teacher, school supervisor, attendance teacher, superintendent, special class teacher, and special education consultant.

7. Consultation with the parents of the child selected for special class placement is often desirable. The conference with the

---

[7] California Administrative Code, Title 5, Education, Section 183.

[8] *Ibid.*

parents will usually be held by the psychologist, the counselor, the special class teacher or the principal or some staff member already having good rapport with the parents. The person consulting with the parents should have a complete understanding of mental retardation and be objective in approach with sympathy regarding the emotional conflicts of the parents. The parents should be invited to meet the teacher and visit the special class periodically for conferences with the child's teacher. The psychologist plays an important role in a selection of pupils for the special class but the final responsibility for placement rests with the administrative head of the school.

It is essential that only those children for whom the special classes are organized be admitted to them. Classes for the educable retarded lose their purpose and value if they become a "dumping ground" for the trainable child, the slow learner, the educationally retarded, and the socially maladjusted. Neither should we allow the special classroom to degenerate into a panacea for all other ills with which the regular classroom teacher does not wish to cope.

The success of the program for the education of mentally retarded pupils is dependent to a great extent on the proper selection of pupils assigned to the special classes. It is to be remembered that a special class is an administrative device for bringing together a group of pupils, who because of a common difficulty, i.e., retarded intellectual development, have a common need for a particular service. The success of a class for mentally retarded children also depends on the homogeneity of the grouping and the number enrolled in the class. The more homogeneous the class, the larger it can be, and vice versa, the more heterogeneous the class, the smaller it should be. Class size should be determined by the variety of children and chronological and mental ages of the children in the group, rather than by a set standard or traditional grade grouping. It is much more difficult for a teacher to organize a group of children with chronological ages from six to sixteen than to organize a group ranging from six to ten. The recommended chronological age range per class should not be more than four years.

The greatest number of today's mentally retarded children attend special day classes. These classes are held in classrooms of the regular elementary, junior high and high schools. One, two or three classrooms in a given school may be designated for special education. A special teacher, trained in the field of a speciality (mentally retarded, emotionally disturbed, etc.), is provided for each classroom.

The junior high and high school students receive training in the core subjects from special teachers in a special classroom. However, they attend shop, art, physical education, home economics, and music in the regular classrooms with the so-called normal children. The elementary children usually have a self-contained classroom program, but share playground activities with the children from the regular classes.

At present this approach to teaching the educable retarded is endorsed and recommended by many authorities. Association with children from regular classes helps the mentally retarded child to become better adjusted socially. It is evident that he will be in contact with more normal people than with his kind during his life's span. Therefore, it is essential that he learns to live peacefully and contentedly with unexceptional children because he must obey the same laws and conduct business as is required in daily living.

APPROACHES TO OVERCOMING INSTRUCTIONAL PROBLEMS OF THE MENTALLY RETARDED

Regardless of a child's intellectual level, there are certain fundamental requirements which must be met if he is to grow up and become an integral part of his community. Among these skills, reading, writing, knowing how to use ordinary language, and compute simple problems are the basic tools in social communication. These subjects must, therefore, be a vital part of the school curriculum for the retarded child, as well as for the average school child.

The fundamental studies need not, however, be formalized, strictly academic processes. Such an approach is generally discouraged in teaching the retarded child. But since reading is one of the skills so highly stressed in special classes, and also because of the difficulty encountered by mentally retarded children in learning to read, a systematic development of reading techniques becomes a matter of paramount importance.

The question is often asked whether the mentally handicapped child can learn to read. The real problem lies in keeping the reading material within the orbit of the child's experience, which is of necessity limited, and simultaneously provide the required cumulative development of basic skills. There is no special method for teaching the mentally handicapped child to read. However some suggestions will be found in Chapter Five. Experience has shown almost conclusively that whatever method is used, it must be a systematic and consistent development of reading techniques, and should be based upon the following specific factors: the reading readiness, the ability of the child, a development of vocabulary, and the techniques of word recognition; the interest created in the child toward the reading material; appropriate selection of reading material; availability of supplementary material.

In testing for reading readiness, the mental age of a child on a verbal intelligence test, such as the Binet,[9] gives some indication of the child's potential. Studies by Bennett,[10] among others, show that as a rule, mentally handicapped children learn to read up to their mental age expectancy in this area, just as children with normal or superior intelligence do. The confidence of the child should be established and held. He should be introduced to book words at his own level and rate of reading, so that this activity will be a pleasure, and not become another frustration. It must be remembered that in most cases the language and environment of these children have been poorer than that of average children, and in addition, their field of experience has been more limited. Since reading requires a background of both experience and language, these lacks must be recompensed by school instruction and school experiences. The time spent in this initial introduction to the informal and incidental uses of reading, until most of the children are ready for it, will be richly repaid by the greater familiarity with oral language which the children will achieve. Accordingly, planned activities rather than reliance upon incidental learning, are essential to upgrade mentally handicapped children in the concepts of reading and language.

----

[9] Alfred Binet and Simon, T.: *Mentally Defective Children*. New York, Longmans, Green and Co., 1914.

[10] A. A. Bennett: *Comparative Study of Subnormal Children in the Elementary Grades*. Contributions to education, No. 510, New York, Bureau of Publications, Teachers College, Columbia University, 1932.

These activities, preliminary to actual reading exercises, should center about the day-to-day experiences of the child, both at home and in the school. The naming and labeling of simple objects will help the child become familiar with symbols and associate them with objects.

Learning to match words or corresponding pictures or colors, using picture dictionaries, preparing scrapbooks, constructing pens for pets, modeling with clay, making charts, all are opportunities for utilizing purposeful communication in keeping with the character of the project. These help the child develop mental maturation and thus, reading readiness.

Children who are mentally handicapped can also be retarded below their capacities, and may have a genuine reading problem, and need remedial care. For example, a mentally retarded child with a mental age of nine who is a non-reader, may be a remedial case and require special attention. Such children have been reported by Hegge.[11] Another way of recognizing this problem is to compare a child's reading ability with his attainments in other fields on standardized tests. If his reading age is well below that in arithmetic, spelling and other subjects, the possibility is that the child needs remedial work in reading.

The remedial program recognizes the specific disability of the child and devises special techniques to deal with this weakness. It also requires that the teaching be raised to a maximum effectiveness. Actually the techniques used for retarded children are the same as those used for pupils of average intelligence. The chief additional requirement of an appropriate remedial program is a general supply of easy reading material, dealing with interesting subjects and well written.

In the field of arithmetic, the child's experience with number concepts and relationships must be as closely akin to his activities as possible. In conducting a study comparing the arithmetical abilities of a group of normal children of the same mental age to a group of mentally retarded children, Cruickshank[12] found the following differences in retarded children: they did not have the

---

[11] T. C. Hegge: Special reading disability with particular reference to the mentally deficient. *American Association on Mental Deficiency*, *39*:297-343, 1934.

[12] Wm. W. Cruickshank: A comparative study of psychological factors involved in the responses of mentally retarded and normal boys to problems in arithmetic. Doctor's Dissertation, University of Michigan, 1946.

ability to grasp advanced and complicated concepts—finger counting and other immature habits were prevalent, their arithmetic vocabulary was more retarded; they were less capable of understanding basic principles and concepts because of their poor insight and inability to generalize.

An interesting study comparing methods of teaching arithmetic to mentally handicapped children was made by Costello,[13] who divided the children into three groups, each taught by a different method. The methods used were: a) socialization, defined as an active, experienced type of activity; b) sensorization, defined as a method in which concreteness or realism of presentation was used, and c) verbalization, defined as the method conventionally used in the schools in which verbal description is used as a substitute experience. She found that the poorest method of instruction for the improvement of attention, association, vocabulary, comprehension, and judgment was the verbalization method. The most successful method was the socialization method which was closely followed, and in some cases exceeded by the sensorization method.

In using the verbalization method, the handicapped child was told the relationship between various measurements. In using the concrete method, the child was told the relationships of measurements in conjunction with concrete demonstrations. The child actually made the measurements, and so saw the relationships. In using the socialization method, the child learned the concepts in relation to a need. For example, a child baking a cake would learn the meaning of a level tablespoon, parts of a teaspoonful, a heaping teaspoonful, and the same differences in cup measurements, thus giving specific meaning to concrete situations. As a result, there was a better grasp of the concepts in other situations as less dependence was placed upon the transfer from theory to practice.

In most cases these children will accept the study of arithmetic readily enough if they are not forced into it too early or too rapidly. It must include the knowledge, skills, and concepts that are familiar to the child and that will be of value to him now as well as in later life. Equally important is the recognition of the special abilities or disabilities which are a component of the retarded

---

[13] Helen M. Costello: The responses of mentally retarded children to specialized learning experiences in arithmetic. Doctor's Dissertation, University of Pennsylvania, Philadelphia, Pa., 1941.

child so that the proper presentations, amount of practice, and amount of emphasis will be in keeping with their own abilities to learn.

It should constantly be borne in mind that since the whole program of the education of mentally retarded children is based on the premise that the prime consideration in his education is to make him acceptable to his fellows, his vocabulary in every phase of study must be limited to the terms familiar to him and used by him in daily living at his stage of development. Such a vocabulary would include words relating to the following terms:

Size—big, small, huge, tiny

Length of distance—inch, foot, yard, far, near, etc.

Other types of measures—dozen, ounce, quart, cup, pound

Amount—more, less, increase, decrease, some, none, each, double, twice, enough, few, many, part, half

Money—penny, nickel, dime, quarter, dollar

Location—up, down, above, below, right, left, across, etc.

Time—early, late, soon, later, day, week, month

This list is of course endless as applied to the daily experiences of the child, and a properly selected list may be of inestimable value to the mentally handicapped child in helping to understand arithmetic concepts.

The general public concept of mathematical functions necessary in life appears to be:

Time—hour, day, week, month and year

Numbers—ability to read and understand those used in the home, house numbers, room numbers, telephone, etc.

Money—most frequently values were under $100

Various units of measures

The mentally handicapped have need for arithmetical concepts from the time when they can handle simple number problems and this need increases with adulthood. Consequently, every classroom activity in which a number situation arises should be utilized to add to the child's meaningful experiences and further his grasp of the concepts. These should be used to give him additional practice in understanding and manipulating numbers in the basic skills. Therefore, the arithmetical needs should encompass the development, understanding, and use of an arithmetical vocabulary; the development of number concepts and skills; the development of the ability to apply number concepts; the development of an understanding of various units of measurements; and the more difficult understanding of fractional parts. This type of activity program, which has as its purpose the development of a rich fund of informal experience with functional use of numbers, becomes an essential background for more formal systematic instruction later on.

It cannot be stressed too much or too often that "individualized instruction is a key to success in teaching the mentally retarded." Each child must work at his own level of achievement and at his own rate of speed in each subject. Let us examine a class of fifteen retarded children and we shall find each child is reading on a different level, each has his own level of problem-solving, of language skills and of social and civic understanding. More than likely we shall find that no child is accomplishing at a given level in all subjects. He may be reading at the first grade level, doing arithmetic on the third grade level and cannot spell at all.

During the process of individualized instruction, the teacher is confronted with the problem of "what to do with the other fourteen members of the class while she instructs number fifteen in reading." The writer has become aware of this fact, mentally retarded children wish to do what their classmates do at a given time, if they are at all capable of performing the same tasks. With regard to their wishes during the reading period, the child who is capable may read silently and ask the teacher words he does not know until it is his turn for individual reading with the teacher. Another child may be asked to locate five words or two phrases from a chart story or from a given page of a story in the book he fondly calls, "my reader."

Example 1. 1) many, 2) monkey—page 16,—name of book.

Example 2. 1) many monkeys—They live—page 25, name of book.

When the child locates the word or phrase, he copies the complete sentence containing them underlining the word or phrase he was told to locate.

During the arithmetic period, all children may be given their assignments on the proper grade level. Some will be using a textbook; others, teacher-prepared work sheets, and some may be only learning to write the numbers 1 through 10, and so on. After the assignments are given out, the teacher assists each child as he asks for help.

Children who are capable of reading social studies and science texts on a given level may profit from experience gained in the following method: assign certain topics (length of topic to be determined by the child's ability and interest), accompanied by a set of teacher prepared questions on the topic. The child reads to find the answers and writes the answers. Most mentally retarded children cannot see any sense to reading science or social studies for discussion but they will read diligently to find the answers to written questions.

Thus, we conclude that a richness of experience with a few essential instructive processes and concepts has been found to be preferable to a "smattering of ignorance" about many things.

Much has been said and written about the needs of special education in terms of curriculum, methods of instruction, types of classrooms and equipment, research and teacher training, but these speakers and writers avoid mention of one of the most important needs in the field today, that of the trained administrator who has a thorough knowledge of special education and an understanding of the exceptional child. This is the untold pathetic state of affairs in special education today in the year of 1963. Something must be done in the near future to correct this sad situation. At the International Seminar on Special Education held in the Hotel Thayer, West Point, New York on August 25, 26, 27, 1960, Dr. Frances P. Connor, Teacher's College, Columbia University, in discussing what special education is, made the following statement:

> "It is in providing for exceptional children that instruction is needed in order to realize their maximum potential. To do this, of course, the teacher needs help. He cannot do the job alone. In addition to educational supervision, he needs skilled personnel to whom he can direct his questions and to whom he can refer his pupils. He needs some 'give and take,' some opportunity to try out what he is thinking, and I believe he needs some people from other disciplines to question him, to determine the reasons behind what he is doing."[14]

---

[14] Frances P. Connor: World Frontiers in Special Education. Proceedings of the International Seminar on Special Education, International Society for Rehabilitation of the Disabled, New York, 1960.

The above quotation has been offered as a testimonial to the necessity and importance of having qualified administrators in the field of special education. All personnel working with exceptional children which includes the superintendent, his assistants, the director of special education, his assistants, school principal, psychologists, speech therapists, counselors and teachers must understand the exceptional child and his unique problems if the educational program is to achieve the highest possible degree of success.

GUIDING PRINCIPLES FOR TEACHING THE MENTALLY RETARDED

Since the mentally retarded has limited capacity for any abstractions, opportunities for first-hand experiences related to his daily life should be provided so that he may be led to see relations between his experiences in school and his experiences outside of school.

The learning situation should therefore be planned so that the child may take active part in the mental, physical, social and emotional experience of the group. Large units related to the home, neighborhood and community, make it possible to teach reading, language, spelling and art work at different levels.

The program should be planned in somewhat larger periods of time. It should be variable and flexible with plenty of purposeful activity. A certain part of the day should be given to social living, life at school, skills, and recreational activities. The program should also be planned in such a way that the slow child may be one of the group, but working at his own level of accomplishment.

The teacher should make certain each child succeeds in many things that he does. Permissiveness of activity is greater than in a regular class and instruction must be more systematic.

The training must start early and continue as long as it is possible to send him to school, for he must be taught a number of things that the normal child takes for granted or learns in his preschool years. For example, the young mentally retarded child must often be taught such simple things as putting on coats and outer clothing. He must be taught to use buttons, zippers, and other fasteners. Sometimes he is clumsy, his fingers do not work well, and many hours of training may be necessary for him to master such tasks. It must be remembered that the educable mentally retarded child's mental age is approximately one half to three fourths his chronological age, and that the speed of learning is much slower than that of the normal child, about two-thirds as much per year. He should be taught to respect those in authority; he should experience the satisfaction of doing things for others and have an attitude of good will toward other people. He should be encouraged to use good manners, to observe small courtesies, and good social habits in his everyday living.

The capacities, interests, and needs of retarded pupils should be considered. In dealing with retarded pupils one will discover that not only are their interests less varied but also that they are handicapped in their ability to learn to appreciate and enjoy more fully the interests they do have. Units of instruction must be organized in such a manner as to provide further development of the interests and needs of each child in accordance with his ability, with the aim of preparing mentally retarded pupils to live a useful social life.

For young pupils, simple units of school work may be organized around social experiences that present an opportunity to discuss and dramatize home, school and community relationships. Older pupils should have an opportunity to engage in many activities related to situations that they will be expected to meet in adult life. Each of these will need to be planned on the level of each child's ability to comprehend. The mentally handicapped pupil can be trained in punctuality, steadfastness, loyalty, cleanliness and other qualities, and thus become an asset to the community. All this takes time, of course, and although the mentally handicapped child may not be able to tell us what eight times ten equals, he will be learning how much change he should receive if he buys a twenty-five cent box of cookies and he gives the grocer fifty cents. To learn about buying in a store the children should visit a store and see what happens there. Then they will make a store in their classroom and take turns being first the buyer and then the grocer. Through such activities as these, they learn practical things such as how to make change, how to meet people, how to express themselves, and so on. They learn by doing. At all ages, emphasis is placed on the practical aspect of his education. He is taught to do the best he can with what he has, at the same time knowing as nearly as possible his limitations. Lessons should be short and repeated often. Repetition is essential and does not seem to become boring to the mentally retarded children. For them learning is a systematic, step by step process.

In the pre-adolescent years, new problems are encountered. The knowledge of right and wrong often comes slowly to mentally retarded youngsters. It will take considerably more explaining to the mentally retarded child that one must be considerate of the other fellow's rights than will be necessary for the normal child. Social problems involving boy and girl relationships must be explained painstakingly and tactfully by the teacher and at times, rehearsed and corrected.

Opportunity for social experiences should be provided to help develop socially acceptable habits. Their inability to pursue advanced academic study or to prepare for trades of a technical nature limits their job opportunities. In order to compete in the labor market for jobs that they can do, it is necessary to get along well with their associates, respect the rights of others, and respect the laws of their country. They must learn how to enjoy leisure hours through hobbies or in fellowship with others in group activities. Social experiences must be an important part of the entire curriculum. These children do not have the ability to deal with abstract concepts and ideas and cannot be expected to master all the academic skills required of pupils whose intelligence is normal. Only skills that will help them to develop into useful adults should be stressed. These should be presented through concrete experiences that are meaningful to the pupils.

"A teacher of mentally retarded children will find the following principals to be of value in planning her program":

1. Provide experience at child's mental level.
2. Help pupils to select interesting activities.
3. Use concrete situations and materials—not abstract.
4. Provide repetitive drill to reinforce instruction.
5. Provide for use of all avenues of learning.
6. Limit periods of formal instruction to short duration.
7. Motivate individual children by capitalizing on their particular abilities and achievements.
8. Use play and dramatization whenever possible to produce interest in instruction.
9. Encourage oral expression.
10. Give attention to abilities—do not try to correct irremedial defects.

11. Help each pupil to evaluate his own work.

12. Provide many group projects.

13. Use an individualized tutoring approach when necessary.[15]

The writers deem number thirteen as one of the most vital steps in the entire program of teaching the educable mentally retarded.

Study of the personality, handicaps, problems and abilities of these children must be done by the teacher. This should be a continuing and constant process. The teacher will need to search for new interests, new approaches and new techniques. She should strive to adjust the school program to meet changing pupil needs. Much of her time will be utilized in searching for materials and situations which will promote her objectives. Curriculum for the mentally-retarded children must be organized according to the nature and needs at each age level and the instruction should be adapted to the growth levels of the children.

Emphasis should be placed upon planning the best education that can be given over a period of nine or ten years rather than the completion of any grade requirements. The information, habits, and attitudes necessary for wholesome participation in community life must be acquired, if at all, during the period of compulsory school attendance since few mentally retarded children remain in school beyond that time. Chronological age, as well as mental age and intelligence quotient, should be a guiding factor in determining curriculum content.

For educational purposes it is wise to divide mentally retarded pupils into three classifications: primary, intermediate, and secondary. The primary group usually consists of pupils with a mental age between three and six and one-half years and a chronological age between six and ten. The intermediate group usually has pupils with a mental age between six and nine and one-half and a chronological age between ten and twelve. The secondary group is composed of pupils with a mental age from eight to twelve and a chronological age between twelve and eighteen years.

The mental age is doubtless the most important single factor for consideration in classification of a pupil, but many other factors including the physical, social and emotional characteristics of the pupil must also be considered. This classification is based

---

[15] Ray Graham: The Illinois Plan for Special Education of Exceptional Children. *The Educable Mentally Handicapped Circular*, Series B, No. 12, p. 17, Springfield, Ill., Supt. of Public Instruction, 1950.

upon consideration of the chronological age of the child and the interests and abilities which are determined by physical maturity. It also takes into consideration the mental age and IQ in that the instruction within the chronological age group should be adjusted to meet the varying capacities of the children.

Certain facts must be taken into consideration as a basis for planning school programs for these children whatever the age group. One of the first is a thorough knowledge of the child's abilities in light of his chronological age. The following table may be of assistance in planning:

	Chrono. Age (Range in Years)	Mental Age (Range in Years)	Capacity (Grade-level)
Primary	6-10	3- 6½	Nursery-Kdgn.
Intermediate	10-12	6- 9½	1-3
Secondary	12-18	8-12	3-6

When children have a mental age below six years, regardless of their chronological age, emphasis should be placed upon pre-reading experiences, such as motor and sensory training, personal hygiene and habit training, improvement of speech, emotional control, rhythm, drawing, and other simple activities at school and in the home. The mental age of twelve years is the probable highest ability to be attained by a mentally retarded child.

While planning the instructional program the teacher should be cognizant of the fact that many of the children in her group do not have and never will attain this level of mental development. The teacher should be very honest with a pupil at all times, in regard to everything, especially his limited ability. He must understand his limitations, accept them and learn to live with them.

Many educators in the field of mental retardation favor a developmental program rather than a remedial version of a normal program for mentally retarded children. The writers feel that good curriculum for these pupils should maintain careful balance between general education and the unit method to acquire basic skills and transfer them to the behavior areas.

SUMMARY

Our educational administration at local, intermediate, and state levels has undergone many distinct changes to provide special educational services for our children and youth.

Many types of educational services can be enjoyed by today's children for the asking. Each state provides special services for children according to their classification:

1. Normal.
2. Emotionally disturbed.
3. Mentally retarded.
4. Physically handicapped.
5. Gifted.
6. Educationally handicapped.

However, the discussion of services has been limited to educational procedures for the mentally retarded. Each boy and girl as a person is worthy and entitled to an education. As a pupil, each has an equal educational opportunity.

The modern public school seeks to provide each child with an equal opportunity to develop his abilities for successful and happy living, both for self-realization and as a member of the group. Education's responsibility to the mentally retarded child is to provide a special program of instruction which offers educational experiences that are worthwhile to him and are within his limitations of accomplishment.

Children having an IQ of between 50 and 75 present an educational problem with which the "average" teacher cannot cope adequately in a class of thirty or more children. The extreme range of behavior, interests, and abilities of these children make severe demands upon the teacher's time and energy. Consequently, she must either neglect the retarded or the larger group of average children. Therefore, it seems sound practice to place the child with retarded intellectual development under a special teacher for the academic phase of his school life.

Adequate diagnosis should be made before placing a child in a special class. The selection of a child for assignment to special classes requires more information than an IQ rating supplied by psychological testing. Findings on physical condition, combined with the results of psychometric examinations, educational achievement tests, social maturity ratings, and a careful study of developmental, social, and family history provide a basis for judging the suitability of a child for special classes. Decisions based upon thorough analysis of this data could change the entire pattern of life for a child. Therefore, it is of the utmost importance that a capable, competent person deal with pertinent information.

Regardless of a child's intellectual level, there are certain fundamental requirements which must be met if he is to grow up and become an integrated part of his community. Among these skills, reading, writing, knowing how to use ordinary language, and knowing how to compute simple problems are the basic tools in social communication.

The fundamental studies need not, however, be formalized, strictly academic processes. Such an approach is generally discouraged in teaching the retarded.

It should be borne in mind that the whole program of education of mentally retarded children should be based on the premise that the prime consideration in his education is to make him accepted and acceptable to his fellows. Individualized instruction is a key to success in teaching the mentally retarded. Each child must work at his own level of achievement and at his own rate of speed in each subject. Some problems in reading, arithmetic, science and social studies, along with suggested solutions, have been discussed in this chapter.

We are confronted today by a gigantic problem which is seldom, if ever, discussed publicly—the lack of trained administrators in the field who have a knowledge of special education and an understanding of the exceptional child. Many at the administrative level seem to attach little importance to special preparation in this field even though they are associated with and are in charge of these programs. A change of attitude toward special children, special teachers, and special education must be wrought before the problem can be solved.

Children learn by doing and this particularly applies to the mentally retarded child. At all ages, emphasis should be placed on the practical aspect of his education. Teach him to do the best he can with what he has and to recognize his limitations. For educational purposes, it has been deemed wise to divide mentally retarded pupils into three classifications: primary, intermediate, and secondary according to chronological age.

However, the mental age is the most important factor for consideration in teaching these children. The writers feel that good curriculum for them should maintain careful balance between general education and the unit method to acquire basic skills and transfer them to the behavior areas.

CHAPTER V

Curriculum Based on Chronological and Mental Age

THE PRIMARY GROUP

CHILDREN of this group are usually six to ten chronologically and will have a mental age of three to six and one-half years. To teach these children to live in a social environment is far more important than to attempt to teach them to read. During this process of social adjustment, the child will be getting ready to read. As he grows intellectually he will approach the task with an enriched background of meaningful experiences, enlarged speaking vocabulary, a lengthened and more stable span of attention and improved muscular coordination. The following experiences can be used to advantage with this group of children:

1. Habit training as emphasis upon personal cleanliness and neatness, proper toilet habits, care of such personal property as coat, hat, overshoes, shoes, etc.
2. Social experiences such as talking about relationships involving father, mother, baby, sister, brother, schoolmates, school safety officers, firemen, policeman, and visiting nurse.
3. Such sense training as recognition of a name when called; matching shapes, colors, sizes and position of objects; picture completion, puzzles; watching natural phenomena such as sky, clouds, trees and sunlight; recognition of things by sound, smell and touch; recognition of food elements by taste; and recognition of primary colors.
4. Speech training with emphasis upon clear enunciation and correction of baby talk, lisping and other speech defects.
5. Muscular coordination exercises such as marching, dancing and outdoor games; the use of large muscles to the accompaniment of musical instruments or singing; exercises such as walking a balanced rail, stepping through the rungs of a slightly raised horizontal ladder and walking over a stile of three or four steps.

6. Nature study that will acquaint the children with common pets, flowers, trees, and seasonal weather changes.
7. Such training as hammering nails into blocks of wood; carrying household articles as needed, stringing spools, beads and buttons; coarse needle work on materials that have a design; cutting paper and cloth according to a pattern to make leaves, flowers, animals, and so on; carrying and stacking large blocks.

These activities and experiences of similar types can be used as the foundation for training in oral language. They can be made more effective if they are integrated into a purposeful program of work planned about a center of interest. Many games and activities of short duration, which children play spontaneously, can be structured for a particular goal. Some improvement may be expected in performing muscular and manual activities. As the child grows older in years, practice improves physical coordination and develops ability to perform useful tasks. The objective of the whole program is to make the individual, however low his intelligence may be, happier and more comfortable as well as useful by helping him to contribute something to the society of which he is a part.

THE INTERMEDIATE GROUP

These children are usually from about ten to twelve years chronologically. They are ready for experiences in reading, writing and numbers. They should be given an opportunity to make progress in these fields according to their several abilities without the sacrifice of much more important social values. Class curriculum is more structural than that of the primary group. It stresses the learning of tool subjects and experiences in the areas of everyday living. The children help plan many of the activities.

THE SECONDARY GROUP

This group consists of children twelve to eighteen years of age chronologically. The secondary class emphasizes the areas of living as the children are preparing themselves for life outside of school. Mentally retarded adolescents are capable of profiting by such instruction and should receive special assistance with:

1. Appreciation of social and civic values and participation in social and civic activities either in the community or school.

2. Manual activities in the shop, the kitchen and laundry, and in a variety of types of occupational experiences.
3. Health, physical training, including sports and games. A child lacking in health cannot do the work of his peers, therefore much emphasis should be placed upon the mentally retarded child's physical condition. Not only should he be taught to observe all the health rules, but he should be placed in the care of a physician, ophthalmologist, orthodontist or whomever might be indicated to improve the child's health.
4. Preparation for homemaking through experiences in the usual housekeeper responsibilities, household budgeting, child care, home beautification and the general repair work so often needed around and in the home.

Any contribution of reading, arithmetic, music, art, literature, science and other content subject to those goals is justifiable provided it is planned on the level of the pupil's ability to comprehend and does not take up the time that should be given to major objectives of a practical nature. Children in the secondary group having a mental age of below nine years will obviously work on primary levels of academic experiences while those having a mental age above nine years will be able to achieve on a higher level. The greater part of their time and energy should be given to those activities that are definitely related to the situations they will face when they leave school. Work of an academic nature should be reduced to a minimum.

The experience type unit carefully balanced by general education would seem to provide the most adequate curriculum. Units of instruction might include the home, the neighborhood, neighborhood helpers, employment, and how to spend income and leisure time. Some retarded children will have an excellent opportunity for success in the hand-skilled or semi-skilled ranks because normal standards will be more nearly attained in physical and social areas than in mental development. The individualized or child-centered approach is essential. Instruction should be a systematic, step by step method using concrete presentation of material. Make the instruction meaningful and useful. Repetition is of primary importance and must be used more frequently than with the normal. This is because there is usually little transfer of training. Development of motivation on the part of the child is essential; stress approval, praise and success.

Primary Level Reading

Chronological Age—6-10   Mental Age—3-6½

Education in the primary grades must take into consideration the fact that mentally retarded children are deficient in language development, speech production and visual and auditory discrimination. In the area of language development emphasis should be placed on increasing the speaking vocabulary, growth in concepts and word meanings, and in improved ability in self-expression. Visual and auditory discriminations, ability to observe and remember accurately, must be developed because these skills are definite reading readiness factors. Speech defects are common in retarded children. Provision of the following can serve a useful purpose:

1. Opportunity for maturation through self help.
2. Development of imagination and expression of ideas and feelings.
3. Opportunity for social development.
4. Ample opportunity to develop intellectual abilities.

READING READINESS

Reading readiness is especially emphasized during the foundation period for formal teaching of communication skills. The following activities may be helpful:

1. Beginning reading readiness (period of rapport).
   a. Provide for and encourage opportunities for the children to speak naturally about things in which they are highly interested.
   b. Telling stories and listening to the teacher relate them.
   c. Dramatization in which simple parts are memorized.
   d. Carrying on telephone conversations.
   e. Increasing the child's vocabulary through gradual introduction of new words related to activities.
   f. Excursions to nearby places of interest followed by discussion of what was observed.
2. Developmental state of reading readiness—developing visual and auditory discrimination and memory.
   a. Visual discrimination activities—

Games involving the finding of likenesses and differences between objects.

Grouping pictures and objects according to similarities and differences.

Matching colors.

Matching pictures with pictures.

Matching words with the same words on a chart.

b. Auditory discriminations—

Blindfold a child and have him identify classmates by the sound of their voices.

Have blindfolded children attempt to name objects in the room which the teacher has tapped with a pencil.

Listening to records which have many common sounds— have the children identify them.

c. Memory—

Teach simple jingles and nursery rhymes.

Ask child to recall experiences which happened in the recent past.

Tell a simple story and have pupil recall the essential parts.

3. Advanced level of reading readiness.

a. Child learns to print his name.

b. He can distinguish many kinds of labels—labels on objects in classrooms, common signs—

thin ice	crosswalk	entrance	girls
keep off	fresh paint	hands off	office
stop, go	coat room	door	push
high voltage	exit	boys	pull

c. Understand street signs.

d. Understand directional signs in theaters and buildings.

e. Use of flash cards with pictures.

f. Understand use of bulletin board.

4. Some other reading readiness activities.

a. Continue to use field trips and audio-visual aids.

b. Establish activity areas in the classroom.

c. Make word cards.

d. Draw pictures and discuss them.

e. Use alphabet picture books for sound of letters.

f. Match dominos.

g. Finger play exercises with music or rhymes.

Intermediate Level Reading

Chronological Age—10-12   Mental Age—6½-8

When a child reaches this point in his education it is wise to ask two things:

1. Is the child ready to read?
2. Does he have a desire to learn to read?

These questions can be answered by two methods: standardized tests and by teacher observation. Some of the reading readiness tests which have proven valuable are:

Gate's Reading Readiness Test
Metropolitan Readiness Test
Monroe Reading Aptitude Tests

Informal teacher-made tests are useful. Various other reading readiness tests may be used. Teacher observations should answer such questions as:

1. How is the child's vision?
2. How is the child's hearing?
3. Is his motor coordination adequate?
4. Is he able to make adequate auditory discrimination?
5. Has he developed adequate language?
6. Does he have fairly good work habits?
7. Is the child socially and emotionally mature?
8. Is he able to follow from left to right?
9. Does he express any interest in learning to read written material?

When a majority of the above readiness signs are present, the child will in all likelihood have achieved a mental age of at least six and one-half years. This is essential before beginning to teach him formal reading. At this stage in development, the children should have had an extensive reading readiness background. Emphasis should now be placed on the more formalized teaching of reading. A slow systematic approach is more likely to be successful.

Children see whole things first and details later. Thus, they are able to learn words without noting the details and phrases without knowing the individual letters. A basic sight vocabulary should be acquired as early as possible to enable the child to attain success in initial reading experiences. It will also increase his comprehension of material in the primary texts.

Using flash cards containing the basic words and employing these words in games and stories is very helpful. The experience chart is a valuable method of building vocabulary. A simple routine to follow is: situation—Sue comes to school telling about a kitten that has been given to her. The class can make a story about Sue's kitten. On the chalk board, the teacher will write the story as told by the children. Short sentences as:

Sue has a kitten.
The kitten is white.
He can say, "Mew, mew."
His name is Puff.

The above is composed of short words and short sentences, all words related to the child's experiences and are within the child's ability. These are the essentials of a good experience chart. The teacher can transpose this material to newsprint or oaktag. The child may copy it for use in his own story booklet. Children can draw or use cutout pictures to illustrate their story books and charts. It is important that they be able to interpret pictures and tell stories about them. Materials and exercises such as these motivate children to begin to read simple books.

Use the Dolch[1] basic word list as a core to develop charts and booklets in the following activities:

1. Holidays.
2. Class health records.
3. Things to do.
4. Daily news.
5. Safety signs and rules.
6. Record of an experiment.
7. Word picture dictionary.
8. Flash card games.
9. Illustrations for stories.
10. Charts, home and class experiments.

Emphasize word attack skills. They enable a child to achieve independence in reading new words. When a pupil has acquired a basic sight vocabulary of fifty or more words, the phonetic approach should be used.

1. Teach sound blending with simple words at first—"CAT," "DOG."
2. Use words from child's own vocabulary to derive sounds which are found in new words.
3. Emphasize words that a child will find in his reading.
4. Remember that words not phonetic in character must be taught by sight.

---

[1] Edward Dolch: The basic sight vocabulary cards. Champaign, Ill., The Garrard Press.

5. Avoid teaching rules—these only confuse mentally retarded children.

Next, increase practice in phonetic word attack skills:

1. Help the child to blend the sounds of letters together softly to pronounce words.
2. Encourage independent word attack.
3. Help children to make generalizations about word sounds.
4. Do not "over-use" phonetic drill.

Other methods related to phonics are structural analysis, learning prefixes, suffixes and syllables. Teachers! Beware of confusing these children by presenting too many ways of attacking words. Do not use any of these to excess.

Secondary Level Reading

Chronological Age—12-18   Mental Age—8-12

The secondary level is the stage at which experience of a broader social nature must be integrated with improved facilities in communication. Depending upon the individual child's level of achievement in reading, the following practical activities are designed to increase efficiency:

1. Development of better reading habits through a wider use and selection of reading materials.
   a. Newspapers.
   b. Magazines.
   c. Use of the library.
   d. Comic books.
   e. Subscriptions to weekly publications geared to interests and reading level of these children.
2. Increase reading range for information and pleasure.
   a. Reading road maps, time tables, directories.
   b. Use of tables of contents.
   c. Use of index in books.
   d. Procedure to withdraw books from library.
   e. Forming book clubs.
   f. Use of dictionary.
   g. Reading warning and danger signals.
   h. Learning to read directions and follow them.
3. Increase the use of word recognition skills.
   a. Use of suffixes and prefixes.
   b. Visual and phonetic analysis.
   c. Encourage practice in independent word attack.

      d. Context clues.
      e. Learn some phonetic rules.
  4. Increase silent reading speed.
      a. Use teacher-made exercises designed to fit an individual need.
      b. Strive for accuracy.
      c. Strive for independence in word recognition.
      d. Make frequent checks for comprehension.
      e. Integrate reading with other tool subjects such as arithmetic, social studies, music, art, etc.

It is not advocated that these subjects replace the reading program but rather to supplement it.

Speed has not been emphasized at the intermediate level but it may prove interesting to experiment with it at the secondary level.

Primary Level Spelling

Chronological Age—6-10   Mental Age—3-6½

Spelling as such is not introduced at this level. It will not be introduced until the mentally retarded child has acquired the equivalent of beginning second grade reading.

Intermediate Level Spelling

Chronological Age—10-12   Mental Age—6½-8

Mentally retarded children need to be able to spell only a minimum of words. Only words that he will use in current life experiences or in adult life should be taught. These should come from his daily experiences so that he has need to learn them. Spelling is closely related to the learning of reading and involves auditory and visual memory and motor ability. Therefore, the teacher must be careful not to teach spelling too early. Some children in this group will not be ready for spelling. A child should be able to work at a second grade level and show some handwriting ability before formal spelling instruction is begun.

A multiple teaching approach seems best. This includes:

  1. Visual method.
      a. Child sees the word.
      b. A variety of places should be used for word presentation—chalkboard, charts, books, labels in the room.

2. Phonetic method.
   a. Child hears the word as a whole.
   b. He hears the word in syllables.
   c. He hears individual letter sounds in the word when possible.
   d. He hears the word in a sentence.
3. Visuo-memory method.
   a. Teacher writes word on chalk-board or on paper.
   b. Teacher pronounces a word clearly and then child says it.
   c. Give the child ample time to study the word.
   d. When he is sure of a word, it is erased and he writes it from memory.
   e. Have him turn the paper over and write it a second time.
   f. Teacher arranges a natural, meaningful situation in which the child uses the word he has learned. Review.
4. In view of the above approach a good method is:
   a. See the word.   d. Write the word from memory.
   b. Hear the word.   e. Use the word.
   c. Say the word.   f. Use the word in context.
5. Other techniques.
   a. Teacher-made flash cards from Dolch's list.
   b. Words chosen from other subjects (reading, social studies, etc.).
   c. Word booklets made by the children.
6. Things to bear in mind.
   a. Spelling instruction should be adapted to: mental maturity of the individual child; the needs of the child.
   b. Begin by teaching one or two words at a time—never more than five.
   c. Avoid meaningless drill.
   d. Frequent review and use of words.
   e. Be sure the words are related to reading and writing lessons.

Secondary Level Spelling
Chronological Age—12-18   Mental Age—8-12

At the secondary level, the above mentioned practices should be continued but expanded to include material of a more practical nature for the child's later vocational life. Some suggestions for expansion of curriculum are:

1. Learning words that will be necessary in letter writing.
   a. Addresses.   c. Enclosures.
   b. Salutations.   d. Dates.

2. Learning words that will be necessary to vocations.
   a. Applications and various forms.
   b. Order blanks.
   c. Receipts.
   d. Money orders.
   e. Withholding statements.
   f. Insurance applications.
   g. Income tax forms.
   h. License applications.
   i. Budgets and accounts, etc.

Words given to these children should be drawn from lists for which they have a need and should be presented by using the above mentioned multiple teaching approach. No word should be given unless the child understands and can use it correctly in a sentence. There is no known work-book which will serve the spelling needs of the mentally deficient people.

ORAL AND WRITTEN LANGUAGE

It has been observed that the one basic skill which is most markedly underdeveloped in our mentally deficient children is that of oral communication. This is the skill upon which the other skills depend. The ability to communicate orally is the main goal of language development for these children. All goals in language development center around the production of clear speech and expression in a variety of social and vocational situations. Classroom experiences will enable a child to increase his speaking vocabulary.

In teaching oral language, these opportunities are valuable:

1. Story telling.
2. Dramatic play.
3. Telling of actual experiences.
4. Discussions and informal "bull sessions."
5. Group projects.
6. Choral exercises.

The teacher should consistently expect a realistic level of clarity of expression. Be careful to emphasize spontaneous, rather than mechanical speech. Before a child can use written language, he must have the ability and background in the use of oral language. When the child feels the need and wants to write about some activity in the classroom, he will be ready to learn the necessary words and phrases. This is related to the teaching of reading and should grow in complexity as the child's ability in reading, spelling and speaking develops.

At the primary level, written language must be relatively simple and emphasize the production of manuscript writing which is neat and clear enough to be read by others. When a child matures and enters the intermediate class, cursive writing should be taught with communicating ideas to others in mind.

On the secondary level, spoken and written language is centered around filling out forms, applying for jobs and letter writing. Approaches involving the use of radio and television type skits prove helpful. Socio-dramas based on situations which have been or will be encountered by the students have been used with success. These involve all the communication skills and are invaluable in drawing together the skills acquired in the tool areas. The following areas in written communication may be taught in varying degrees or difficulty depending upon the individual child.

1. Writing the simple declarative sentence.
   a. Ask questions which must be answered with sentences.
   b. Teach simple punctuation such as period at the end of statements, question marks at the end of questions.
   c. Any sentence must begin with a capital letter.
2. Instruction in grammar.
   a. Use examples of correct and incorrect grammar, help children identify them.
   b. Have pupils list errors they have made in correct usage and write the corrections.
3. The written paragraph.
   a. When a child has learned to write sentences, give him ample practice in putting them in proper paragraphs.
   b. Help him to write about experiences, movies, pictures, games he has played or seen, etc.
4. Establish understanding of simple letter-writing forms.
   a. Give practice in letter-writing to friends and relatives.
   b. Letters of application for jobs (business forms).
   c. Thank you notes, other formal notes.
5. Writing of labels on bulletin board of exhibits and other materials.
6. Keeping of written records of weather, attendance, health checks, etc.

What should the graduate of a secondary level class for E.M.R. (educable mentally retarded) children be expected to have learned in the area of communication skills? Mental age is the key to answering the question. The pupil whose chronological age is almost twice as much as his mental age will have achieved but a second or third grade reading ability. After he leaves school he will find that reading material written at his level is practically non-existent and he will tend to forget what he has already learned. However, reading for information and protection will still be possible. The child whose mental age is about three-fourths of his chronological age may be reading at the fourth or fifth grade level and will therefore be able to read the newspaper and some magazines.

In the areas of spelling and writing it is expected that most of the pupils will be able to write simple letters and complete commonly used forms. They should be able to locate names in a telephone directory and words in a dictionary. Of all the communication skills, oral language is most important because it is the one most widely used by these children. Therefore, much emphasis should be given to development of a simple, suitable vocabulary. The purpose and importance are to provide means of expression and communication; to equip the child better to communicate with others; to develop listening skills and to stimulate auditory and visual memory; to promote better personal, family, community, and social adjustment; to promote a sense of need for speech and to help him develop verbal concepts.

DEVELOPING NUMBER SKILLS

In arithmetic as in other areas the slow learner is not ready as early as is the normal child. He cannot progress as rapidly nor grasp the concepts as soon. But during his school years he can develop sufficient maturity to learn enough arithmetic to be functional in family and community life. The acquisition of the basic essential number skills is necessary to help mentally retarded children to become successful members of society. A special class teacher asks, "What are the arithmetic skills which adults find most useful?" A study by G. M. Wilson reported by Kirk and Johnson[2] gives at least a partial answer. This study shows that arithmetic problems encountered by four thousand adults in a period of two weeks were:

1. Eighty-three per cent of these were concerned with the purchase and disposition of goods.

[2] Samuel A. Kirk and Orville Johnson: *Educating the Retarded Child.* New York, Houghton, Mifflin Co., 1951, p. 281.

2. Six per cent with the use of money but not related to No. 1 above.
3. Six per cent dealt with quantitative measurements (lengths, widths, weights, amounts).

Most of the processes used were multiplication, addition, use of common fractions, making out or understanding accounts, and the use of simple denominate numbers. It seems that the minimum arithmetic requirements in adult life are relatively few, but nonetheless, they are important. Needed concepts are those related to:

1. Time.
2. Money and accounts.
3. Simple fractions.
4. Units of measurement.
5. Practical problems of buying, selling, and saving.
6. Basic arithmetic processes of addition, subtraction, multiplication and division.

Retarded individuals are limited in the amount and type of arithmetic which they can learn. Special education instructors must take this into consideration and teach only the basic essentials in a systematic, concrete manner so as not to discourage and overburden them. Few retarded children will ever go beyond the fifth grade level in this subject. The majority of them achieve between the third and fifth grade level.

GUIDING PRINCIPLES IN TEACHING ARITHMETIC TO THE MENTALLY RETARDED

According to Kirk and Johnson, some of the more important principles of teaching arithmetic to the mentally retarded are:

1. Find the level where the child can succeed and have him proceed at his own speed.
2. Present all material in a simple, precise, and understandable manner always keeping in mind the slower learning ability of the children and pacing the material to the child's learning rate.
3. Give ample individual help and attention (encouragement).
4. Use concrete materials as often as possible.
5. Teach in easy one-at-a-time systematic steps with repetition.
6. Develop understanding, then accuracy, then speed.
7. Provide motivation.

8. Teach essentials only.
9. Establish individual standards for the quality of work which each individual pupil will strive to attain.
10. Inasmuch as possible, guide transfer from concrete to abstract.
11. Use objective test data to measure pupil progress.
12. Be patient, understanding, and sincere.
13. Use a systematic, not individual approach.
14. Do not over-stress arithmetic fundamentals—emphasize the development of problem solving skills.[3]

Special class teachers find that by excessive drill some mentally retarded children can become adept in addition, subtraction, multiplication, and division skills. In simple problems requiring arithmetic reasoning, these same pupils are unable to apply their knowledge of arithmetic fundamentals. Drill is very essential but it must not replace training in arithmetic reasoning where they are given opportunity to solve meaningful, concrete oral and written problems.

ARITHMETIC READINESS FOR THE RETARDED

Arithmetic cannot be learned until the pupil has some understanding of quantitative thinking. The mentally retarded child is deficient in the functions, abilities, and achievements which are necessary before a child is ready to learn arithmetic. Before formal arithmetic can be undertaken, the child must have the ability to think in terms of quantity, count and understand number concepts, recognize simple grouping such as one and two, and understand and recognize written numbers.

Primary Level

Chronological Age—6-10   Mental Age—3-6½
Grade Expectancy—Nursery and Kindergarten

Some educators have postulated that children go through four stages in arithmetic readiness:

1. Object stage—they will count crayons, pencils, blocks, chalk, coins, etc.
2. Picture stage—they will count pictures.

---

[3] Samuel A. Kirk and Orville Johnson: *Educating the Retarded Child.* New York, Houghton, Mifflin Co., 1951, p. 165.

3. Semi-concrete stage—they will count dots, circles, marks, things that represent objects, and so on.
4. Number symbols—they will recognize, recall, and use the Arabic numbers 1, 2, 3, 4, 5, 6, 7, 8, 9, 0.

When a child has learned to count, read and write numbers, and has developed a rationalization of the number system, the teacher should present addition. To understand this concept, a child must realize that addition is not a counting on but a "putting together." If a mentally retarded child is to learn the addition idea, he must be taught from the beginning to use it. Otherwise he will continue in the object stage and will not understand why he should bother to learn addition combinations. Sometimes a mentally retarded child can learn simple combinations such as $2 + 3 = 5$ even though he does not write the numbers at this time. Number games are excellent motivators to develop the before mentioned stages.

Informal arithmetic at the primary level should consist of experiences introducing:

1. Time—today, tomorrow, yesterday, week, month, year, hour, and appreciation of the clock as a helper.
2. Money—experience with actual coins, comparisons as to size, color, design and value.
3. Temperature—cold, hot, warm, cool, used to describe kind of day, feel of the room, comparison of foods (ice-cream, soup).
4. Weight—light, heavy—comparing weights of various articles used by the children.
5. Sizes—big, little, too big, too little, observation of different sizes of clothing (shoes, coats, etc.).
6. Fraction concept—whole sheet of paper, half of apple, quarter of a pie, etc.

At the end of this period the accomplishments should be:

1. Ability to count at least ten objects, pictures, and semi-concrete objects (such as dots or lines).
2. Can write Arabic numbers: 1, 2, 3, 4, 5 and understand meaning of these symbols.
3. When using concrete objects, i.e., blocks, dominoes, etc., he can arrange combinations to five.
4. Has a fair quantitative vocabulary.
5. Knows his own age.
6. Knows own address, can tell if he cannot write it.

Intermediate Level

Chronological Age—10-12   Mental Age—6½-8
Grade Expectancy—1-3

The intermediate level shows a transition from the incidental and informal approach to one which is more formal. The mentally retarded child's accomplishments should include most of the following:

1. Advanced counting—they should learn to count to at least 100, beyond if possible. Counting is the foundation of addition, but stress the difference between rote counting (rhyming off) and rational counting (counting objects).
2. Number facts—learn as many as possible of the 81 number facts or combinations which summate from 2 to 10.
3. Subtraction—the child learns that the subtraction concept is a separating or taking away. Teach the 81 subtraction facts which correspond to the 81 addition facts. Flash cards and number games are excellent aids. Some suggestions for comprehension of taking away or separating are:
   a. Take two objects from a group of not more than five objects.
   b. Take away a given number of objects from a group of not more than ten objects.
   c. Borrowing, take away a group of objects from a group of more than ten. Example—Bill had eleven crayons, Jim borrowed six, five left.
   d. Play store—buy different items that requires change from a dime.
4. Pupils should learn to count by 2's, 5's, and 10's.
5. Making change—children should learn to make change for 25c, 50c, and $1.00 if possible.
6. Measures—facility in use of pints, quarts, inches, feet, yards, pounds, dozens; is a skill that should be developed at this stage (use actual measures).
7. Writing numbers—pupils should learn to write the Arabic numbers to 100.
8. Problem solving—give ample opportunity to use arithmetic fundamentals in solving practical, one-step problems. This will be done orally until reading skills are established.

The expected maximum accomplishments at the end of this period are:

1. Ability to count, read and write numbers to 100.
2. Know his birthdate, house number and telephone number.
3. Read prices on articles for sale.
4. Find pages in books.
5. Read numbers on clocks and classroom doors.
6. Know meaning of first, second, third, —to tenth.
7. Count to 100 by ones, twos, fives and tens.
8. Solve simple oral and written problems.
9. Use the calendar and read days of week and month.
10. Read and write numbers used in daily school work.
11. Use foot ruler and yardstick.
12. Use measures, such as gallon, quart, pint and one cup.
13. Knowledge of simple fractions, $\frac{1}{4}$ of a pie, half an apple, $\frac{2}{3}$ cup of water, etc.
14. Weigh purchases in pounds and half-pounds.
15. Count money and make change in units up to one dollar (penny, nickel, dime, quarter and half-dollar).
16. Play number games such as simple arithmetic, dominoes, checkers.
17. Tell time, hours of day, noon hour, time for recess, time to go home, meal time, time for bed, etc.

Secondary Level

Chronological Age—12-18   Mental Age—8-12
Grade Expectancy—2-6

The secondary level will emphasize "social arithmetic." The children should learn about saving money, paying taxes, banking, insurance, leases, mortgages, and so on. It must be pointed out that all of these children will not be capable of understanding these facts.

Mentally retarded children become more adept in using arithmetic fundamentals at this level. Children who have an IQ of 50 or above should be able to use the addition process before leaving school. Addition is second only to multiplication in terms of frequency of use in adult life. At this time the children who are capable of doing so have "mastered" the multiplication combinations and processes. They must understand what they are doing and not feel that they are applying tricks with numbers.

Subtraction is third in place of importance to an adult in social usage of arithmetic. The most frequent use is in making change. During the years before the mentally retarded reaches the mental age to master subtraction, he will have many experiences that teach the subtraction principle. Example: remainder or "how much" is left? The difference or comparison of ideas (how much will I save if I buy a dress marked down from $19.98 to $15.95?).

There are few needs in the life of a mentally retarded child for division of numbers larger than 12, 24 and 36. Little time should be spent with this process. Few instances occur in the classroom when the child is faced with the need for division. The trained teacher will capitalize on such occasions when they do occur. Sharing equally in the cost of a classmate's birthday cake, ice cream for a special treat or of a special book for the class are comprehensive methods to discover the use of division.

Accomplishments at the end of the secondary level should include most of the following:

1. Ability to count in any ordinary situation the pupil will meet.
2. He can add four digits and carry.
3. He can subtract four digits and borrow.
4. He knows multiplication tables up to nines, can multiply two digits by two digit numbers.
5. Use simple fractions.
6. Draw simple figures, circles, squares, diamonds, triangles, etc.
7. Can read thermometers.
8. Tell time correctly and use calendar.
9. Some conception of distance.
10. Knows money terms and values.
11. Can keep a budget account of his spending.
12. Has an understanding of the services of a bank, make out deposit slips and write checks.
13. Uses telephone directory, read time table, use of various licenses, birth certificate, etc.
14. Know where and how to get help for situations beyond his ability, such as filing an income tax return.

In all probability this is the last opportunity the mentally retarded child will have for formal instruction in number concepts. Many students of this age group will probably attend class only part time because they will have part time jobs or will be receiving "on the job" training. This will be advantageous because arithmetic applicable to their jobs may be used.

WRITING

The writing program for any school must be adequate in scope and well adjusted to the maturity levels, abilities and developmental needs of the pupils taught whether they be in a special class or regular class.

Purpose

1. To deepen interest in learning to write.
2. To promote the orderly development of the requisite attitudes and skills.
3. To help pupils to overcome difficulties in learning to write by studying carefully the nature and causes of their difficulties and providing appropriate help in each case.
4. To encourage pupils in the use of writing for meeting personal needs, as an aid to learning and as means of self-expression.
5. To prepare pupils for more advanced stages of development in the use of handwriting in social and civic life.

A. Readiness: The preparatory activities should take place as far as possible during the pre-reading period. The early training in writing and reading should begin at about the same time.

A child acquires mental readiness through experiences that reveal the value of handwriting and promote interest in learning to write.[4] The child acquires readiness through activities that enable him to learn to control muscles and to hold writing tools.

Some suggested activities are:

1. Swinging the arm in a circle.
2. Building with the blocks.
3. Modeling and drawing.
4. Holding of stick, pencil, chalk or crayon between fingers and thumb and making circles or straight lines in air.
5. Making circles and lines in sand or dust with a stick.

As these activities proceed, other useful types of experiences may be provided. The teacher may write the names of the pupils on their desks, books, or some other belongings or the name of the day of the week on the blackboard each morning, together with a list of things to be done.

---

[4] William S. Gray: *The Teaching of Reading and Writing.* Chicago, Scott Foresman, 1956, p. 211.

These activities should be continued until the child expresses keen interest in learning to write and has attained sufficient motor control to hold the writing tools and engage in the larger movements required.

B. Chalk Board: The child's first experience in learning to form the letters should be on the board as chalk is easier handled and he can make larger circles and marks. Later when the forms of new letters are to be mastered let him trace the letter and other characters on the board at first. Then make him a model. Example: 0, let him practice making it by himself but be ready to help him with his difficulties and the correction of his errors. These activities should be continued until the child has learned to hold his chalk and has attained motor control sufficient to make circles, marks and characters fairly well.

C. Pencil and Paper: When children begin to write at their desks on paper, the large size lead pencils of good length and with soft lead should be used. Children should be taught to adopt a good posture in writing.

The act of writing should begin in a situation which has meaning and purpose to the child. The item to be written may be his name or the day of the week. As a compelling motive for writing develops, the teacher may place on the blackboard a clear copy of what is to be written. At first, do not demand too much of the pupils in reproducing the models on the board. The result is that the character, letters, or words are perceived and reproduced largely through the child's own efforts and often quite inaccurately. Through continued practice more and more details are observed and the written forms become more accurate and regular. Handwriting difficulties do not appear to be peculiarly associated with mentally retarded children.[5]

D. Manuscript: The use of manuscript has spread rapidly during recent years. This is due to the fact that it can be learned more easily and written more legibly and rapidly. The manuscript letters resemble printed ones. It is, therefore, of considerable use during the first few years of an educable mentally retarded child's school life. Many educable mentally retarded children never change to cursive writing because manuscript is easier

---

[5] W. C. Kvaraceus: Handwriting needs of the mentally retarded children and of children in regular classes. *Elementary School Journal*, 280:42-44, 1955.

for them. On the other hand, some of these children can do cursive writing exceptionally well.

E. Cursive: When shall we help a child change from manuscript to cursive writing? A question that has bedeviled teachers almost since the introduction of manuscript writing in this country. Its strongest advocates answer, "Never!" Just abandon the cursive.[6]

However, cursive writing continues to be used in our culture. It remains personally distinctive and children do learn it. In relation to most things we attempt to teach, we have almost come to accept as fact that children must eventually learn cursive writing. Readiness is basic to learning; therefore, it would seem only common sense to be guided by the same idea when we attempt to decide at what point we should teach children cursive writing.

How shall we recognize a child's readiness to begin cursive writing? The child should show sufficient control of fine muscles:

1. To direct a pencil in forming recognizable lines other than simple circles and straight lines.
2. To control the pencil in following movements from form to form with some evidence of rhythm.

Be able to do some co-ordinated movements without extreme tensing of muscles and without evidence of emotional disturbance.

Be able and willing to make large letters other than tight, cramped and very small ones.

Be able to write all letters small and capitals in manuscript without too much deliberation or uncertainty as to form.

Should show awareness of cursive writing repeatedly expressing interest in attempting it.

Should be emotionally mature enough that he can experience a few failures and repeated partial successes without becoming upset.

As children make progress in learning to write, teachers should note daily the nature of their individual difficulties and should help each child according to his needs after a careful study of his state of general development, motor control, mental age, physical defects, background of experience, and home environment. It is particularly important that a child should not be required to re-

---

[6] Lucy Nulton: Readiness to change from manuscript to cursive. *Elementary English,* *32*:382-383, 1955.

produce exactly the prescribed style of handwriting if it presents unusual difficulties for him.[7]

SUMMARY

Children that comprise the "primary group" are usually six to ten chronologically and have a mental age of three to six and one-half years. The "intermediate group" children are about ten to twelve years chronologically and have a mental age of six and one-half to eight years. The "secondary group" consists of children twelve to eighteen years of age chronologically whose mental ages are approximately eight to twelve years. Most of this chapter discusses reading, spelling, arithmetic and suggested procedures for teaching them according to chronological and mental age. The remainder of the chapter deals with handwriting for all three of the above mentioned groups.

---

[7] Gray: *op. cit.*, p. 219.

CHAPTER VI

Social Studies, Health and the Fine Arts

DEVELOPING CIVIC AND SOCIAL SKILLS

The Educable Mentally Retarded Child as a Part of His Community

IT is indeed elementary to observe that the child whom we have described as being educable mentally retarded will, with proper teaching, usually grow up to be an effective member of society. Although his participation in the community may be limited, he will participate in its economic life and he may exercise his right to vote.

Considerable thought should be given to how he can become qualified to carry out his role in society. A realistic approach should be given to the development of social and civic skills and the understanding of them. In most respects his needs and abilities in this area will not differ greatly from those of a normal child. Frequently the difference is in degree rather than in kind.

When employing the term "social skills" we obviously are considering the development of traits and habits which have to do with establishing and maintaining satisfactory personal relationships. These associations may be person to person as in making friends or person to group relationships such as in the home, church, classroom or club.

We usually consider "civic skills" as being part of social skills. The reason for giving the term special emphasis here is because it is crucial for every person to think in terms of his responsibility as a citizen. As a good citizen he is not always expecting personal gratification; rather he is learning those things necessary in an orderly society. In other words, he not only learns to participate in activities which are satisfying but he also learns to exercise restraint. He learns to enjoy his own rights and also to respect the rights of others. For purposes of simplification there will be no division of "civic" and "social" skills in this chapter, but the reader will note that both are integrated into the suggested activities at various levels. This serves a two-fold purpose; first simplification and second, careful integration of activities which when completed, results in an individual who is happy in his role as a person and as a citizen.

The types of activities suggested in the following pages must be suited to mental age; therefore, adaptation to primary, elementary and secondary levels should be made by the teacher.

The following suggestions are offered:
1. How the teacher may assist in social adjustments.
2. The child in his community.
3. Personal goals.

How the Teacher May Assist in Social Adjustment

The writers believe that the child is the center of the educative process. School, plant, equipment, teaching materials, supplies, and available community resources are all tangible elements of an environment which is designed for learning. Out of this atmosphere should come education that is meaningful, complete as possible and especially fitted to the needs and abilities of each mentally retarded child in the group. Social adjustment can be improved by good practices in education. In the education of the mentally retarded child the teacher occupies a position secondary only to that of the pupil. Take the most expensive books, materials, aids and equipment that can be purchased; place these in a specially designed, modern classroom; add a teacher who is cool, aloof, unfeeling and mildly kind, even though properly credentialed, it becomes immediately obvious that this class will show little progress.

The teacher must have a particular kind of aptitude for working with this type of child. The writers feel that some of the more important qualities are: kindness without maudlin sympathy, sincerity, honesty, acceptance, ability to listen and console, and quality of helping each child to feel secure, loved, wanted, and that he belongs. This teacher must be creative in various ways. Situations must be created to allow the children to succeed as well as to soften the extreme feeling of defeat when they fail. They must be helped to accept failure because later in life many situations of this nature will arise. Mentally retarded children should not be over-protected; they must learn to rely on themselves.

The teacher can help promote social adjustment through sound practices, procedures and demonstrations. Kirk and Johnson have provided an excellent summary of procedures affecting social adjustment.

1. Well-planned activities decrease unacceptable behavior.
2. Self-direction should be encouraged.
3. Successful programs for children are based on the children's interests and experience.
4. Materials of instruction should be selected with care.
5. Instruction should begin with simple material.
6. Familiar material aids instruction.
7. Gradual introduction of new situations avoids misbehavior.
8. It is advisable to avoid abstract materials and utilize concrete ones.
9. Variety of methods and materials is recommended.
10. Routines of the class should be kept simple.
11. Out-of-class activities should be correlated with activities within the classroom.
12. Instruction should be individualized.
13. It should be recognized that all behavior, adequate or inadequate is caused.
14. Emphasis should be placed on successful accomplishments.[1]

The management of behavior is of great importance in the total adjustment of the mentally retarded child. In the classroom the child develops habits and attitudes that will carry over into everyday life. The teacher can assist him in developing the type of behavior which will help him meet many situations. Kirk and Johnson offer the following suggestions for behavior management:

1. Make positive statements rather than negative.
2. Use encouraging rather than discouraging statements.
3. Use specific rather than general statements.
4. Use placement requests rather than scoldings.
5. Be consistent in requests.
6. Use substitute suggestions rather than negative commands.
7. Use unhurried directions rather than negative commands.
8. Give the child a choice in activities.

---

[1] Samuel A. Kirk and Orville G. Johnson: *Educating the Retarded Child.* New York, Houghton, Mifflin Co., 1951, pp. 326-330.

9. Keep teacher verbalism to a minimum.
10. Use manual guidance to aid verbal suggestions.
11. Avoid issues with the children.
12. Avoid making threats.
13. Avoid anger in the presence of the children.
14. Isolate hyperactive children when necessary.
15. Stimulate shy and withdrawn children.[2]

Discuss the classroom rules and problems with the children. When they understand reasons and solutions to problems they are more likely to co-operate with the teacher.

The Child in His Community

Frequently, children with retarded intellectual development have not had the opportunity to develop satisfactory personal relationships in the home or the neighborhood. Unfavorable comparison with others, rejection by parents and peers and the general attitude of the public toward them will produce an individual who must be educated so that he can find a more adequate place in his own environment. It is fundamental that instruction be so organized as to present the community to the child in a concrete and practical manner. The following suggested topics may be adapted to suit particular situations at the primary and intermediate levels.

1. The home:
   a. Members of the family.
   b. Respect for others in the home.
   c. Relationships in the home.
   d. Social life in the home.
   e. Homemaking.
   f. Relationship of home to other homes in community.
2. Foods:
   a. Producing our food.
   b. How to keep foods: food processing, food conservation, distribution of food (stores).
3. The neighborhood:
   a. Other homes in the neighborhood.
   b. Respect for others in the neighborhood.
   c. Making friends and playmates.

[2] *Ibid.,* pp. 330-334.

d. The neighborhood grocery, drugstore, etc.

e. Location of places of importance and interest such as post office, fire, bus and train stations, and airport.

4. The community:
   a. Transportation (various types as air, land, water, etc.).
   b. Public buildings and their functions.
   c. Places of interest, zoo, parks, museums, etc.
   d. Factories and industries.

The following units may be adapted to use at the secondary level or some specific topic may be presented to the intermediate level.

1. The World of Work:
   a. Why people work.   f. Mining.
   b. Work and how it applies to the child.   g. Manufacturing.
   c. Family occupations.   h. Trade.
   d. Agriculture.   i. Transportation.
   e. Forestry and fishing.   j. Communication.

2. The Child's State:
   a. History of the state.
   b. Agriculture in the state.
   c. Animals (domestic and wild).
   d. Natural resources and climate.
   e. Recreation in the state.
   f. The people and their government.
   g. Communication in the state.
   h. Transportation in the state.

3. The Nation:
   a. Its capital.
   b. Why we have national government (details very briefly).

For the secondary class who is in its last year of attendance, the following units are applicable:

1. You and Your Friends:
   a. Need for friends.
   b. How to choose a future husband or wife.
   c. Legal requirements for marriage.
   d. How to choose friends.

2. Choosing a Home:
   a. Types of dwelling.   d. Location.
   b. Price.   e. Furnishings.
   c. Family needs.

3. Care of Home:
   a. Household routines.   d. Care and use of home appliances.
   b. How to clean.   e. Care of building and grounds.
   c. Repairs.   f. home safety.
4. Thrift:
   a. Sources of income.   d. Savings.
   b. Family expenses.   e. Insurance.
   c. Budgeting.   f. Credit buying.
5. The Family and the Community:
   a. Co-operating with neighbors.
   b. Joining community groups.
   c. Responsibility of community to you.
   d. Your responsibility to the community.
   e. Local laws and regulations.
   f. Recreational facilities in the community.
   g. Sanitation facilities in the community.
   h. Health facilities in the community.
   i. Police facilities in the community.
   j. Fire facilities in the community.

It must be remembered that in discussing the foregoing topics, adaptation and materials should be in accordance with the child's mental age. The teacher should be flexible in constructive lesson plans related to the community. She should analyze the community in which the child lives and try to plan instruction with the following points in mind.

1. What is the child's present knowledge of his community?
2. What does he need to learn about his community which will be of practical use to him later?
3. What elements of knowledge will help to enrich his life?
4. Does he need to change his attitudes toward the community or its individual members?
5. Encourage constructive attitudes which are not presently developed.

Through careful analysis it is possible to build sound knowledge and acceptable attitudes with effective social and civic skills emerging in the process.

Personal Goals

In planning an educational program for any child, we should ask three fundamental questions. How does he feel about himself? How does he relate to others? What does he want to do or become? More often than not, the mentally retarded child is confused in his thinking about these questions. He may not be certain how he feels about himself. A series of frustrating relationships may make him wonder if he relates to others at all well. Preoccupation with unsatisfactory personal relationships may have precluded his giving much thought or attention to what he would like to do or what he is capable of doing to earn a living. The wise teacher will not attempt to undo or solve problems of the past but will direct all effort toward achieving good personal goals such as these:

1. Attend to personal grooming to insure cleanliness and neatness.
2. Maintain courtesy toward everyone.
3. Respect the rights and privileges of others.
4. Try to understand other people's attitudes.
5. Curb selfishness.
6. Be friendly and kind toward others.
7. Co-operate in worthwhile projects.
8. Be loyal.
9. Set good spiritual and ethical standards.
10. Do all tasks well.

Remember that progress toward these goals may be slow and limited. Nevertheless, the positive values which can accrue are worth the time, effort and patience which the teacher may need to put forth to help the mentally retarded child to achieve them. "We learn by doing" and this is especially true for mentally retarded children. Personal goals will become habits of behavior only if practiced consistently at school, at home, and in the community.

The following standards will serve as a measure:

1. Are we as teachers, through our attitudes, procedures and techniques, demonstrating to the pupils the best possible social adjustment patterns?
2. Are we helping him to understand and become a part of his community?
3. Are we assisting him in developing and achieving personal goals which will contribute to his total progress in becoming a useful, stable member of society?

In a discussion of the development of social and civic skills, it is obviously impossible to outline procedures which would be appropriate for the many varying communities of any given state. A teacher will need to exercise ingenuity and imagination in order to develop a suitable program for the educable mentally retarded.

DEVELOPMENT OF SKILLS FOR HEALTHFUL LIVING

Health is one of the chief objectives of education today. The teaching of health requires different and specialized skills because "health" is more than a subject; like arithmetic it does not mean merely to impart knowledge—it often means changing attitudes and practices toward better and more satisfactory living. Health is more than physical well-being; it is the thinking, feeling, acting human being; it is the condition of the mind and spirit as well as in body. The goals of health education are the same for all children but the curriculum for mentally retarded children should be specially designed to fit the needs of each individual child. Good health enables these children to put forth more energy in developing their potentialities. A good health education program is based upon the philosophy that all children have the same basic physical and psychological needs; that all children need an adequate and balanced diet, sufficient rest and sleep, a comfortable temperature, and activity when well rested; that all children need to be loved and wanted, to have a reasonable independence in managing their own lives and in making their own decisions; to feel a sense of achievement that comes from making things and doing jobs; to win the appraisal of others for what they are and do; and to feel that they are worthwhile individuals who reasonably meet their own inner standards. Helping these children fulfill their physical and psychological needs is the task of parents, teachers and community, each working co-operatively and understandingly toward a common goal. The characteristics of a healthy child are:

1. He gives an impression of physical fitness, emotional stability, vigor and vitality.
2. He takes an interest in life, appears happy and contented.
3. His skin is clear and the color in his cheeks increases following outdoor play.
4. His teeth are sound and regularly spaced with cavities treated.

5. He gains in height, weight, and other bodily measurements. Growth may fluctuate but overall he shows a measurable gain.
6. His appetite is good and elimination satisfactory.
7. He has no remedial defects or has adjusted himself to his handicaps.
8. He has good functional posture and handles his muscles and body appropriately for his age.
9. He has strength and energy sufficient for work and play.
10. He sleeps well and during sleep recovers satisfactorily from fatigue.
11. He sees and hears well with any deficiencies corrected.

A good health program includes:

1. The teacher's observation—
   a. General appearance and behavior—
      Physical signs: excessive thinness, excessive overweight, very small or very large in build for age, pallor, weary expression, poor posture, dark circles or puffiness under the eyes.
      Behavior: acts tired, is easily irritated, makes frequent trips to toilet, has persistent nervous habits, is subject to fainting spells or frequent nose bleed, gets short of breath after mild exertion or climbing stairs, appetite poor.
      Complaints: feels tired, doesn't want to play, has aches or pains, feels sick at stomach, feels dizzy.
   b. Hair and scalp.
   c. Ears.   f. Nose.
   d. Eyes.   g. Throat.
   e. Mouth and teeth.   h. Skin.
2. Vision tests—
   a. The Snellen Chart for visual acuity at 20 feet is used to test acuteness of vision of school children.
   b. Wheel chart for detecting astigmatism.
   c. Other testing devices—The Massachusetts Vision Test and the "telebinocular."
3. Hearing—
   a. Audiometric testing: the pure-tone audiometer is designed upon principles similar to those used in constructing radio sets.
   b. Whisper test: a whisper can usually be heard in a quiet room by a person of normal hearing at a distance of

twenty to thirty feet, depending upon the loudness of the whisper.

   c. The watch-tick test: a loud-ticking watch may be substituted for the residual whisper as a rough-and-ready hearing test.

   d. Other tests: the coin test and the acumeter tests.

What Should Be Taught

1. Needs: The majority of slow-learning children come from homes where sanitation and hygiene are at the lowest ebb. These children as a group are physically below par, they are more susceptible to disease, are in greater need of corrective exercises, have lower vitality, show a greater need for good nutrition, and in general are more seriously in need of medical attention. The special class teacher should try to bring about an improvement in the health habits of this group both at home and school.

2. Methods: Health habits can be taught at any age and at any time. Situations are continuously arising both inside and outside the classroom which call for correction or suggestion from parent or teacher. Health training need not be arranged and presented in an order of increasing difficulty. Most of its items should be taught all the time and in correlation with other subjects.

Health habits should begin at home, but the teacher is likely to find her progress in establishing good health habits handicapped by indifference and lack of co-operation in the home. The teacher must supervise health habits in as many situations as possible; "toothbrush drills, daily, not weekly showerbaths, and health committees, or 'inspectors.'" The elementary teacher is at an advantage in supervising many of the health habits of her pupils during the lunch hour. Vigilant supervision and careful individualized instruction will prove most effective in bringing about improved conditions in habits of personal hygiene.

Subjects for class discussion:

1. The nature of bacteria (germs), spread of germs and virus, extermination of germs, prevention of diseases caused by them.
2. Growth-height and weight charts, relation to health and corrective measures.
3. Sleep—importance to health, proper amount, need for regular sleep, proper sleeping conditions.

4. Posture—correct sitting and standing postures, corrective exercises, use of posture charts and mirrors.
5. Food—balanced diet, food value, merits of simple and substantial food, temperature, importance of cleanliness in the regular handling of food, thorough mastication, regular hours for eating, necessity for water.
6. Exercise—relation and importance to health, need for outside exercise daily, dangers from over-exercising.
7. Good toilet habits—proper elimination, regularity in relation to diet and exercise.
8. Care of the mouth—importance of clean mouth, mouth washes and how to use them.
9. Care of teeth—structure of the teeth, importance of sound teeth, kind of toothbrush, chewing to keep teeth in good condition, twice yearly visits to dentist, local dental clinics.
10. Care of the eyes—protect them from strong light, dust and eye strain, correct distance between eyes and work, glasses and use.
11. Care of the ears—how to cleanse, testing of hearing and corrective measures if necessary.
12. Care of nose and throat—dangers of breathing through mouth, need for cleanliness, sore-throat beginning of many diseases, colds and coughs, tonsils and adenoids, proper use and care of a handkerchief, precautions necessary.
13. Care of the hands—clean hands are important in the hygienic care of the rest of body, care of the fingernails, how to protect the hands from chapping, precautions: do not handle food without first washing hands, keep hands out of mouth and eyes.
14. Care of the skin—bathing, care of wash basin and bathtub, individual towels and wash cloths.
15. Care of the hair—shampooing, use of the brush and comb, treatment for dandruff.
16. Clothing—garments appropriate to varying temperatures, woolens, cottons, etc. and their use in protecting the body, roomy and comfortable, cleanliness, need for frequent airing and changes, garments of washable materials next to body.

Mental Health

Mental health is a measure of a person's ability to shape his environment, to adjust to life as he has to face it and to do so with a reasonable amount of satisfaction, success, efficiency and happiness.

Points to note:

1. Most social maladjustments result from a feeling of insecurity.
2. In overcoming feelings of inferiority and developing a wholesome personality, it is highly important that the child be successful in his undertakings and that he develop special skills in some field.
3. The timid normal child is apt to substitute excessive reading and day-dreaming for aggressive activity.
4. Children with inferiority conflicts may develop traits opposite to original characteristics.
5. Instead of facing realities, some children evade them in various ways—temper tantrums, sulkiness, invalidism, forgetfulness, sleep, hysteria, rationalization and criticism of other people.

Some indications of maladjustment in children are:

1. Aggressive behavior—temper outbursts.
   a. Defiant, over-aggressiveness.
   b. Resistance to authority.
   c. Disobedience—quarrelsome, fighting, boasting.
   d. Rejection of school routine.
   e. Always wanting to be the leader in activities or to pursue own methods of work.
   f. Contentiousness, poor sportsmanship.
   g. Overactivity, delinquency, truancy.
2. Withdrawing behavior—shyness, timidity, cowardliness.
   a. Anti-social, solitariness, unable to make friends.
   b. Extreme docility, over-dependence on adults or on routines. Sensitive to criticism.
   c. Feelings easily hurt.
   d. Fearfulness, suspiciousness.
   e. Pedantry, over-diligence in schoolwork.
   f. Inability to carry responsibility.
3. Somatic manifestations.
   a. Nail-biting, finger-sucking.
   b. Pencil-chewing, facial twitching.
   c. Blinking of eyes, infantile behavior.
   d. Unestablished toilet habits.
4. Educational problems.

    a. Difficulty with reading despite normal intelligence and vision.

    b. Difficulties with arithmetic.

5. Speech difficulties.

    a. Pseudo stuttering.

    b. Infantile speech.

The principles of mental hygiene should help the teacher to:

1. Aid the child's personal adjustment and social interaction with other children.
2. Assist him to achieve an integrated personality.

The child's ability to learn can be aided by:

1. Encouragement and approval from teacher and parents.
2. Knowledge that children grow at different rates and learn in different ways.
3. By providing him with inner strength and security.
4. Understanding that some difficulties are due to some home problem.

The teacher helps the child:

1. To gain a sense of accomplishment and responsibility.
2. To make personally satisfying and socially approved adjustments in many situations.
3. By understanding each child.
4. By satisfying the basic needs for security, affection, recognition, approval and a sense of belonging.
5. By treating each child in a kindly, impartial and considerate manner.
6. By striving to attain a spirit of friendliness and success.

Methods to improve the identification and diagnosis of personality difficulties:

1. Observation: 1) note the child's behavior patterns, 2) note any unusual responses.
2. Interview: a planned and purposeful conversation. Objective: to provide the child with the feeling that the teacher is a friend who understands him and is interested in his personal and social happiness.
3. Achievement tests: Rorschach method, The California test of personality, The Detroit "Telling What I Do" test, The Vineland Social Maturity Scale, and others.

4. Reports (informal): an outline that will bring together meaningful data.
5. Sociograms: a chart that teachers may use to determine the nature of the child's social relationships with peers.

Children are quick to sense the feelings of others. Teachers and parents who are loving, kind, sympathetic and understanding but firm and set up behavior limitations, will provide the child with skills to become secure, happy and to adjust to life. They are more likely to develop these desirable traits:

1. Obedience.
2. Good manners.
3. Good humor.
4. Cooperation.
5. Perseverance.
6. Loyalty.
7. Tolerance.
8. Orderliness.
9. Self-control.
10. Self-reliance.
11. Thrift.
12. Honesty.
13. Trustworthiness.

Needless to say, children with behavior problems are easily detected, but children with emotional problems minus overt behavior problems are not always easy to locate. But in the life of both types, the teacher plays a significant role in moulding their personality, helping them to modify their behavior, and adjusting to life as they must face it in adulthood.

DEVELOPING ARTISTIC EXPRESSION AND APPRECIATION

Art, music, rhythm, dramatics and dance are important elements in a curriculum designed for mentally retarded children. They are excellent approach media for release of tensions. They provide opportunity for successful experiences as well as:

1. The development of better motor coordination.
2. The creation of new interests.
3. The development of avocational activities for later life.
4. The fostering of group and other socializing activities.

Probably the most important of all is the provision of opportunity for the mentally retarded to find self-expression. The teacher should not lose sight of the excellence of these media for child study. Careful observation gives the teacher new insight into the needs, interests, and activities of each pupil. Often the retarded child has difficulty in expressing himself in language. Frequently, music, dance, art and play can become alternative avenues of expression. Creative activities are also useful in helping children build self-respect through the feeling of accomplishment and success.

Certainly the major objective of a school program for the retarded is the development of happy, well-adjusted, and contributive members of society. A rewarding sense of achievement in music and art will do much to increase the happiness and social competence of these people. In the development of cultural competencies in the mentally retarded child, the objective of greatest meaning for the child is the rewarding sense of achievement, an increased happiness. Art and music provide many opportunities for group activity and other socializing activities.

Music: The value of music in varied forms can scarcely be overestimated. Through it may come the release of pent-up emotions, the development of an innate ability on the part of some, and the sheer joy of singing, playing or listening on the part of all. Music is a means of expression of which no one is utterly deprived and it should be used to make the child happy through appreciation and participation.[3]

Most mentally retarded children enjoy singing even though some may be limited to humming a tune. The child's ability in this field usually excels his academic accomplishment.[4]

Those who do have ability in the field of music obtain much enjoyment out of life in society with others and at times contribute much to the enjoyment of others. This satisfaction is priceless in giving the child confidence, a feeling of being a part of society and of contributing something. It is just as important to educate the mentally retarded child to be happy and efficient in social relationships as it is to prepare him to earn a livelihood.

Methods of Teaching Music to Mentally Retarded Children

Rote singing is best for mentally retarded and slow-learning children. Songs of suitable length with content within the experience of the child should be chosen. Simple folk songs, singing games, songs popular at social gatherings, patriotic and national anthems, favorite melodies and popular, suitable song hits are best.

Rhythmic expression is latent in most slow-learning children.

[3] Ethelyn Stinson: *How to Teach Children Music.* New York, Harper, 1941.
[4] Elsie H. Martens: *Curriculum Adjustment for the Mentally Retarded.* Washington, D. C., Federal Security Agency, Bulletin No. 2, 1950, pp. 52-53.

They should be encouraged to clap hands, walk, march, skip, and run to the accompaniment of music. Imitative and creative rhythmic expression may be introduced through the specific unit projects. Singing games and folk dances can be used for the entire group.

Rhythm and harmonica bands provide learning situations. In classes for mentally retarded children will be found many non-singers. Most of these non-singers have become so because of lack of concentration and inattentiveness in other grades before assignment to a special class. The teacher should place each of these children near one who can carry a tune and keep the pitch. Encourage each child to listen and to follow the melody.

Music provides an opportunity for a variety of experiences upon which a rich background can be built. Music should be correlated with unit projects. Theoretical music should not be taught.

Suggestions for learning:

1. Discussion.
    a. What kind of music do you like?
    b. What kind of music do you dislike?
    c. Do you know the names of any musicians?
    d. How many musical instruments do you recognize?
2. Listening to radio, record-player or watching television.
3. Activities.
    a. Development of rhythm bands.
    b. Singing of popular songs.
    c. Provide opportunity for children to use various instruments.
    d. Folk dancing and singing games.
    e. Study of pictures of instruments.
    f. Rote singing.
    g. Exercise to music aids in rhythm development.
    h. Listen to all types of music.

Music and songs should be used often during the day as a relief from academic routine. These "break periods" should be only a few minutes in duration. Many recorded selections which are beyond their singing ability yet within their listening comprehension should be presented.

Music for the mentally retarded should include:

1. Daily singing of songs.
2. Listening.

a. Rhythms.
b. Appreciation.
c. Quiet and bodily activities.

In the proper atmosphere, under a warming influence, most children will learn to love music. Thus, music can become a kind of improved speech as meaningful as talking.

Dancing for Special Class Children

Dance is essential for wholesome development of mentally retarded children and opportunity should be provided to express themselves through this art in a well-planned program. The primary class may sing and move to singing games. The intermediate and secondary groups may derive a great deal of pleasure from using rhythm instruments and responding rhythmically with free expression through movements of bending, bobbing and turning as they play the music. Any child who is capable may participate in the regular school band or orchestra with the regular class children. The record player brings to the classroom all forms of recorded sounds, thereby providing dance music for any group of mentally retarded children.

Dance-plays create a wide range of self-expression experiences for these children. Example: the teacher improvises at the keyboard or finds simple appropriate music to represent characters in such stories as "Peter Rabbit" or "The Three Pigs."

The teacher may tell the story of Peter Rabbit while she sits at the piano and plays:

Eighth notes in middle register—Peter hopping.
Two sixteenth notes in high register—Peter nibbling lettuce.
Half-notes in bass—Mr. McGregor's foot steps.
Sixteenth notes up the keys—Peter running away.

The children may act out the story. This encourages imagination, memory and concentration as well as releasing tensions.

Dramatics

The logical outcome of imitative play is dramatic expression which constitutes an enjoyable part of the recreation of retarded children whether they are in the audience or acting upon the stage. Some points to be remembered in dramatics for the mentally retarded are these:

1. The plot must be simple with much action.
2. Lines must be easily understood.
   a. Discuss lines before production.
3. The mentally retarded enjoy several types of activities.
   a. Puppetry.
   b. Formal play.
   c. Creative dramatics.

Teachers often make this statement, "With so much concern directed toward reading, there is no time left for frills such as drama." On the contrary, free dramatic expression can be a great aid to verbal confidence and understanding when associated with much of the reading material. It is of paramount importance that mentally retarded children be provided with opportunities for free oral expression from the earliest years throughout their entire school life.

A mentally retarded child, regardless of age, tends to think in terms of some type of action. When his family buys a new car, he comes to school and speaks about the car to his teacher. He does not use descriptive terms such as color, size or model, but how fast it will go and, "Daddy drives our new car to work." It is logical to assume that dramatic action is an effective method of teaching.

Art

Whoever engages in art activities must make use of the intellect. Care must therefore be exercised by the teacher to see that the child does not attempt to do things that are too different lest he begins to fail in art also.[5]

1. Techniques and skills should be taught in purposeful and meaningful situations.
   a. Constructing gifts, games and models.
   b. Pictures of things seen or with which they are very familiar.
   c. Drawings depicting common activities such as eating lunch.
   d. Decorating the room.

---

[5] Ruth Crawford: Art for the exceptional child. *National Elementary Principal,* 30:25-26, 1951.

2. Art should be used as a method of expression in correlation with other class activities.
   a. Illustrating stories and rhymes.
   b. Correlation of symbols and number experiences.
   c. Connection of oral language and expression with handiwork.
   d. Illustration of home and community.
3. The child should not be deprived of manipulative experiences because of his awkwardness and coordination.
   a. Begin with simple manipulation of objects, feeling of textures and experimenting with materials.
   b. Proceed to drawing and painting, cutting and pasting.
   c. As his skill increases, due to improved coordination, neatness and accuracy will follow.

Some art activities correlated with other subjects as used by the writer:

1. Charts
   a. After a field trip children draw pictures to represent what we saw. Under each picture they print simple words, phrases or sentences.
2. Booklets—made by cutting and pasting pictures from magazines, catalogs and nursery (gardening) ads. Children who prefer may draw their own pictures if they are capable. Here are some suggestions for booklets:
   a. The flowers we know.
   b. Very familiar vegetables.
   c. The fruits we know.
   d. Some farm animals.
   e. The zoo animals we saw.
   f. The birds we know.
3. Picture cards for teaching A B C's and sounds
   a. Use tag board size 20″ x 20″, place a letter such as "A" in upper left hand corner. Paste several pictures of objects that begin with "A" "a" and some pictures of objects that begin with other letters. The children identify all objects that begin with "A." Repeat this process with all letters of the alphabet, making a card for each. The children and teacher work together on this project, selecting, cutting and pasting the pictures.
4. Picture cards for teaching words
   a. Assist children to cut out small pictures and paste on 3″ x

5″ cards. Teacher prints name of object on another card of same size with "flo-master" pen. Children match pictures with proper name word cards.

5. Arithmetic ideas

   a. Learning to count by twos. Draw on the chalkboard or on paper, pig heads showing both ears. Count the ears. Other versions of twos may be used. The pig ears seem to work best with most mentally retarded children because of the simplicity of the drawing.

   b. Count by fives. On paper or chalkboard the children draw their hands showing brightly colored nails. Count fingers by fives.

   c. Count by tens. Shape eggs from various colors of clay, then place by tens in baskets made from cottage cheese or sherbert containers.

   d. Learning addition and subtraction combination 1-10. On a piece of tag-board 36″ x 36″ the teacher draws a large tree with numerous branches. Cut slots at the end of each branch. Tack the board to easel-type stand. The children draw, color and cut out many leaves for the tree. Joe may place two green leaves and one red leaf on the tree. How many in all? Sue puts on five yellow leaves and Billy takes off two. How many are left? And so on.

6. Health and safety

   The children enjoyed this project immensely. Tack on the bulletin board seven yards of white butcher paper, 30″ wide. Draw lines on the paper, dividing it into seven one-yard spaces. At the top of each space, place one of the following titles:

   a. We keep clean.
   b. We dress.
   c. We eat.
   d. We work.
   e. We play.
   f. We rest.
   g. We keep safe.

   Children cut pictures from magazines to depict each subject. Then they paste in proper space under the correct heading. Example: a. we keep clean—use pictures of children washing faces, brushing teeth, shampooing hair, cleaning nails.

7. Science unit (how the sun helps us)

   Place a work table against the wall centered under a large

window in the classroom. Cut a ten-inch diameter circle from yellow construction paper to make the sun. Paste this near the top of the window. Cut paper strips 1" wide by 8" and 10". Paste them alternately around the sun to represent rays. At the bottom of the window paste strips of green paper ½" by 5" long to represent grass. Cut trees and flowers from seed catalogs or make from colored paper and paste among the grass blades. Above the plants paste bees and butterflies. On or near the grass paste ants and grasshoppers. Place the classroom aquarium containing fish, snails, etc. in the center of the work table. Encourage the children to bring their turtles, parakeets, white mice or other small pets to school for a few days stay on the table.

Any teacher can use his or her own ideas and ingenuity to make this project an enjoyable experience to show the children the relation between sun, earth and living things.

   8. Social studies
      a. Use sand table to build a farm. Children may make clay animals or cut them from picture books and put cardboard stands on the bottom. Lincoln logs make fine buildings.

All the above activities are merely suggestions to serve as guide lines in the art approach to helping the mentally retarded in the classroom. Successful art activities can help children build self-respect through the feeling of accomplishment.

SUMMARY

Considerable thought should be given as to how mentally retarded children can become qualified to carry out their role in society. In most respects their needs and abilities will not differ greatly from those of normal individuals.

Social skills refer to the development of traits and habits which have to do with establishing and maintaining satisfactory personal relationships. Civic skills are usually considered as being part of social skills; no division of "civic" and "social" skills is made in this chapter. This serves two purposes: one of simplification and the other of careful integration of activities which when completed, results in an individual who is happy in his role as a person and as a citizen.

The teacher can assist in promoting social adjustment through sound practices, procedures and demonstrations. Management of behavior is of great importance in the total adjustment of the mentally retarded child. In the classroom he develops habits and attitudes that will transfer into everyday life.

Often, children with retarded intellectual development have not had an opportunity to develop satisfactory personal relationships in the home or in the neighborhood. It is fundamental that instruction be so organized as to present the community to the child in a concrete and practical manner. This chapter suggests many topics which may be used for this particular purpose.

Health is more than physical well-being; it is the thinking, feeling, acting human being; it is the condition of the mind and spirit as well as the body. The goals of health education are the same for all children but the curriculum for mentally retarded children should be especially designed to fit the needs of each individual child. A good health education program is based upon the philosophy that all children need an adequate and balanced diet, sufficient rest and sleep, a comfortable temperature and when well rested, activity. All children need to be loved and wanted; they need to have a reasonable independence in managing their own lives and in making their own decisions; they need to feel a sense of achievement that comes from making things and doing jobs; they need to win the approval of others for what they are and to feel that they are worthwhile individuals who reasonably meet their own inner standards.

Art, music, rhythm, dramatics and dance are important elements in curriculum designed for mentally retarded children because they provide for release of tensions and, more important still, they provide opportunity for the mentally retarded child to find self-expression. This chapter sets forth suggested procedures for teaching the fine arts to mentally retarded children.

SELECTED REFERENCES

Abel, Theodora M.: Resistance and difficulties in psychotherapy of mental retardates. *Journal of Clinical Psychology, Monograph Supplement*:9-11, April 1953.

Allen, Amy A.: Let us teach slow learning children. *Division of Special Education, State Department of Education,* Columbus, Ohio, 1955.

Baker, J.: *Introduction to Exceptional Children.* New York, Macmillan Company, 1953.

Baker, H. J.: *Introduction to Handicapped Children*. Third edition. New York, Macmillan Company, 1959.

Barnett, C. D. and Cantor, G. N.: Discrimination set in defectives. *American Journal of Mental Deficiency*, 62:334-337, 1957.

Barr, Martin W.: *Mental Defectives: Their History, Treatment and Training*. Philadelphia, P. Blakiston's Son and Company, 1913.

Baumgartner, Bernice B.: *An Approach to an Experimental Program for Educable Mentally Retarded Children*. Albany, University of the State of New York, 1960.

Benda, C. E.: *Developmental Disorders of Mentation and Cerebral Palsies*. New York, Grune and Stratton, 1952.

Bender, L.: *Aggression, Hostility and Anxiety in Children*. Springfield, Illinois, Charles C Thomas, 1953.

Bennett, A. A.: Comparative study of subnormal children in the elementary grades. *Contributions to Education*, No. 510. New York, Bureau of Publications, Teachers College, Columbia University, 1932.

Bennett, A.: Reading ability in special classes. *Journal of Educational Research*, 20:236-238, 1929.

Bensberg, G. J.: Concept learning in mental defectives as a function of appropriate and inappropriate attention sets. *Educational Psychology, 49*: 137-147, 1958.

Binet, Alfred and Simon, T.: *Mentally Defective Children*. New York, Longman's, Green and Company, 1914.

Blodgett, Harriet E. and Warfield, Grace J.: *Understanding Mentally Retarded Children*. New York, Appleton-Century-Crofts, Inc., 1959.

Bond, G. L. and Fay, L. F.: A comparison of good and poor readers on the individual items of the Stanford-Binet scale, forms L and M. *Journal of Educational Research, 43*:475-479, 1950.

Bower, Eli M.: The emotionally handicapped child and the school. *Exceptional Children, 26*, September 1959.

Brand, H., Benoit, E. P. and Ornstein, C. N.: Rigidity and feeblemindedness: an examination of the Kounin-Lewin theory. *Journal of Clinical Psychology, 9*:375-378, 1953.

Burton, A.: Psychotherapy with the mentally retarded. *American Journal of Mental Deficiency, 58*:486-489, 1954.

California Administrative Code, Title 5, Education, Section 183.

Cantor, C. N. and Stacy, C. L.: Manipulative dexterity in mental defectives. *American Journal of Mental Deficiency, 56*:401-410, 1951.

Capabianco, R. J.: Quantitative and qualitative analysis of endogenous and exogenous boys on arithmetic achievement. *Monograph of Social Research in Child Development, 19*:101-142, 1954.

Carrison, D. and Werner, H.: Principles and methods of teaching arithmetic to mentally retarded children. *American Journal of Mental Deficiency, 47*:309-317, 1943.

Clarke, Ann M. and Clarke, A. D. B.: *Mental Deficiency, The Changing Outlook*. London, Methuen and Company, 1958.

Clarke, A. D. B. and Clarke, A. M.: Pseudo-feeblemindedness—some implications. *American Journal of Mental Deficiency, 59*:507-509, 1955.

Connor, Frances P.: World frontiers in special education: proceedings of the international seminar on special education. *International Society for Rehabilitation of the Disabled,* New York, 1960.

Connor, Leo E.: *Administration of Special Education Programs.* New York, Bureau of Publications, Teachers College, Columbia University, 1961.

Costello, Helen M.: The responses of mentally retarded children to specialized learning experiences in arithmetic. Doctor's Dissertation. Philadelphia, University of Pennsylvania, 1941.

Crawford, Ruth: Art for the exceptional child. *National Elementary Principal, 30*:25-26, 1951.

Cruickshank, W. M.: Arithmetic work habits of mentally retarded boys. *American Journal of Mental Deficiency, 52*:318-330, 1948.

Cruickshank, W. M.: A comparative study of psychological factors involved in the responses of mentally retarded and normal boys to problems in arithmetic. Doctor's Dissertation. Ann Arbor, University of Michigan, 1946.

Cruickshank, W. and Johnson, G. O.: *Education of Exceptional Children and Youth.* Englewood Cliffs, New Jersey, Prentice-Hall, Inc., 1958.

Cutts, Norma and Mosely, Nicholas: *Teaching the Bright and Gifted.* Englewood Cliffs, New Jersey, Prentice-Hall, Inc., 1957.

Daly, Flora M. and Henderson, Robert A.: Education of mentally retarded minors in the public schools of California. *California State Department of Education, XXXVIII*:8, Sacramento, October 1959.

Davis, Kingsley: Final note on a case of extreme isolation. *The American Journal of Sociology, 57*:432-437, 1947.

Dinsmore, M.: Teaching reading to the brain-injured child. *American Journal of Mental Deficiency, 58*:431-435, 1954.

Dolch, Edward: *The Basic Sight Vocabulary Cards.* Champaign, Illinois, Garrard Press.

Dunn, L. M.: A comparison of the reading progress of mentally retarded and normal boys of the same mental age. *Monograph of Social Research and Development, 19*:7-99, 1954.

Ecob, Katherine G.: Deciding what's best for your retarded child. *Mental Health Materials Center, Inc.,* New York, 1956.

Ellis, N. R. and Distefano, M. K.: Effects of verbal urging and praise upon rotary pursuit performance in mental defectives. *American Journal of Mental Deficiency, 64*:486-490, 1959.

Encyclopedia of Educational Research. Monroe, Walter S., Ed. New York, Macmillan Company, 1950, pp. 1247-1260.

Engle, T. L. and Hamlett, I. C.: Comparison of mental defectives and normal children in ability to handle clock and calendar situations. *American Journal of Mental Deficiency, 58*:655-658, 1954.

Everybody's child, the mentally retarded. *Health, Education and Welfare Programs.* Olympia, State of Washington, 1961.

Ewerhardt, P. J.: Reading difficulties in subnormal children. *American Association of Mental Deficiency, 43*:188-193, 1938.

Featherstone, W. B.: *Teaching the Slow Learner.* New York, Bureau of Publications, Teachers College, Columbia University, 1951.

Featherstone, W. B.: *The Curriculum of the Special Class.* Published with the approval of Professor Paul R. Mort, Teachers College, New York, Columbia University, 1932.

Foale, M. and Paterson, J. W.: The hearing of mental defectives. *American Journal of Mental Deficiency, 59*:254-258, 1952.

Font, M.: Some clinical applications of the Rorschach technique in cases of borderline deficiency. *American Journal of Mental Deficiency, 54*:507-511, 1950.

Freeman, F.: *Theory and Practice of Psychological Testing.* New York, Holt, Rinehart and Winston, 1955.

Gallagher, J. J., Benoit, E. P. and Boyd, H. F.: Measures of intelligence in brain damaged children. *Journal of Clinical Psychology, 12*:69-72, 1956.

Gann, E.: *Reading Difficulty and Personality Organization.* New York, King's Crown Press, 1945.

Garton, Melinda Dean: *Teaching the Educable Mentally Retarded, Practical Methods.* Springfield, Illinois, Charles C Thomas, 1961.

Gates, A. I.: *Improvement of Reading.* New York, Macmillan Company, 1935.

Gibson, R.: A tentative clinical classification of the special types of mental deficiency. *American Journal of Mental Deficiency, 54*:382-393, 1950.

Gilmour, D.: The rh factor: its role in human disease with particular reference to mental deficiency. *Journal of Mental Science, 96*:359-392, 1950.

Goldstein, K.: *Language and Language Disturbance.* New York, Grune and Stratton, Inc., 1948.

Goldstein, K.: *The Organism.* New York, American Book Company, 1939.

Gothberg, L. C.: The mental defective child's understanding of time. *American Journal of Mental Deficiency, 53*:441-455, 1949.

Graham, Ray: The Illinois plan for special education of exceptional children. *The Educable Mentally Handicapped,* Circular Series B, No. 12, p. 17, Springfield, Illinois, Superintendent of Public Instruction, 1950.

Gray, Wm. S.: *The Teaching of Reading and Writing.* Chicago, Illinois, Scott, Foresman and Company, 1956, p. 211.

Greene, E. B.: *Measurement of Human Behavior.* New York, Odyssey Press, 1941.

Guertin, W. H.: Differential characteristics of the pseudofeebleminded. *American Journal of Mental Deficiency, 54*:394-398, 1950.

Guertin, W. H.: Mental growth in pseudo-feeblemindedness. *Journal of Clinical Psychology, 5*:414-418, 1949.

Gunzburg, H. C.: An experimental approach to the improvement of reading of educationally subnormal boys. *Special Schools Journal, 37*:77-86, 1948.

Gunzburg, H. C.: Experiments in the improvement of reading in a group of educationally subnormal boys. *Journal of Mental Science, 94*:809, 1948.

Gunzburg, H. C.: Maladjustment as expressed in drawings by subnormal children. *American Journal of Mental Deficiency, 57*:9-23, 1952.

Gunzburg, H. C.: The significance of various aspects in drawings by educationally subnormal children. *Journal of Mental Science, 96*:951-975, 1950.

Gunzburg, H. C.: The subnormal boy and his reading interests. *Library Quarterly, 18*:264-274, 1948.

Hafemeister, N. R.: Development of a curriculum for the trainable child. *American Journal of Mental Deficiency, 55*:495-501, 1951.

Harrison, S.: A review of research in speech and language development of the mentally retarded child. *American Journal of Mental Deficiency, 63*:236-240, 1958.

Hart, Evelyn: How retarded children can be helped. Pamphlet No. 288. New York, Public Affairs Committee, September 1959.

Heath, S. R.: A mental pattern found in motor deviates. *Journal of Abnormal Social Psychology, 41*:223-225, 1946.

Heck, Arch O.: *The Education of Exceptional Children.* New York, McGraw-Hill Book Company, 1953, pp. 329-373.

Hegge, T. G.: Special reading disability with particular reference to the mentally deficient. *American Association on Mental Deficiency, 39*:297-343, May 1934.

Hermelin, B. F.: Studies of learning and trainability in imbeciles. Unpublished A.B. Thesis. University of Reading, 1956.

Hilliard, L. T. and Kirman, Brian H.: *Mental Deficiency.* Boston, Little, Brown and Company, 1957.

House, B. J. and Zeaman, D.: Visual discrimination learning in imbeciles. *American Journal of Mental Deficiency, 63*:447-452, 1959.

Ingram, C. P.: *Education of the Slow-learning Child.* New York, The Roland Press, 1953. Also third edition, 1960.

Interpretation of mental retardation to the community. *California State Department of Education,* Sacramento, November 1958.

Jastak, J.: The endogenous slow-learner. *American Journal of Mental Deficiency, 55*:269-274, 1950.

Jordan, Thomas E.: *The Exceptional Child.* Columbus, Ohio, Charles E. Merrill Books, Inc., 1962.

Jordan, Thomas E.: *The Mentally Retarded.* Columbus, Ohio, Charles E. Merrill Books, Inc., 1961.

Justa, Sister Mary: Meeting the reading needs of the slow-learner. *Journal of Education, 137*:13-15, October 1954.

Katona, G.: *Organizing and Memorizing.* New York, Columbia University Press, 1940.

Kephart, N. C.: *The Slow Learner in the Classroom,* Columbus, Ohio, Charles E. Merrill Books, Inc., 1960.

Kingsley, H. and Gary, R.: *The Nature and Condition of Learning.* Englewood Cliffs, New Jersey, Prentice-Hall, Inc., 1957.

Kirk, Samuel A.: *Teaching Reading to the Slow-learning.* Boston, Houghton, Mifflin and Company, 1950.

Kirk, S. A. and Johnson, G. O.: *Educating the Retarded Child.* Boston, Houghton, Mifflin and Company, 1951, pp. 165, 281, 326-334.

Krause, Arnold and Stolzfus, Grant: *Forgotten Children.* New York, National Association for Mental Health, 1957.

Kvaraceus, W. C.: Handwriting needs of the mentally retarded children and of children in regular grades. *Elementary School Journal, 280*:42-44, 1955.

Lavalli, A. and Levine, M.: Social and guidance needs of mentally handicapped adolescents as revealed through sociodrama. *American Journal of Mental Deficiency, 58*:544-552, 1954.

Laws and regulations relating to education and health services for exceptional children in California. Sacramento, California State Department of Education, 1960.

Lerrigo, Marion O.: The mentally retarded and the church. *International Journal of Religious Education,* December 1958.

Lowenfeld, V.: Self-adjustment through creative activity. *American Journal of Mental Deficiency, 45*:366-373, 1941.

Mackie, Romaine: Exceptional years for exceptional children. *School Life, 40*:8-10, 1958.

Mackie, R. P. and Dunn, L. M.: College and university programs for the preparation of teachers of exceptional children. *U. S. Office of Education,* Bull. No. 13, 1954.

Mackie, R. P., Dunn, L. M. and Cain, L. F.: Professional preparation for teachers of exceptional children: an overview. *U. S. Office of Education,* 1959.

Maisner, E. A.: Contributions of play-therapy techniques to total rehabilitative design in an institution for high-grade mentally deficient and borderline children. *American Journal of Mental Deficiency, 55*:235-250, 1950.

Martens, Elsie H.: Curriculum adjustments for the mentally retarded. Washington, D. C., Federal Security Agency, Bull. No. 2, 1950, pp. 52-53.

Magnifico, L.: *Education for the Exceptional Child.* New York, Longmans, Green and Company, 1958.

McBride, R., Kaplan, J. and Hall, M. A.: Community planning to meet some of the social needs of the mentally retarded adult. *American Journal of Mental Deficiency, 58*:331-336, 1953.

McClelland, D.: *Readings in Motivation.* New York, Appleton-Century-Crofts, Inc., 1955.

Mowrer, O. H.: *Learning Theory and Personality Dynamics.* New York, The Roland Press, 1950.

Nulton, Lucy: Readiness to change from manuscript to cursive. *Elementary English, 32*:382-383, 1955.

Peckman, Ralf A.: Problems in job adjustment of the mentally retarded. *American Journal of Mental Deficiency, 56*:448-453, October 1951.

Perlstein, J. A. and Hood, P. N.: Infantile spastic hemiplegia, intelligence and age of walking and talking. *American Journal of Mental Deficiency, 61*:534-543, 1957.

Preparation of mentally retarded youth for gainful employment. Washington, D. C., U. S. Department of Health, Education and Welfare, Bull. No. 28, 1959.

Reynolds, B. and Adams, J. A.: Psychomotor performance as a function of initial level of ability. *American Journal of Psychology, 67*:268-277, 1954.

Ross, C. C. and Stanley, J. C.: *Measurement in Today's Schools.* 3rd Ed. Englewood Cliffs, New Jersey, Prentice-Hall, Inc., 1954.

Roulle, E. N.: New horizons for the mentally retarded: when a school looks at the problem as a whole. *American Journal of Mental Deficiency, 59*:359-373, 1955.

Sarason, Seymour B.: *Psychological Problems in Mental Deficiency.* Third edition. New York, Harper and Brothers, 1959.

Schaefer-Simmern, H.: *The Unfolding of Artistic Activity.* Berkeley, University of California Press, 1948.

Simpson, Roy E.: Education of mentally retarded minors in public schools in California. *California State Department of Education, XXVIII*: 8, Sacramento, October 1959.

Stacey, C. L. and deMartino, M.: *Counseling and Psychotherapy with the Mentally Retarded.* Chicago, The Free Press, 1958.

Stinson, Ethelyn: *How to Teach Children Music.* New York, Harper and Brothers, 1941.

Suggested activities for mentally retarded children. *California State Department of Education, XXI*:2, Sacramento, January 1952.

Terman, L. and Merrill, M.: *Measuring Intelligence.* Boston, Houghton, Mifflin and Company, 1937.

The slow learner in secondary schools. *New Jersey School Teachers Association,* Year Book. Plainfield, New Jersey, 1961.

Thorne, F. C.: Counseling and psychotherapy with mental defectives. *American Journal of Mental Deficiency, 52*:263-271, 1948.

Tizard, J.: The effects of different types of supervision on the behavior of mental defectives in a sheltered workshop. *American Journal of Mental Deficiency, 58*:143-161, 1953.

Town, C. H.: An investigation of the adjustment of the feebleminded in the community. *Clinical Psychology, 20*:42-54, 1931.

Van Riper, C.: *Speech Correction.* 3rd Ed. Englewood Cliffs, New Jersey, Prentice-Hall, Inc., 1956.

Vaughn, C. L.: Classroom behavior problems encountered in attempting to teach illiterate defective boys how to read. *Journal of Educational Psychology, 32*:339-350, 1941.

Wallin, J. E. Wallace: *Education of Mentally Handicapped Children.* New York, Harper and Brothers Company, 1955.

Yepson, L. N.: Counseling the mentally retarded. *American Journal of Mental Deficiency, 57*:205-213, 1952.

Young, Kimball: *Personality and Problems of Adjustment.* New York, Appleton-Century-Crofts, Inc., 1952.

Chapter VII

The Education of the Severely (Trainable) Mentally Retarded

B EFORE 1950, very little was done for severely mentally re- tarded children and although a great deal has been accom- plished in the few years since, progress is still hampered by the widespread view that only the educable retarded can benefit from education. It has been estimated that one out of every 250 per- sons in the United States, or more than 600,000 persons, is in this group of retardates. One study conservatively concludes, "It ap- pears that for every thousand school-age children there are one to two trainable mentally handicapped children in the community and one trainable child in an institution."[1]

From an economic standpoint, the greater the number of these individuals assisted in their own communities, the greater the sav- ings in institutionalization costs to society. Considering the hu- manitarian point of view, every child should be given the oppor- tunity to use his capabilities regardless of their limitations.

In 1955, thirteen states had permissive and six had mandatory legislation to provide education for trainable mentally handi- capped children. In contrast to the nineteen states recognizing the needs of the trainable, there were forty-six states providing for the needs of the educable retarded.[2] By 1958, forty-seven states had one or more state schools, thirty-six had one or more day schools, and thirty-seven had one or more private boarding schools for the mentally retarded.[3] However, all of these schools do not admit the trainable. Furthermore, many of them have age limits and fees curtailing registration.

According to the Directory of the American Association on

---

[1] M. A. Wirtz and Richard Guenther: The incidence of trainable mentally handi- capped children. *Exceptional Children, 23*:175, 1957.

[2] Special education of exceptional children. *School Life, 38*:7-10, 1956.

[3] *Education and training facilities, a directory for exceptional children.* 3rd ed. Porter Sargent, Mass., 1958, pp. 95-151.

Mental Deficiency,[4] forty-five states claim no restrictions as to type or degree of mental defective accepted in at least one of their state schools. This report further indicated that the total of seventy-six of these schools may admit trainable children.

Professor Goldberg of Columbia University has pointed out some important aspects of the problem of education for trainable children.[5] He estimated that 22,000 trainable children received schooling in 1956-57. This represents school-age children in the United States for that school year. He further stated that, "There are four main classes of schools for the 'trainable' child in the United States today:

1. Public day schools and classes.
2. Private day schools and classes.
3. Public residential schools.
4. Private residential schools."[6]

The present trend is toward keeping the trainable child in the home and community and providing special education for him in the public school. Not only is there a pressing need for more schools and classes for these children, but there is also a need for a "Life-Plan." Education and guidance for children from six to sixteen years of age is insufficient for the trainable. Since the state and federal governments have been so reluctant to provide training for the severely retarded child, "Many parents felt compelled to organize their own classes in church basements or community centers wherever they could obtain free space for a few hours a day."[7]

San Francisco, St. Paul and St. Louis were among the first cities to provide classes for the trainable. By 1950, California, Pennsylvania and Wisconsin, followed by a few other states, began making provision for the trainable in state legislation. However, the classes thus opened were never sufficient to warrant closing the parent-

---

[4] Neil A. Dayton, comp.: Listings of public and private schools and homes for the retarded. *Directory of the American Association on Mental Deficiency*, 1956, appendix A, pp. 19-100.

[5] I. Ignacy Goldberg: Current status of education and training in the United States for trainable mentally retarded children. *Exceptional Children, 23*:146-154, Dec. 1957.

[6] *Ibid.,* p. 149.

[7] Cornell Capa and Maya Pines: *Retarded Children Can Be Helped.* New York, Channel Press, Inc., 1957, p. 52.

sponsored schools. The numerous parent groups have banded together to form the "National Association for Retarded Children." All the problems of providing education for trainable children are not solely the problem of the parents. They are also problems of the community.

Parents can inspire and lead in building programs for these children but their success depends entirely on the support of people around them—teachers, social workers, doctors, legislators, clergymen and neighbors. These people must implement what parents have already proven; mentally retarded children, both educable and trainable, can be helped.

CLASSROOM TRAINING FOR THE SEVERELY MENTALLY RETARDED CHILD

A training program for severely mentally retarded children necessitates sufficient flexibility to permit adaptation to the individual child's level of growth and development. In many instances, limited learning has been previously acquired through the erratic process of trial-and-error with no awareness of cause-and-effect and consequently, with very little satisfaction from achievement. It is important to recognize and accept these children at the level of their respective mental and social development and to provide more adequate opportunity for consistent integration of proficiency in the various learning areas experienced by young, normal children of equivalent development ages.

The severely mentally retarded child (IQ below 50) is referred to as the trainable child; he usually profits very little from formal schooling but is capable of being trained to work with the hands. Many people in this category earn their living as maids, dishwashers, janitors, busboys or boxmakers when they reach adulthood.

The trainable child comes to school with his own individual capacity to participate and grow in an educational program. He is a combination of biology and culture molded by people and events. His condition has been determined by genes, prenatal and post-natal environment, and his ability to learn from experiences.

Cruickshank describes the trainable as being the mentally handicapped who are, "unable to profit or adjust to the offerings of the public school program because of extremely low ability."[8]

---

[8] Wm. M. Cruickshank and G. O. Johnson: *Education of Exceptional Children and Youth.* Englewood Cliffs, N. J., Prentice-Hall, Inc., 1958, pp. 45-46.

All skills are acquired through practice with noted progress from gross accomplishment to more refined and discriminatory adeptness. This is more obviously seen in attainments from muscular development, but the identical process is applicable to communication skills with oral language and ultimate symbolization in writing. This basic principle is applicable to all instructional and training procedures in the areas which are delineated in this chapter as objectives to affect more acceptable personal and social adjustment for these children who are not considered to be of educable mind.

All aspects of training should be meaningful to the child in his daily life at home and in his neighborhood experiences as well as within the classroom situation. To attain optimum results, it is essential that the teacher concern herself with individual appraisals and to recognize and understand the heterogeneous groupings we have in respect to chronological age, mental age, emotional stability and degree of organic impairment, as well as family attitudes. These considerations necessitate marked modification of the conventional teaching methods in the more homogeneous regular school class. There will be greater need for specific goals with constant repetition in teaching procedures and an ever awareness of concrete association as the limited means to learning for it is generally accepted that these children are incapable of abstract conceptual thinking.

The design of an appropriate training program for severely mentally retarded children has necessitated development, modification, and revision of basic curriculum guidelines with anticipated continued change on the basis of teacher observations and experiences in the classroom. With the primary training objectives of teaching severely retarded children to function socially at a higher level in the immediate environment, cognizance is taken of the fact that certain training procedures will be applicable to more than one of the following areas:

1. Personal routines.
2. Health routines.
3. Care of property.
4. Safety routines.
5. Play performance.
6. Social adjustment.
7. Language development.

The intent of this chapter is to serve as curriculum guidelines to assist each teacher of severely mentally retarded children in developing a program of instruction adaptable to the capabilities and developmental levels of individual children within a particular group.

Personal Routines

The objectives are to develop proficiency in care of self, to instill a sense of personal social responsibility, thus enabling the child to adjust better to his home and community environment.

Activities
1. Care of clothing.
   a. Removing wraps.
   b. Folding and hanging wraps.
   c. Lacing and tying, brushing and polishing shoes.
   d. Washing, ironing, mending and sewing buttons on clothes.
2. Eating habits and table manners.
   a. Taking turns asking the Blessing over food.
   b. Proper handling of food, food on plate, plate on table.
   c. Eat slowly, keep food in mouth.
   d. Passing and serving food.
   e. Learning to say "please" and "thank you."
   f. Proper use of silverware.
   g. Importance of the table napkin and its use.

Health Routines

The objective is to develop daily health habits and to instill a sense of need for personal cleanliness.

Activities
1. Personal grooming.
   a. Clean hands, teeth, nails, hair, clothes, shoes and importance of daily bathing.
   b. Teach child how to use faucet for washing hands.
   c. Advise older children on shampooing and setting hair.
2. Care of nose and mouth.
   a. Use of handkerchief and tissues, covering mouth when sneezing or coughing.
   b. Encourage child to keep mouth closed, hands away from face and fingers out of nose and mouth.
3. Proper attire.

    a. Wear proper clothing according to the weather.

    b. Keep properly clothed and decent.

4. Proper attitude toward food and eating.

    a. Learning seven basic foods and how to prepare healthy foods.

    b. Developing proper attitude toward nutritional foods.

    c. Taking small bites and masticating with mouth closed.

    d. Emphasizing desirability of pleasant atmosphere during meals.

5. Rest.

    a. Teaching need for retiring early and getting plenty of rest.

6. Use of restroom.

    a. Assign definite time period, if possible, for toilet needs.

    b. When necessary for child to visit restroom at irregular intervals, teach proper way to request permission.

    c. Encourage cleanliness in restroom.

7. Attitudes towards doctors, dentists, nurses.

    a. Attempt to establish a friendly relationship between child and doctors, dentists and nurses.

8. Physical exercise.

    a. Plan time outdoors (weather permitting) playing ball or other games, marching, racing, jumping rope or other like active games.

Care of Property

The objective is to instill a sense of responsibility for personal possessions, to teach proper regard for school and other public property; and to respect property of others.

Activities

1. Personal possessions.

    a. Training in care of clothing and personal belongings with emphasis on both appearance and economic values.

    b. Care of pets, i.e., feeding and handling.

2. Public property.

    a. Play equipment.

    b. Classroom equipment.

    c. Care of supplies in daily use.

    d. Public buildings, parks and playgrounds.

3. Property of others.

    a. Respect for and care of belongings of others.

    b. Appropriation is stealing.

Safety Routines

The objective is to teach recognition of simple precautions and train children to obey safety rules.

Activities

1. Safety at home.
   a. Cautious use of electrical appliances.
   b. Danger in falling.
      Getting in and out of bathtub.
      Going up and down stairs.
      Climbing upon things.
      Playing in windows.
2. Safety in car or bus.
   a. Staying on seat at all times while vehicle is moving.
   b. Never play with door handles or instrument panel.
   c. Never put head, arms or legs outside moving vehicle.
   d. Never get into car of stranger.
3. Safety on the street.
   a. Obeying traffic signals.
      Crossing street with green light only.
      Waiting on curb for the light to change.
      Looking all directions before crossing street.
      Walk, never run across street.
   b. Ability to give name, address, phone number in event one is lost.
   c. Danger in riding bicycle or sled, or skating in street.
   d. Danger in running toward a ball which is rolling into or toward the street.
   e. Awareness of dangers of icy sidewalks or steps.
4. Safety at school.
   a. In the classroom.
      Proper use of scissors, hammer, sticks, etc.
      Consideration for safety of others, avoid throwing objects.
      Danger in pushing or shoving.
   b. On the playground.
      Proper use of playground equipment.
      Danger of throwing sand in eyes, etc.

Play Performances

Many skills and behavioral attitudes are developed through play performance, some of which include: language development (the child communicates much more freely in the relaxed atmosphere of playtime); large muscle development and improved motor co-ordination (games should include those which improve walking, running, climbing, and hand co-ordinations); development of natural rhythms and harmonious movement, e.g., encouraging the enjoyment of rhythmical music; and development of social skills, learning rules, taking turns, sharing and learning fair play and cooperation (the acquisition of such skills enables the child to participate in the play of normal children, thereby providing opportunity for more acceptable social adjustment).

Objectives

1. To give the child self-confidence by helping him to develop concentration.
   To develop better coordination and muscular control.
   To learn to derive pleasure in cooperation.
   To provide opportunity for relaxation and release of tensions.
   To stimulate the lethargic and calm the over-active child.

Activities

1. Directed play.
   a. Indoor activities.
      Singing and rhythm games.
      Peg-boards, puzzles, clay.
      Musical chairs, thimble, pussy-cat, pop goes the weasel.
      Bean-bag, horse-shoes and bouncing ball.
      Story games and finger play.
      Playing with dolls, house-keeping.
      Blowing bubbles.
      Matching games.
      Structural play situations such as grocery store, host and hostess and guests, shoe shop, etc.
   b. Outdoor activities.
      Dodge ball.
      Jump rope, tether ball.
      Hide plastic eggs and blocks.
      All kinds of ball games.
      Sand-box.
      Crawling through barrel with ends removed (going through the tunnel game).
      Train trip (chairs used for engine and cars).

Relay races.

Hide and seek.

Sharing playground equipment.

2. Free play—a time for undirected but not unsupervised play should be included in the daily schedule. Materials for such free play should be available for the child to utilize in such manner as his imagination and capacities may allow. We should keep in mind the three stages of play development which are indicative of mental and special growth of the child.

   a. Solitary play wherein the child can amuse himself in some manner with no desire for companionship in play and with indifference as to what play others are engaged in.

   b. The next stage "parallel play," will find two or more children engaged in the same occupation such as playing dolls or stacking blocks on the floor, but still not working together.

   c. The highest stage, "cooperative play" finds the children playing with dolls, acting as the mother of a sick child with another being doctor or nurse treating the infant, or the children with blocks may put them together to make a train with an engineer or passengers.

3. Free play activity.

   a. Hollow blocks (8″ x 4″ x 16″). These are used for houses, trains, boats, furniture, rows of sidewalk, etc.

   b. Large boxes, various sizes, but large enough to crawl into, through and over.

   c. Hand puppets (unbreakable dolls), blankets and beds, peg-boards and mallets, blocks and rods, beads, clay, scissors, magazines from which pictures may be cut or merely observed.

   d. Nurse and doctor kits, cowboy equipment, toy rakes, shovels and hoes.

   e. Chalk-boards and chalk, paints, brushes and crayons (these materials should not be given at one time).

Social Adjustment

Social adjustment is the ultimate goal for trainable retarded children as well as for the educable retarded, and work in all other areas should have the aim of making the child more "socially acceptable." Better speech, better personal habits, respect for property—these things are part of a specific training to enhance the social acceptance of the child. The objective is to help the child become more acceptable to others. This can be attained by working toward a better social adjustment and by developing various behavioral skills such as learning to control temper tantrums, learning to take turns, and to share and learning to play social games.

Objective

1. To develop an understanding of the child's role in the home and his contributions to the family group.
2. To make the child more acceptable to the neighborhood by helping him to react in a socially acceptable manner and to respect private and public property.
3. To develop a feeling of belonging through interaction of individuals in a group setting such as church, restaurant, grocery or other public places.
4. To teach the child how to act toward other people, relatives, those in authority, younger people and babies.
5. To acquaint child with neighborhood, crossing streets, how to mail a letter and other simple errands.

Activities

1. Field trips.
   a. Preliminary planning of trips to places that have a direct and indirect influence on the daily activities of these children.
      —Tour of all the school buildings.
      —To various places in the community—bakery, grocery, theatre, shopping centers, church and others.
      —To learn to know community helpers—fireman, policeman, water works, gas plant, electric plant, etc.
      —These may be broadened to include industries, train trips, factories—all these may be actual trips.
   b. Social drama, act out the things seen on the field trips.
      —Choose daily tasks—housework, discussion of things they can do at home.
      —Put toys and belongings in proper places.
      —Lunch period offers one of the best opportunities for improvement in the social acceptability of the child, simple good manners, learning acceptable table manners, table conversations and similar things.

—Show love and appreciation for others.

—Use of television to learn how to behave in public.

—Play barber shop.

—Understand value of money (when playing grocery store have children earn money they spend).

—Birthdays—furnish learning opportunities which are carried over into neighborhood activities. The children learn to find pleasure in giving as well as receiving.

Language Development

It has been observed that the one basic skill which is most markedly underdeveloped in our "trainable" children is that of oral communication. It is felt that this is the skill upon which the other skills depend. Therefore, concentration on the development of basic language skills and on enlarged vocabulary is strongly recommended. The purpose and importance are to provide means of expression and communication; to equip the child better to communicate with others; to develop listening skills and to stimulate auditory and visual memory and discrimination; to promote better personal, family, community and social adjustment; to promote a sense of need for speech and to help the child develop verbal concepts. Conversation implies more than communication of wants or needs to the parent or teacher. It is to listen while others speak. Such topics as these may be introduced to encourage group participation: "What we saw on the way to school," "what we did last night," "what we had for breakfast," "who is wearing something new," "what will we do when we go home?"

Activities

1. Morning exercises.
   a. Children help plan duties of the day.
   b. Singing.
   c. Salute to the flag.
2. Story hour.
   a. The story should be simple, short and concrete in form. A slide projector and film strip story is very good. Use eye and ear gate together. Discuss every showing.
3. Speech games.
   a. Designed to provide training in formation of vowels, diphthongs and consonants.
   b. Designed to help children overcome speech defects.

4. Free group plan.
   Designed to encourage intra-child association, self-expression, and spontaneous intra-child communication.
5. Sharing period.
6. Organized social play.
   a. Host and hostess games and others.
7. Music period.
   a. Rhythm, dramatizing songs, singing and listening.
8. Arts and crafts period.
   a. Drawing, painting, ceramics, and needle work.

Perhaps it would be wise, at this time, to examine the practical application of the daily routines suggested in the beginning of this chapter. For this purpose, the description of the children and their actual class routines as given by the teacher is used below.

Since it would not be feasible to cover the entire school year, routines to be used were chosen at random for each month over a period of six months. The descriptions and records and any expression of opinion contained herein are to be regarded as that of the teacher. They have neither been accepted nor refuted by authority.

A TEACHER'S REPORT OF CLASSROOM PROCEDURES
(Used with a group of five severely retarded children)[9]

Description of the Children

1. Jeanie (C.A. 11)

Hair—fine, quite thick, could be attractive if neat, often matted in back, straggling over face.
Eyes—crossed, objects must be held very close to be identified.
Nose—constant drainage, frequent sneezing.
Ears—unusually small.
Neck—fat, short, bowed.
Trunk—very fat, otherwise normal.
Arms—apparently normal.
Legs—very thin.
Hands—slightly plump, dimpled and pretty. Often held up with fingers spread.

---

[9] Marian G. Pfeifle: A neighborhood school for trainable children. Unpublished Master's thesis. Reno, University of Nevada, 1960.

Feet—apparently normal but not held straight in walking, toed out.

Skin—texture and color seem normal on face and hands, but legs are mottled, red and purple. Hands look blue at times.

Posture—poor. Sits with legs apart, shoulders slumped, head hanging or slumps down on arms, upon anything handy—a chair, a desk or a person.

Motor control—walks and runs slowly and for short distances only with feet turned out at a wide angle. Has learned to skip with one foot only. Afraid to jump over a rope six inches from the ground. Can walk down or up stairs with use of alternate feet but may not unless reminded. Likes to dance and has some sense of rhythm but also remembers routines in simple dances. Afraid of losing balance, cannot stand on one foot or walk a chalk line putting one foot ahead of the other. With hands has trouble coloring, cannot keep within a margin or follow a dotted line. Can write 1 and 0. Can cut with scissors but not along lines. Can swing, but is afraid to go high. Will not try the slide or climb on the monkey bars.

Speech—numerous articulation difficulties.

2. Lorrie (C.A. 16)

Hair—rather fine with slight natural curl, frizzed occasionally by mother or older sister, later permanently curled.

Eyes—round and slightly "bugged out," also slightly slanted. Sight poor, objects identified only at close range.

Nose—small, otherwise normal.

Mouth—open often with tongue visible. Much mouth-breathing, yet nose not blocked by colds. Lower lip often pushed out to mutter or pout.

Head—flat in back.

Trunk—about normal.

Arms—short and rounded resembling those of a very young child.

Legs—shorter in proportion from the knee downward.

Hands—small, plump, with short fingers.

Feet—small, but apparently normal.

Skin—yellowish, dry.

Posture—poor. Head forward, shoulders sagging, slight forward lean as though carrying a pack. Often walks with arms dangling forward.

Motor control—quite skillful. Runs fast, plays ball well, dances well, dances independently, interpreting music. Climbs, slides, swings high, jumps and jumps rope. With hands cuts, pastes, colors, draws and writes with skill.

Speech—articulation difficulty and stuttering.

3. Ray (C.A. 11)

Hair—fine, not too thick, always neatly in place.

Eyes—very slight slant. Often red and sore-looking, with crusting on lids and in corners.

Nose—constant drainage, heavier at times. Apparently never used for breathing.

Mouth—always open usually with tongue prominent.

Neck—short and fat.

Head—flattened in back.

Trunk—apparently normal.

Arms—apparently normal.

Legs—apparently normal.

Feet—toed in.

Skin—normal and healthy looking.

Posture—poor. Head forward, shoulders sag, toes turned in.

Motor control—fairly skilled in walking, running, throwing, catching, climbing, and sliding. Very gentle and dainty in use of crayons and pencils but strokes are not smooth or straight. Works puzzles well and builds well with blocks.

Speech—as well as usual articulation difficulties, makes "slushy" sounds. Cannot manage fricatives. Very difficult to understand speech.

4. Marnie (not mongoloid type) (C.A. 17)

Hair—coarse, blond, naturally curly. Could be beautiful, but cut too short making the child's head look too round and small for her body.

Eyes—small, half-closed, wears glasses.

Nose—nothing unusual, colds rare.

Mouth—sometimes open, not always.

Neck—short and fat, beneath double chin.

Skin—constantly covered with eruptions on face and neck.

Trunk—seems short. Very obese. Shoulders sloped.

Arms—very fat and lazy. Cannot reach behind at waist or to back of neck. Seldom raised even to shoulder level.

Hands—plump and pretty but feeble and lacking in skill. Child palms objects rather than picking them up.

Legs—child has had one or more operations and hip has a pin in it. Knees seem to knock together and one leg may be shorter as there is a noticeable limp.

Feet—wide and fat, but appear normal.

Posture—poor. Head down, shoulders rounded.

Motor control—pitiful. Walks very slowly by choice. Cannot run at all, but has a strange hurried walk with head bobbing and arms flapping and knees jerking. Learned to get on and off chair. Takes stairs with hand rail bringing two feet together on each step like a very young child. Has gained enough confidence to go up or down four steps without a hand rail or someone helping.

Speech—has high-pitched voice, whining but not loud. Can pronounce many words correctly, but has careless pronunciation, perhaps heard at home. Uses some baby talk and frequently mutters meaningless syllables, as "tassah" or "wassah." Rather like a parrot coming out with sentences or phrases that are correct, but have no relation to the given situation.

5. Susie (C.A. 8)

Hair—coarse, black, straight and unruly. Never neat. Clutched together with string or rubber band and masses of bobby pins placed at random. Long enough to reach well over the shoulders, but held up while wiry ends escaped from the pins hang about her face.

Nose—frequently runny.

Mouth—open, tongue showing. Breathes through mouth.

Skin—yellow. Whole appearance Oriental.

Trunk—perhaps slightly short. Not over fat, waistline proportionally too large.

Arms—apparently normal.

Hands—plump, childish and pretty. Has some strength in fingers, pinches occasionally, causing pain. Could cling to mother or father and require considerable pull to get free.

Legs—apparently normal.

Feet—apparently normal.

Motor control—rather like that of a four-year-old. Walks and runs well. Takes stairs like a very young child but requires no help. Can beat time to music and learns simple dance routines steadily.

Speech—can talk a little, but does not seem to want to. Has articulatory difficulties but much of her baby talk can be corrected.

From these descriptions, it will be seen that the children could not be called grotesque. In fact, if their weight were trimmed down and they were well-groomed, they could pass as normal in appearance.

The test scores on the Vineland Social Maturity Scale were 51, 54, 55 for three of these children. No score could be obtained for two of them since their immaturity made testing impossible.

DAILY PROGRAM

9:00—Opening exercises.

1. Teacher and children exchange greetings and children greet one another.
2. Children remove wraps and hang them neatly. The teacher or children help those who are still unable to manage alone. (Those who need help are given instruction individually, usually when an assistant is directing some activity with the others.)
3. Flag salute.
4. Attendance is checked and all sing "Good Morning."

9:10—Show and tell.

1. Children take turns showing interesting things brought from home or telling about activities of the previous evening, or the weekend. If they have nothing better to relate, they tell what they had for breakfast. (This activity encourages speaking and listening.)
2. Neatness check. Attention is called to signs of neatness and cleanliness. Children respond with compliments and suggestions for good grooming are made by teacher and pupils.

9:30—Language.

1. Story or poem is read or told to children. (The same one is repeated many times.) It is illustrated with colored pictures, cut-

outs for flannel board, stand-up cut-outs, models, toys, puppets, view-master reels, filmstrips or movies.
2. Questions are asked about the story.
3. Depending on the amount of time available and the attention of the children, any or all of the following may be used that day or on succeeding days:
   a. The teacher retells the story omitting words that the children try to add.
   b. The teacher retells the story, omitting several words at the end of each sentence and the children try to complete the sentence.
   c. The teacher begins the story then asks what happened next. She uses stand-up or flannel board cut-outs to illustrate what she is saying and the children select the cut-out for the part they tell.
   d. The story is dramatized by the children.

9:50—Music or rhythm.

1. Singing game with or without music accompaniment.
2. Marching, skipping or dancing to music.
3. Choral speaking or finger play.

10:00—Speech training.

1. Speech cards are used according to individual needs.
2. Games are used to give practice to consonant sounds, in nonsense syllables.
3. Rhymes are repeated or games are played that dramatize simple sounds.
4. Listening games are played.

During the above period, the children sit together and take turns. If they become bored with watching and listening, they may engage in some quiet activity such as stringing beads, coloring, or looking at a book.

10:15—Exercises and games.

1. Exercises requiring the use of large muscles are given.
2. A game requiring the use of large muscles is played. (It may be played indoors or outdoors.) Or a simple folk dance may be enjoyed.

10:30—Health or social studies.

1. Health or safety lessons are given.
2. Training in neatness of person and surroundings.
3. The children are given a daily reminder of the need for courtesy and fair play.

These lessons may include the use of pictures, stories, dramatizations and conversation.

10:40—Recess.

Recess is supervised carefully and may be spent in free play. A teacher-directed game or a walk in the vicinity of the school. It is spent outdoors.

10:55—Snack time.

1. Lavatory period.
2. Children take turns playing host or hostess or they may choose to work as a group. They set the table and serve water or juices and crackers.
3. Snack time is regarded as a "party" and relaxation and conversation are enjoyed.

11:15—Arts and crafts.

1. A new activity is presented each day, but old, familiar, easy-to-do activities are also available for those who cannot be encouraged to try the new.
2. Children are encouraged to finish any work they start.
3. The children are helped to tidy up after work and are urged to help one another as needed in washing hands or unbuttoning smocks.

11:45—Prepare for dismissal.

The children help put away the materials used during the day, then put on wraps, etc.

Dismissal.

DAILY RECORD OF CLASS PROCEDURE AS KEPT BY THE TEACHER

Monday, September 21

Jeanie held the flag while I said the pledge and the children mumbled the words with me. Began teaching them a "good morning" song. Tried to get the children to clap in time to some music played on the record player. The children were to watch and try to keep in time with me as well as listening to the rhythm. Not too successful at first.

Gathered in a circle for a story. "The Three Bears." I had told the story once and the children did not seem to understand it. I told it a second time that day and they repeated after me what each bear said. This time, I used colored cut-outs of Goldilocks, the bears, the forest, the house, the table, chairs and beds. While telling the story, I asked the children to finish the sentence such as, "This soup is —." Later, Jeanie and Ray each had a turn at putting the pictures up for the others to tell what was happening. When Lorrie put the pictures up she told the story too, and then she would ask someone to join in or to answer any questions. When it was Jeanie's turn and she was the first to want to tell the story, she asked me to sit in her place. She wanted me to be the pupil while she was being "Teacher." Marnie did not contribute anything but her presence. Well, perhaps more than that! She watched. She listened.

We used jig-saw puzzles next. Ray does them quickly. He did two and started a third one. He gave up on that one because it was too hard. I had told him that it was a hard one but he had insisted on doing it. Lorrie, after being coaxed, worked one puzzle. She was slower than the others. Jeanie worked one puzzle also. Marnie had to be helped. She got one or two pieces of the "Dog" puzzle together by herself, probably by luck. She couldn't seem to tell when a piece did not fit into a space and the color and picture meant nothing to her.

The class went for a walk up the street. Saw pipes being removed from a big truck to the roadside. Sat on someone's lawn to watch. Marnie wouldn't sit down. Jeanie had a cold and had no handkerchief. Gave her a Kleenex and she threw it on the ground after using it. Told her about trying to keep our city clean.

After returning to school, I put out drawing paper hoping to get the children to make or draw something we had seen on our walk. Ray drew two wheels with a line across which did to some extent represent a trailer.

Friday, September 26

It was Ray's turn to hold the flag, but Jeanie wanted it. Because she was refused, she sulked in a corner. I brought her over to stand with the others. She stood till we were halfway through the pledge; then she went to the couch and lay down.

In "Show and Tell," Lorrie had some cards to show. Jeanie came over right away as if nothing had happened. She knew which were kings, queens, or jacks and she sometimes counted correctly on the other cards. She usually counts, "1, 2, 4." This time she said, "1, 2, 3, 4."

The teacher's assistant came and took some of the children into another room so that I could work with one child at a time. Lorrie said all the "s" pictures with only a few mistakes. Then she went with the assistant and worked on sewing cards.

Instead of a directed game, I let the children have "free play" in the yard, Lorrie played on the swing. She hoisted herself up on the bar at the top. She often does that; she can do many things, and might be good at tumbling and dancing.

Ray and Marnie played with the doll house. I had put all the furniture in the right rooms for the fun of it. They came over after I sat down and they emptied most of the rooms. Then they stacked the furniture with no idea of what each object was or what each room was.

Jeanie sat and played with a toy machine gun or just sat. At snack time she started digging into the crackers, as usual.

Lorrie insisted on pouring the juice and spilled it.

Upon returning to class, we got out the finger paint—red and yellow. Lorrie liked it so well she sang and worked away by herself. Jeanie and Ray quit without even spreading the paint over the paper. When I tried to interest Jeanie in making some marks on the paper, she refused and became angry and sullen. She had her hands full of thick paint, so I said, "Oh, don't get paint on my dress!" She immediately reached out and touched my dress, putting a big lump of yellow on it. Then she looked at me with a sneering expression as if to say, "So what are you going to do about it?" I slapped her hand and told her that was naughty. Presently, I went to help her get the paint off her hands and she was all cheerful and chatty as if nothing had happened. While the children were painting, some observers came to view the children. One went to each child and did some of the work for them instead of letting them do it for themselves.

Earlier, with speech cards, I showed Ray a picture of a baby on its back with its feet in the air. He didn't know what it was. He said, "Squirr'," meaning "squirrel!" I told him what it was. Then he turned the card over and said, "Beebee si' do'" (the baby is sitting down).

Jeanie gets many words right. She is very anxious to do this work. She likes to play "teacher" too.

Friday, October 3

Tried to get Marnie to say "pig." No response. Ray couldn't sound "g," so I asked him to feel my throat while I said it. It didn't register. In "News," Jeanie told about her sister going downtown with her mother and getting a new skirt.

At recess, Jeanie, Ray, and I went for a walk up the street. We saw a boat and a trailer. Lorrie wouldn't come.

When we played the game, "What did you see?," in which a number of objects are shown, then covered with a cloth, Lorrie remembered seven of them. Jeanie remembered four, and Marnie one. It was an accomplishment for Marnie to remember something and say it. She usually talks about wholly unrelated things. Whereas, I had shown seven or eight objects to the other children, I only showed three to Marnie. These were a box, a top, and a boat. She remembered the boat. I showed her objects again and asked her to name them after me. She said, "box" and "boat," but she just mumbled "top." Then I put some scissors with the other objects and covered them. I pointed to where the scissors were and said, "What's there?" She said, "I threw the scissors away." Later she said "box" when I pointed then, "scissors" (or her version of the word). When I tried the box, the scissors and a spoon, she couldn't say "spoon" right and she wouldn't even try to say "scissors."

Thursday, October 30

Ray's mother was to bring ice cream. She came half an hour late. Lorrie's mother brought her to school but she was not in costume. She did not bring anything to the party either. I asked the mother to take her home and dress her in something that resembled a costume since all the others were wearing the Halloween costumes, even masks. The mother left with her, but soon the child returned dressed just as she was when she left. A friend came to help with the party and she brought her four year old son and the small baby. The children enjoyed playing games with the little boy. Lorrie picked up the baby several times, although she had been told not to do so. She was very disagreeable about playing games, too. It took some effort to get her to participate, yet once she took part, she had fun. We played London Bridge, Round and Round the Village, Fairies and Brownies, Spin the Bottle (this was Jeanie's idea) and we danced Hansel and Gretel.

We had decorated for Halloween with the things the children had made. There were favors for everyone, and witchhat place-cards on baskets of candy. The children squealed at the sight. They could not read their own names, so they had to be shown where to sit. Lorrie started griping; she didn't want to sit by Ray. Then she sulked and complained because she couldn't pass every-thing or she wanted to choose when something was passed to her, such as a dish of ice cream or a glass of juice, even though they were all alike. When the plate of cake was passed, she hovered over the plate for some time; then she reached for the one farther-est from her. To eat, she turned sideways on her chair, lounged with her right arm across the table, and her back was against the wall.

Marnie did not remove the paper cup from the cake before attempting to eat it. She pushed the lot into her face and made a mess of crumbs. She spooned into the ice cream without holding the dish and it slid out of the container onto the table. Jeanie, sitting next to her, reached over and put it back on the dish. This caused Lorrie to roar with laughter. She thought that Jeanie was taking Marnie's ice cream, and she hoped to see Jeanie punished. Later I heard Lorrie say, "I ha'e you, Jeanie." (I hate you.) She was really in a foul mood.

Jeanie and Ray allowed me to show them how to remove the paper cups from the cake. I started it for them and they finished.

All the children had three helpings of ice cream. Most of them had three heavily iced cakes and two iced cookies. They ate all the sandwiches too, in spite of the fact that each child's mother had told me that her child would eat only such-and-such a sandwich! However, few of them were willing to drink apple cider. Lorrie stood up at the table to see what everyone else had in case she was missing something. She has a nasty habit of demanding things. She says, "I want this" or "Give me that," without so much as a "please."

When it was time to go home, some parents could not handle their children. They raced outside, romped, and ran hither and yon, but would not get into the cars. I finally went outside and told the children to obey their parents. Meanwhile, they had lost their baskets of candy while running wild.

Wednesday, November 5

In number work, Ray still counted "1, 2, 5." We reviewed the story of "The Three Bears," then dramatized it. An observer came and Ray showed her what he could do in work and play. He could spin the hoop, do the Hansel and Gretel dance, name the colors, and answer well in the listening games. He wanted to play "The Three Bears" again. He chose the lady observer to be Goldilocks, and he was baby bear. Once was not enough. We played it again and he was Goldilocks—he knew how to play the part too—and he asked the observer to be father bear. He was the happiest I have ever seen him while he was acting out this story. Marnie was beginning to get something of it. I had to tell her what to do. Lorrie and Jeanie were absent, and Ray shone as never before.

At snack time, Ray and Marnie took turns serving; Ray was first, and he waited till our guest sat down, then he served her first. Marnie was fascinated by the guest. She kept turning to stare at her and smile. Marnie was very excited. She did a lot of ducking of the head and shoulders. She often grabbed her knees or flipped her skirt. Once when standing, she flipped her skirt above her waist.

When the snack was over, we went for a walk. We saw a quail on the roof of a house. Ray was interested. Everytime we hear a bird singing, Ray says, "Ear birdies" or "Birdies schling." We saw a Siamese cat on the dirt road. I called it. Ray called it too, saying "Tlee, tlee," for "Kitty, kitty." I told him he might frighten the cat away if he walked toward it. He said, "Baby," meaning it was a kitten. He then walked slowly and carefully toward it—the cat stayed put and let him pat it. He was very gentle with it. But with dogs, he may pat them then suddenly jump up and take a swing at them. Then he whimpers and cowers when the dog jumps, barks, or growls back at him. I have tried to teach him how to approach a dog. I think he is beginning to learn.

Ray's cold is still bad even though his mother contends it is better. She sent him to class without any Kleenex. I suggested that it may be wise to keep him at home a few days. No response.

Marnie's table manners were terrible today. She palmed the cookies and pushed her hand flat against her mouth to get the cookie in. This she was doing very rapidly, pushing whole cookies into the mouth and bolting them before the others had time to take one bite of theirs. I showed her how to hold the cookie with her fingers. She could do it.

Monday, November 17

At snack time, just as Jeanie started to put the pink cloth on the table, two visitors came.

Lorrie was in the hall sulking because I had scolded her. First she would not get herself and her things off the table when we wanted to set it. She would not help lift any of the school things from the table although this is a part of the expected routine. Her purse was on the table and I had been asking her for days to put it with her coat as I did since we had so little room on the table. When I finally raised my voice, she reluctantly got up and removed one book, leaving all the other things for someone else to remove. She kicked the table as she rose and knocked our sack of beads to the floor. I shouted, "Lorrie! Now look what you have done!" She yelled back, "I di'n to it!" and ran from the room. I picked up all the beads. Ray put the other things away. Jeanie went and washed her hands as soon as I asked. She returned and put out six napkins. I asked her if she had the right number, to please count to be sure. At first she said, "1, 2, 1," and then we started again. I pointed to the children and said, "1, 2, 3, 4," so she did it right. She removed one napkin and gave it to me. She hesitated, then removed another. I said, "Is that right now?" She said, "Yeah." I can't be sure she really knew. Next she put out crackers and in a huge quantity. I poured the water, and asked the visitors if they would like some. They declined. After hearing me offer the water, Jeanie did get the idea of offering them a cookie.

The children grabbed every cracker on the plate. While I discussed school supplies with the visitors, the children went into the adjoining room and played with the hoop. All except Marnie, that is; she stayed in the classroom and stared at us.

Tuesday, November 25

Ray brought a tiger to school. I had been trying to get him to say "tiger." He always called it "tiker" or "ti'er." Today he said it right! After many tries for better pronunciation, he finally was able to say, "I got tiger a' birsday." Just as I was ready to leave for the day in a hurry to keep an appointment, everything was put away and locked up, Lorrie decided that she wanted a coloring book from among the pile of things she leaves at school every day. I told her I had no time to get it. She whined, she begged, and she sulked. But I would not get it. After all, she must learn to ask before the door is locked. Furthermore, she had left it there for weeks and had others at home. She was only trying to delay us. I decided it would do her some good to be refused for once.

When we got outside, Ray's mother was not there in her usual manner of being late. It was then necessary to ask the lady across the street to look after Ray till his mother arrived. Lorrie asked me to give her a ride home. I told her I did not go her way and that I had any appointment anyhow. She turned on an ugly scowl and yelled, "I will not come to school tomorrow."

Wednesday, December 10

Jeanie's father dropped her at my house at 8:00 o'clock this morning on his way to work because her mother couldn't bring her to school later. I had already eaten breakfast. She asked for a cookie and wanted to know when I was going to make breakfast. I explained that I had eaten. She talked a great deal and followed me about. I went into the bathroom to brush my hair and I closed the door. When she called to me, I told her I would be out soon. Then she yelled at me; I came out and told her gently, "You know when someone is in the bathroom, you should not keep calling to them. The nice, polite thing to do is to wait till they came out. Okay?" She said, "Okay," and smiled. Later, she said, "I 'ike 'ou." I did not answer immediately and she asked, " 'ou 'ea me?" (you hear me?) "I 'ike 'ou." I said, "Yes, that's nice. I like you, too." Then she went on, "I 'ike 'ou, I 'ike my fathew, bu' I do' 'ike my momma. My momma no 'ike me. I no 'ike 'ew." I changed the subject because I didn't know what was best to say. I can be patient and kind to her because I only have her around for a short time. If I were her mother, perhaps I would get tired and cross quite often then she would not like me either. I am not sure how to explain the situation to Jeanie.

Friday, December 19

We had one last practice for the program and the children got the tables ready for the party. The parents were invited and were to sit at the tables after the program and be served by the children. We covered the tables with white paper and Ray and Jeanie trimmed the paper with potato prints of Christmas trees. I cut out the shapes for them and they stamped them in green paint. We needed a star for the top of the tree and I had expected Lorrie to be able to make one. Each time I had tried to get her to do it before, she had been too busy doing something else. Today, she did not arrive until it was time for the guests to arrive. She came in with her mother. I was disgusted with her mother. I asked her why Lorrie had not come in time for school. She said, "I thought the invitation said to come at 10:30." I said, "Yes it did. But the invitation was for guests, not for the ones giving the party. Who did you think was going to get things ready? Did you think I was going to do everything? This party was supposed to be given by the children for their parents. This is what school is all about. We have been trying to teach the children to do things. Setting tables and serving are things they should learn to do. Besides, I have been depending on Lorrie to help with work the other children are unable to do. We needed her to make a star for the tree. Now we have none. And she did not finish your gift." I feel sure she wouldn't appreciate the child's gift anyhow. She only stammered, "Oh, I didn't know. I thought these last few days they would not be having lessons and so they were not very important."

I asked Lorrie to finish the gift for her mother. She was not dressed for the party (repeat of the Halloween costume business). She did nothing to help and went to sit with her mother as if she was a guest instead of a hostess. The mother left at 11:00 a.m., then the father came. Neither of them cared about what the children had done in preparation for their visit. They talked to the other guests, even while the children were singing Christmas carols. Jeanie only makes noises when singing, wouldn't even say the words she did know. Ray stood and scratched his leg. Lorrie tried to imitate some of the ladies she sees on television—she went through various silly poses and made faces and Marnie grinned and bounced.

The tables were all ready for the parents and it would have been friendly and pleasant for them to sit with the children. But they refused to budge from the seats along the wall. This meant the children had to do something that we had never practiced— carry glasses and plates, walk up and down the line. There were two rows of chairs and the children could not get between them. Jeanie, who brought the drink and was therefore supposed to serve it, got tired of carrying it and began to bawl like a calf and spilled part of it. The guests did not wait for everyone to be served before beginning so they were ready for more before the children had had time to even sit down, much less take a bite. When everyone was finally served, Jeanie sneezed in her ice cream and began to howl again. This caused her to spill the ice cream all over her dress. The father tried to mop it off with his handkerchief. The mother did not assist her. I went to the aid of the father. Lorrie had been told the thermos jar was too difficult for her to manage and that I would fill the glasses. As soon as I was occupied with Jeanie, she turned the spigot on but was unable to close it. Rather than call out for assistance, she allowed it to run. Ray called me to look at Lorrie. By the time I found out, there was a real mess to clean up.

Even though her disobedience had caused all this she did not offer to help with the cleaning. Her father arose at once, left, taking Lorrie with him.

Marnie's and Ray's mothers stayed and helped me clear away the mess.

Monday, January 5

When I arrived at school, Marnie's taxi was there, and Jeanie and Lorrie were in it too. They all tumbled out apparently glad to see me after the Christmas vacation. Lorrie came running and kissed me. Jeanie came slogging along behind her and I gave her a hug. She began yelling for me to look at her new red gloves and red purse. This caused Lorrie to push in to show me her new black patent purse.

Meanwhile, Marnie had plodded along the sidewalk nearby and she was looking on. As soon as I could get a word in, I called to her, "Hi, Marnie! Did you have a good Christmas?" She nodded and smiled taking a step toward me; she fell from the edge of the sidewalk. Lorrie and I tried to lift her up but Marnie just left her feet lying limply on the ground. As we pulled, she slid along on her seat in the dirt. Then I bent one of her knees slightly so that the foot was flat on the ground and pressed one of mine against it. Now she could not slide forward. We finally succeeded in getting her to her feet. I asked if she had hurt herself but she just looked blank. Then we went into the classroom. I thought Marnie had regressed during vacation. She seemed unable to do anything. She was very lifeless but did throw the bean bag once and walked around twice in "London Bridge." She did not sit down until she was handed a chair. She stood by the piano for singing, while the other children are always so tired they sit. At snack time she handed out the glasses and passed the cookies. While eating she spilled two glasses of water. We went out for a short walk; we didn't go far because of the bad weather. She came with us but walked unusually slowly. Her mother was half an hour late in picking her up after school. She sat with me in my car while we waited. When her mother came, she had so much difficulty in getting out of my car that I went over and told her mother about the fall. During the evening the mother called and said, "Marnie had a sprained ankle." Why didn't she tell me her ankle hurt? She didn't cry or let me know in any way that she was suffering pain.

A new girl came today. Her name is Susie. The mother works and since her father is unemployed, he brought her. He held her on his knee and she clung to him like a leech. Every time he tried to leave, she shrieked and kicked and tore at him, so that he sat down again and looked sheepish and helpless. I finally told him that children often do this but if he would just go, she would soon stop crying. He was willing to try it but he could not pry her loose. I put my arms about her and he pulled her hands off and ducked out fast. I held her for a few seconds and then let go. In no time at all she was fine. She followed me about like a puppy.

I attempted to teach her our new dance and she seemed to enjoy it. When she wanted to go to the washroom, she made odd whimpering sounds in my ear. I only guessed at what she was telling me. Her father had said she could go by herself but she was wearing tight slacks that were fastened with a safety pin which she could neither undo nor do up. I assisted her with the pin problem.

Thursday, January 8

Only three children present.

For activity time, I suggested that the children choose whatever they wanted from the truck. Lorrie selected a puzzle, but Ray just sat. Susie whispered some odd syllables in my ear and she pointed vaguely away so I assumed she wished to go to the washroom. This time I tried leaving her and went back to see if the others needed help. She ran right out after me with her clothes all undone. It was necessary for me to return and remain in the restroom with her. While I was helping her with her slacks, she grabbed one of my earrings and yanked it off. I yelled, "Ow! That hurt." She giggled madly. When I tried to show her how to wash her hands (it is too bad parents don't teach their children at home), I pulled up her sweater sleeves saying, "I'll pull these up so they won't get wet." She looked at me and reached her arm over as far as she could putting her sleeves above the elbow under the tap. I said, "Say! Look what you're doing!" I laughed so she would know I wasn't angry because I thought it was an accident. She grinned and put her arm under again. Later in the morning she snatched one of my fingers and really twisted it. I cannot believe she wants to hurt me because she appears to like me since she constantly clings to me and follows me about.

She chomps her teeth which reminds me of a rattlesnake. As soon as I mentioned this to her, she did it more often and giggled about it.

Lorrie said her mother was coming and bringing crackers. She came and talked for more than half an hour while the children stood about open-mouthed, listening. They couldn't follow the conversation but they could tell from the tone of our voices that we were angry. She said she wants her child to be happy so if the child does not want to come to school, she does not have to. I asked her if she considered that a child at nursery school or kindergarten should be asked if she wants to go to school. Do parents go by the child's opinion of what is best for him? She said that that was different. I said, "It is not one bit different. Your child's mental age is that of a kindergartner at best. She cannot think or judge any more than a kindergarten child." She offered no argument for that, so she tried another attack. She said that she had been fighting with her family all year because they did not want her to send Lorrie to this school. She said that the only reason she had sent her was because she felt she owed it to the person who had worked so hard to have the class established. Her main question was, "Did we have sufficient enrollment to keep the class if she took Lorrie out?" I said sharply, "Never mind about the school. What about Lorrie? Do you have a better school for her to attend?" "Oh, no," she said. "She would just stay home." "Would she have someone to teach her or be a companion to her? Would she have other children to play with her?" "Oh, no. She would be alone. She likes to be alone." "Fine! So nothing at all is better than what we have to offer her! That sounds insulting to me."

She floundered about with profuse apologies. By way of explanation, she told me that her daughter, being older than the other children, was losing all she had gained at the previous school. I asked her to consider this: suppose you lived in an area where the only school was a rural school. Would you say that your daughter should stay home because she was in the highest grade and was the oldest there? The only school would be better than no school, wouldn't it? The teacher would instruct the children according to their grade and ability to learn, wouldn't she?" She said, "That's different." I tried to show her that the situation is almost identical, but she could not see it. As well as I was able to tell from her remarks, the complaint must be that Lorrie did not think the school was good—she was not "top dog" at all times. Also, she did not bring home an abundance of ditto sheets, full of crayon color, nor did she have a number book to color in.

I finally told her that I was thoroughly disgusted. What hope is there for children when the parents feel this way? She left saying that she had not meant to upset me. What had she meant to do? I was so agitated that I went to the piano, hoping to calm down with the music. Lorrie came and sat beside me. I looked at her and said, "Oh, Lorrie, to think that you don't want to come to school anymore. I like you and want to help you." She said, "I 'ike you. I do' wannt weave you. I do' wanna weave you." I put my arms around her and held her tight. She did not leave the class.

February 14

We had our Valentine Party. Marnie's mother and I brought home-made cookies and cakes. The others sent Dixie cups and store candies. The parents seemingly have no time for their severely retarded children. Not one child was dressed for a party. Evidently the parents do not regard school parties worthy of consideration. Yet what other parties do these children have an opportunity to attend? Jeanie had a dirty face and Ray, as well as having a dirty face, was wearing a filthy shirt. He had several days' spillings of egg on it and it looked as if it had been rolled in the dirt for hours. Marnie is always clean and attractively dressed. Susie has never had her hair parted—if, indeed, it was ever combed. It looks as if a four year old had clutched it together.

The children seemed to enjoy the party. Mrs. P. came to help and she brought some extra valentines for the children. She and I had made a valentine box. (Lorrie said that she had never seen one before.) We had decorated the room with hearts and cupids, and the table with valentine place mats, napkins, and candy baskets. The favors were red and white blowers. The children loved these, especially Susie, after I taught her to blow hers out. It wasn't easy. She didn't want to have anything to do with it. I finally persuaded her to try. Once she learned, she didn't want to stop. She seemed to prefer it to the food. She laughed each time she blew. When the children were ready to go home, we put their favors, candy, and valentines in bags. Susie refused to allow her blower to be put into the bag. She carried it in her hand.

Wednesday, February 25

Ray had a dirty face again and was wearing a dirty shirt. His hands apparently had not been washed since snack time yesterday morning; they still had finger paint on them.

We used "We Read Pictures" again. The children made sentences about various pictures in the book. Lorrie usually understands and Jean does when she isn't having one of her moods. Ray needs prompting. For example:

Lorrie: "I see Sally. I see Sally an' Puff. I see Sally an' Puff jumpin'. I see Jane an' Sally eatin' somethin' an' a stan' " (and they're standing). Her sight is very poor and she was not able to tell that the children in the picture were eating ice cream cones.

Jeanie: "I see Sally." Then she points to the next picture, saying, "Iss one? (yes) I see Sally an' a kitty. Sally an' a kitty jumpin'."

Ray: "Sane. (No, that is the big girl's name.) Sa'y. (Now, the next one.) Ki'y (And who's this?) Sa'y. (Say "I see . . ." and tell us what you see.) See Ki'y. See Sa'y."

Each time he says a word, he jerks his head forward.

Susie and Marnie did not respond. Lorrie told me that her mother's kitchen was pink and blue so she wanted to make a potholder in those colors. She worked diligently. I helped her to start; then she finished all except the edges by herself.

Jeanie put three loops on her frame, made a wry face, and pushed the work away.

I told the children not to touch the record player or the records, because they were borrowed. As soon as my back was turned, Jeanie tried to pull out the plug. It was in tight so she broke it by jerking hard. I did not know she had done it. She pointed and said, "Pfffft!" Then she held her finger, saying, "Ught!" It was not until I went to disconnect the plug that I realized what she had been trying to tell me. There had been sparks and she was shocked. She received a spanking as well. These children must learn discipline the same as any other child.

Today Susie played the triangle for me. She also stood up and waved her arms as if she were conducting.

Suddenly Jeanie decided to call a meeting. She hammered on the top of the table with a xylophone stick to call the meeting to order. We all sat down. Jeanie asked each of us to come forward and speak. When I came at her request, she said, "What 'ou doin' 'day?" Our speech was to be an answer to her question. When she called our visitor she pounded on the table impatiently, saying "Talkin'! Talkin'!" (in other words, "start talking"). Mrs. C. began to talk. But Jeanie soon tired of her speech and told her "no mo' a's 'nough. Si' down." Then she called Ray. He squirmed, he put his head down, he whimpered but could not talk. She told him to sit down. He did so gladly.

Friday, March 13

Ray and Jeanie have red, crusted eyelids again. When they arrived this morning, Ray's hands were filthy and Jeanie had dirty hair—something like porridge sticking all in her hair. After all the others had told what they had for breakfast, it was Marnie's turn.

Marnie: "Some eggs. I th'ow them away. Throw m' eggs away!" (She rocked and laughed as she told it. Jeanie was disgusted and she hit the table.)

Marnie: "Who's there?" (The children laughed.)

Teacher: "What else did you have for breakfast?"

Marnie: "Some meat. I th'ow it away, too. My sister an' me an' Tootsie." (She has no sister, and Tootsie is the dog.) "Tootsie go' n' take me for a ride. I'm gonna go bye-bye to Tis-tis. I saw my sister."

Some time ago, our regular table had been taken away and replaced with a very, very low table. It was necessary to cut wooden blocks to raise the table so we could sit at it. Now our low table had disappeared. What next for a change of daily routine?

Tuesday, March 17

Today was our St. Patrick's Day party and only Marnie and Jeanie came. While I trimmed the room for our party, they worked puzzles. Jeanie tried to put the truck puzzle together. She usually works impatiently. She slams a piece down and gives it a shove one way. If it does not fit, she shoves it another way. Then she casts it aside and grabs another piece. I gave her some suggestions, but as usual, she would not follow them. She grumbled trying to make out that something was wrong with the puzzle so that it would not go together. I assured her that all the pieces would fit. She turned on a very determined look and held up the piece showing the side boards. This she planked down on top of the truck bed which she had placed on top of the truck. She said, "See? No go." I said, "Yes, it will. That's the top of the truck that you're holding. You need to move the other piece down." She became more stubborn, saying "no!" Then she threw the whole thing into a box and snatched up another puzzle. This was "Humpty-Dumpty." She scattered it on the table. I watched. The head was placed properly and I praised her for the good start. She proceeded to put all the wall bricks in next, helter-skelter. There was no space under the body for the head. She was irritated to find that the other pieces couldn't be jammed in hurriedly. I removed the bricks. Then, taking the colored pieces of Humpty-Dumpty, I showed her how quickly and easily they could be fitted in if the wall were left till last. I said, "See, these pretty colored pieces? You know they belong to Humpty-Dumpty, so why not put them in first?" She agreed with a murmured "Oh, 'eah" (yeah). I removed the pieces and urged her to try. She put the right hand where the left should go and tried to force it into place.

Thinking it best to change the activity at this point, I went to the piano and the children followed.

SUMMARY

Very little was done for the severely retarded before 1950. It has been estimated that one out of every 250 persons, or more than 600,000 persons in the United States belong to this group of retardates. The present trend is toward keeping the trainable child in the home and community and to provide special education for him in the public school. Not only is there a pressing need for more schools and classes for these children, but there is also need for a "Life Plan." Education and guidance for children from six to sixteen years of age is not enough time for the trainable.

A training program for the severely mentally retarded children necessitates sufficient flexibility to permit adaptation to the individual child's level of growth and development. It is important to recognize and accept these children at the level of the respective mental and social development and to provide more adequate opportunity for consistent integration of proficiency in the various learning areas experienced by young, normal children of equivalent ages of development.

The severely mentally retarded child (IQ below 50) is referred to as the trainable child; usually he profits very little from formal schooling but is capable of being trained to work with the hands. He is a combination of biology and culture molded by people and events. His condition has been determined by genes, prenatal and post-natal environment and his ability to learn from experiences. All skills are acquired through practice with noted progress from gross accomplishment to more refined and discriminatory adeptness. All aspects of training should be meaningful to the child in his daily life at home and in his neighborhood experiences, as well as within the classroom situation.

To attain optimum results, it is essential that the teacher concern herself with individual appraisals and to recognize and understand the hetergeneous groupings we have in respect to chronological age, mental age, emotional stability, and degree of organic impairment; as well as the family attitudes. There is a greater need for specific goals with constant repetition in teaching procedures and an ever increasing awareness of concrete association as the limited means to learning; for it is generally accepted that these children are incapable of abstract conceptual thinking.

With the primary training objective of teaching severely retarded children to function socially at a higher level in the immediate environment, certain training procedures will be applicable to more than one of the following areas:

1. Personal routines.
2. Health routines.
3. Care of property.
4. Safety routines.
5. Play performances.
6. Social adjustment.
7. Language development.

Practical application of these routines as used in the classroom, description of the children and their daily schedule are discussed in the last half of this chapter.

SELECTED REFERENCES

Anderson, Ruth Babb and Hottel, John V.: *Program for Severely Mentally Retarded Children.* Nashville, State of Tennessee Department of Education, 1957.

Baker, Harry J.: *Introduction to Exceptional Children.* New York, The Macmillan Company, 1955.

Barr, Martin W.: *Mental Defectives: Their History, Treatment and Training.* Philadelphia, P. Blakiston's Son and Company, 1913.

Baumgartner, B. B.: *Helping the Trainable Mentally Retarded Child.* New York, Bureau of Publications, Teachers College, Columbia University, 1960.

Blodgett, Harriet E. and Warfield, Grace J.: *Understanding Mentally Retarded Children.* New York, Appleton-Century-Crofts, Inc., 1959.

California State Department of Education: Laws and Regulations relating to education and health services for exceptional children in California. Sacramento, State Department of Education, 1960.

Capa, Cornell and Pines, Maya: *Retarded Children Can Be Helped.* New York, Channel Press, Inc., 1957, p. 52.

Clarke, A. M.: *Mental Deficiency: The Changing Outlook.* London, Methuen and Company, 1958.

Clarke, A. M.: Teaching imbeciles industrial skills. *Cerebral Palsy Bulletin, 6*:14-18, 1959.

Cleugh, M. F.: *Teaching the Slow Learner in the Special School.* New York, Philosophical Library, 1961.

Connor, Francis P. and Goldberg, I. Ignacy: Opinions of some teachers regarding their work with trainable children, implications for teacher education. *American Journal of Mental Deficiency, 64*:658-670, 1959.

Cruickshank, Wm. M. and Johnson, Orville, G.: *Education of Exceptional Children and Youth.* Englewood Cliffs, New Jersey, Prentice-Hall, Inc., 1958.

Cruickshank, Wm. M.: *Psychology of Exceptional Children and Youth.* Englewood Cliffs, New Jersey, Prentice-Hall, Inc., 1955.

Culbertson, E.: Patterns of hostility among the retarded. *American Journal of Mental Deficiency, 66*:421-427, 1961.

Daly, Flora M.: A report on the public school programs for severely mentally retarded children. Sacramento, California State Department of Education, August 1958.

Dayton, Neil A., comp.: Listings of public and private schools and homes for the retarded. *Directory of the American Association of Mental Deficiency,* Appendix A., pp. 19-100, 1956.

Dolch, Wm. E.: *Helping Handicapped Children in School.* Champaign, Illinois, Garrard Press, 1948.

Dunn, Lloyd M. and Hottel, John V.: The effectiveness of special day class training programs for severely (trainable) mentally retarded children. *Peabody College Research Series in Mental Retardation,* Nashville, Tennessee, George Peabody College for Teachers, June 1958.

Educational and Training Facilities, A Directory for Exceptional Children. Third edition. Boston, Porter-Sargent, 1958, pp. 95-151.

Goldberg, I. Ignacy: Current status of education and training in the United States for trainable mentally retarded children. *Exceptional Children, 23*:146-154, 1957.

Goodenough, Florence L.: *Exceptional Children.* New York, Appleton-Century-Crofts, Inc., 1956.

Graham, Ray and Seigle, Dorothy: A guide for establishing special classes for the trainable mentally handicapped. *Illinois Department of Public Instruction,* Circular Series B-1, No. 12, Springfield, 1955.

Guilford, J. P.: *The Structure of Behavior.* New York, Wiley, 1949.

Hafemeister, N. R.: Development of a curriculum for the trainable child. *American Journal of Mental Deficiency, 55*:495-501, 1951.

Hill, Arthur: Special education serves them too. *School Life, 44*:55-61, 1962.

Hill, Arthur S.: The forward look: the severely retarded child goes to school. Washington, D. C., U. S. Department of Health, Education and Welfare, Bulletin No. 11, p. 54, 1952.

Hilliard, L. T. and Kirman, Brian H.: *Mental Deficiency*. Boston, Little, Brown and Company, 1957.

Hottel, John V.: Tennessee experimental program of day classes for severely mentally retarded (trainable) children. Nashville, Tennessee, George Peabody College for Teachers, 1957.

Hudson, Margaret: Procedures for teaching trainable children. *Council for Exceptional Children, Research Monograph No. 2,* Washington, D. C., N. E. A., 1960.

Johnson, G. Orville: *Training Program for Severely Mentally Retarded Children.* Albany, New York State Interdepartmental Health Resources Board, January 1958.

Jordan, Thomas E.: *The Exceptional Child.* Columbus, Ohio, Charles E. Merrill Books, Inc., 1962.

Jordan, Thomas E.: *The Mentally Retarded.* Columbus, Ohio, Charles E. Merrill Books, Inc., 1961.

Certificate Handbooks. Topeka, Kansas, Kansas State Department of Public Instruction, January 1959.

Kephart, N. C.: *The Slow Learner in the Classroom.* Columbus, Ohio, Charles E. Merrill Books, Inc., 1960.

Levinson, Abraham and Bigler, John A.: *Mental Retardation in Infants and Children.* Chicago, Illinois, The Year Book Publishers, Inc., 1960.

Magary, James F. and Eichorn, John R.: *The Exceptional Child, A Book of Readings.* New York, Holt, Rinehart and Winston, Inc., 1960.

Magnifico, L.: *Education for the Exceptional Child.* New York, Longmans, Green and Company, 1958.

McPherson, Marian White: Learning and mental deficiency. *American Journal of Mental Deficiency, 62*:870-877, 1958.

Michal-Smith, H. and Kastein, Shulamith: *The Special Child.* Seattle, Washington, New School for the Special Child, 1963.

Nisonger, Hershel W.: Status of community training facilities for children with severe mental retardation. *American Journal of Mental Deficiency, 59*:335-337, 1954.

Pfeifle, Marian G.: A neighborhood school for trainable children. Unpublished master's thesis. Reno, University of Nevada, 1960.

Pollock, P. and Pollock, M.: *New Hope for the Retarded.* Boston, Porter-Sargent, 1953.

Riese, H.: Academic work with an eleven year old girl with an IQ of 41. *American Journal of Mental Deficiency, 60*:545-551, 1956.

Rosenzweig, L.: Report of a school program for trainable mentally retarded children. *American Journal of Mental Deficiency, 59*:181-205, 1954.

Rothstein, Jerome H.: *Mental Retardation Readings and Resources.* New York, Holt, Rinehart and Winston, Inc., 1961.

Roulle, E. N.: New horizons for the mentally retarded: when a school looks at the problem as a whole. *American Journal of Mental Deficiency, 59*:359-373, 1955.

Sarason, S. B.: *Psychological Problems in Mental Deficiency.* Revised edition. New York, Harper and Brothers, 1953.

Special education of exceptional children. *School Life, 38*:7-10, 1956.

Staff of the bureau for mentally retarded children, social communication for the trainable mentally retarded child. New York State Department of Education, Albany, New York.

Trapp, E. P. and Himelstein, P.: *Readings on the Exceptional Child.* New York, Appleton-Century-Crofts, 1962.

Tredgold, A. F.: *A Textbook of Mental Deficiency.* Seventh edition. Baltimore, Williams and Wilkins, 1949.

Williams, Harold M. and Wallin, J. E. Wallace: Education of the Severely Retarded Child: A Bibliographical Review. Washington, D. C., U. S. Department of Health, Education and Welfare, Bull. No. 12, 1959, p. 24.

Williams, Harold M.: The Retarded Child Goes to School. Washington, D. C., U. S. Department of Health, Education and Welfare, Pamphlet No. 123, p. 24.

Williams, Harold M. and Dunn, Lloyd M.: Teachers of Children Who Are Mentally Retarded. Washington, D. C., U. S. Department of Health, Education and Welfare, Bull. No. 3, 1957, p. 97.

Wirtz, M. A. and Guenther, Richard: The incidence of trainable mentally handicapped children. *Exceptional Children, 23*:175, 1957.

Wirtz, Mervin A.: The development of current thinking about facilities for the severely retarded. *American Journal of Mentally Deficient, 60*:492-507, 1956.

Section Three

THE MENTALLY RETARDED AND THEIR ENVIRONMENT

The two remaining chapters relate to the home and community of the retarded child. Chapter Eight illustrates family life and Chapter Nine discusses community influences and attitudes.

CHAPTER VIII

The Mentally Retarded Child and His Family

BEFORE THE CHILD IS BORN

BEFORE children arrive, a firm base for satisfying family life in the days to come must be built by the parents. Happy parents do not think of themselves as perfect, thus they do not expect perfection from any child they may bring into the world. Nevertheless, parents look forward with pleasure to "showing off" their children. Oftentimes it gives them a second chance to make up for the success and achievement they wished to attain. The child is an extension of themselves. In some cases the child may be looked upon as an insurance against want and loneliness in old age. The unborn child is to mean something special to both father and mother. Even though there may be some little misgiving, normal people do not anticipate being the parents of handicapped children.

Kazier[1] reminds us that "In many ways, a child represents to the parent an extension of his own self. . . . When the baby is born, the mother's wish to be loved is partially transferred from her own person to that of the baby. To the father, a normal child is often an affirmation, at least in part, of his own sense of success. The capacity to produce unimpaired offspring is psychologically and culturally important for the parents' sense of personal adequacy."

THE IMPACT OF THE INITIAL REALIZATION

Probably the largest number of parents feel at the time of birth of their child that their offspring is normal.[2] Unless the mother is informed, it is only later, as development lags, that the mother suspects abnormality. Then still later, in recapitulating, the mother

---

[1] A. Kazier: Casework with parents of children born with severe brain defects. *Social Casework,* 1957.

[2] A. Hersh: Casework with parents of retarded children. *Social Work,* 1961.

realizes that she suspected rather early that the child was different. In talking to her physician or other counselor, she may say, "He was *just* different." "He was too still," "He was like a lump of clay." Hersh[3] says he has known some mothers who fought the world on behalf of their child, almost because they knew too soon that the child was different. "They had a secret that acted as a bond between self and child. The invasion of the outer world and its harsh realities could be climaxed in no other way than a pitched battle in which their struggle to maintain the cherished secret was waged." Salnit[4] thinks the mother's reactions to the knowledge that her child is mentally retarded is "similar to the expression of grief for a lost child"; e.g., the sudden loss of an expected baby. "Feelings of loss; intense longings for the desired child; resentment of the cruel blow that life's experience has dealt; and the guilt that the defective child may evoke by representing the consequence of unacceptable feelings or thoughts."[5]

The parent may at first feel hostile to the pediatrician at his announcement of his diagnosis. What the parent would really like is an announcement that the baby is perfect, but he would settle with a statement that the baby is normal. "If in fact, the parent produces an obviously defective, handicapped child, the first reaction is denial of the fact. The parent then becomes anxious, and with development of a feeling of guilt she begins a search for ways to defend against the anxiety or to remove the state of guilt."[6]

The initial impact of the realization that all is not well with their child results in a reflection of disappointed hopes in parents, a possible fight against the handicap, a bewilderment in what to do, even qualms concerning capacity to help the child. "Each parent responds to the handicapped child according to his or her own psychological make-up. There is no measuring stick with which to gauge the suffering, and resentment. . . . What a particular child means to a parent is a highly individual, deeply personal matter, bound to be colored by that parent's own early life experiences with his own parents, by his feeling toward wife or husband and

---

[3] *Ibid.*, Hersh.

[4] A. J. Salnit and M. H. Stark: Mourning and the interpretation of mental retardation. Paper presented to the American Orthopsychiatric Assoc. meeting, New York, March 25, 1961.

[5] *Ibid.*, Salnit.

[6] *Op. cit.*, Hersh.

by his feelings toward himself and the child must bear the weight of all these combined feelings."[7]

THE ATTITUDE OF THE PARENT

The attitude of the parents toward their mentally retarded child determines the success or failure of family life and the life of the child. The attitude of the parent is highly individual; it represents the total of what parents have experienced, how they feel about the immediate problem, and what they anticipate about the child's future. Ross[8] has noted two extremes in the attitude of the parents of an exceptional child. First, an attitude of over-compensation in which the child supposedly will be all right if he receives love; *viz*, he will be all right even against scientific opinion. This attitude often blinds parents to the needs of the child. Second, an attitude of denial in which both parents treat the child as though he were normal. They expect or demand of the child the general behavior of a normal individual, even expect him to meet the competition of normal children in a classroom.

The genesis of parental attitudes can be traced to the pleasant or unpleasant memories in and out of school. Attitudes toward an exceptional child are also influenced by neighborhood and community reaction. The feelings of siblings may also be a potent factor. In any case parents can be assisted more quickly if the specialist giving the assistance can determine the attitude of parents toward the situation. The use of attitude scales will be of real value in the future. For example, from the remarks of numerous parents of mentally retarded children, Farber[9] constructed the following scale which he thought listed items of increasing impact:

1. I felt it was the biggest tragedy of my life (item of least impact).
2. I was very bitter and miserable.
3. I went to pieces; my world fell apart.
4. I felt the whole world was against us.
5. I avoided telling relatives.

---

[7] Helen Ross: The handicapped child and his family. *Crippled Child*, 4:11-59, Feb. 1953.

[8] Helen Ross: The handicapped child and his family. *Crippled Child*, 4:11-59, 1953.

[9] B. Farber: Effects of a severely mentally retarded child on family integration. *Monographs of Social Research Child Development*, 24:2: serial 71, 1959.

6. I felt somehow that it was my husband's fault (item of highest impact).

ATTITUDE AS REFLECTED IN TYPES OF FAMILY CRISES

The presence of a mentally retarded child in a family can be considered a crisis of a disrupting or frustrating nature only if the family members consider it so. There is no crisis if family members define their situation as normal. When mentally retarded children are considered normal by the family even though specialists consider them otherwise, no crises exist.

Farber[10] describes two kinds of crises, the tragic crisis and the role-organization crisis. In the tragic crisis, the aims, aspirations, and anticipated happy family life are frustrated. The condition of the child is regarded by the parents as an uncontrollable event preventing fulfillment of their hopes and aspirations. Parents are unhappy and frustrated. Accordingly, they tend to direct hostility toward the child. Even though the parents feel hostile toward their mentally retarded child, however, various factors prevent them from acting aggressively against it. For example, the parent does not regard the child as having become intentionally retarded. The parent may even blame himself for the child's condition.

The extent of the crisis appears to be determined by the cultural and socio-economic status of the family. In families of high socio-economic status, for example, there is a tendency for individuals to give conformity to expectations and obligations priority over expression of impulsive personal gratification. Since attainment of long range goals are important in the families of high socio-economic status, they are likely to feel the presence of a mentally retarded child as a real tragedy.

THE CULTURAL DILEMMA

The birth of a handicapped child places the family in a cultural dilemma. The dilemma stems from contradictory values and attitudes with which the culture, or more specifically the society, invests in the handicapped child. Our American society holds strongly to the view that to be a parent is a good thing. Unfortunately to be the parent of a handicapped child is a bad thing. Historically, our highly competitive, industrialized, materialistic

---

[10] *Op. cit.*, Farber.

society tends naturally to disapprove of those individuals who will not be able to maintain standards. It follows, therefore, that the parent who is highly conscious of social standards of behavior will tend to have a difficult time.[11]

Parents in the middle or upper class usually have great ambitions for their children. Such parents, accordingly, have difficulty in overcoming their frustration and disappointment in having a mentally retarded child. "The ideal parents are usually those who, while sufficiently intelligent to appreciate the needs of the child and to have insight into his difficulties, do not have great ambitions, and so they do not constantly display disappointment.[12]

These parents look upon their child as a gift for which to be thankful whatever his condition; they appear even to be rather fatalistic in their outlook.

Some societies apparently do not produce emotional conflict and frustration in parents of mentally retarded children. Wallin[13] for example, reports a high level of social acceptance of the retarded in Peruvian society. The pre-communistic society of the Chinese is described by Buck[14] as being an ideal one for the mentally retarded child. Among the Hutterite sect of the Northeastern United States and Canada, "There is considerable social acceptance of mentally defective persons. Feelings of rejection by parents exist, but they are usually well repressed. Other children are punished if they ridicule or take advantage."[15] Studies of English families on the other hand, indicate that the conflict is as great as in American society.[16]

An analysis of data by Farber[17] showed that the presence of a retarded boy in lower-class families had a more acute effect on the

[11] G. H. Zuk: The cultural dilemma and spiritual crisis of the family with a handicapped child. *Exceptional Children*, 28:405-408, April 1962.

[12] K. S. Holt: The home care of mentally retarded children. *Pediatrics*, 22:744-755, 1958.

[13] E. Wallin: Social and cultural aspects of mental retardation. *Proceedings of the Institute for Nurses on Mental Retardation*. New Jersey, State Dept. of Health, 1960.

[14] Pearl Buck: *The Child Who Never Grew*. London, Methuen Pub. Co., 1951.

[15] J. W. Eaton and R. J. Weil: *Culture and Mental Disorders: A Comparative Study of the Hutterites*. Glencoe, Ill., Free Press, 1955.

[16] K. S. Holt: The home care of mentally retarded children. *Pediatrics*, 22:744-755, 1958.

[17] B. Farber: Effects of a severely retarded child on family integration. *Monographs of the Society for Research in Child Development*, Serial No. 71, 24:2:76-81, 1959.

parents' marriage than the presence of a retarded girl. In middle-class families, however, the sex of the retarded child was not related to the degree of marital integration of parents. These results were presumed to stem from differences in parental expectations of the life-careers of boys and girls and from the greater stress placed on sex differences among lower-class families than among middle class families. As the severely retarded boy grew older, he generally had an increasing disruptive effect on his parents' marriage.

THE EMOTIONS AND THE PARENT

Despair, withdrawal, regression, personality disorganization, hostility, shame, and guilt are all terms used to describe the emotional behavior of parents of severely handicapped children. The threat to the parent of having produced a child severely retarded may be so great that he may not be able to carry out even the most urgent of parental responsibilities. As Jordan[18] has pointed out the initial shock may be so prolonged as to interfere with functioning at home and community. Parents have been known to try to leave their baby at the hospital indefinitely; or after the baby is taken home, to devote so much time to the child as to cut off themselves from other life experiences. Other parents have denied the child's needs for special treatment or have neglected the child physically.

Fathers appear to be more removed, less emotionally involved, more objective, and less expressive of their feelings than do mothers. "Fathers who have not yet achieved or are currently working through their separation from their own fathers appear to have a particular problem with their retarded child. . . . A retarded son, however, may create a real puncture in the male ego unless the father is well established as father and husband. This problem is often expressed in aggressive and disapproving action. More subtle and difficult is the father who smothers and denies the boy his own manhood. Adolescence is particularly stormy, but affords some basis for confrontation and identification between father and son."[19]

---

[18] T. E. Jordan: *The Mentally Retarded.* Columbus, Ohio, Charles E. Merrill Books, Inc., 1961.

[19] A. Hersh: Casework with parents of retarded children. *Social Work,* 1961.

The three major emotions found in parents of the mentally retarded are disappointment, anger, and guilty. Many mixed emotions exist, all quite involved psychologically. To understand the inner drives and motivations of the mother, it is necessary to understand the elementary principles of maternal-child relationships. Disappointment arises from an awareness that the child will not be able to fulfill all of the fond hopes and expectations that have been built up even before the child is born. Eventually, the disappointed parent becomes a stoic, accepting individual, who, in spite of her burden, patiently guides and protects her child through the pitfalls of the world, or she develops a deep rejection for her child and for the people whom she feels helped contribute to her plight.

Anger is usually directed first at the child as the obvious source of disappointment and frustration; later, anger is directed toward someone else (for example, spouse, in-laws, or physician) or even toward self. Anger toward the child may take the form of extreme feelings of rejection and desires to get rid of the child. Bice[20] has reported cases of parents who revealed to him their desires to get rid of the child. Two extreme statements he quotes are: "to put it mildly, we all have moments when we could crown these children," and, "I never really planned to kill my child, but I have thought of how much easier it would be if he died; my religion is the only thing that keeps me from killing my child."

It is true that the child may be frustrating and the community may be rejecting. These elements of reality contribute to parent's hostile feelings. Furious hostility has been noted in parents toward social workers or to the pediatrician for neglect of duty. Just as occasionally occurs in grief and mourning, the "bereaved either makes unreasonable demands or else hardly seems to know what he wants, and often becomes irritable and ungrateful to those who try to respond."[21]

Feelings of guilt arise from the need of parents to deny that they are angry at the child. Many parents blame themselves for what has occurred to the child; they may feel they are being

---

[20] H. V. Bice and Phyllis F. Bartelme: Statement of parents of exceptional children: the cerebral palsied. Trenton, N. J., the authors, 1953.

[21] J. Bowlby: Grief and mourning in infancy. *Psychoanalytic Study of the Child.* New York, International Univ.'s Press, Inc., 1960, Vol. XV.

punished. Guilt ordinarily overlays and inhibits anger; it is a mechanism whereby anger is diverted from the child to the parent herself. In other words, parents feel a need to deny that they are angry at the child and turn the anger inward at themselves.

At this point it is well to distinguish a feeling of shame from a feeling of guilt. "Guilt, or self-reproach, is based upon internalization of values, notably (one's own) parental values, in contrast with shame, which is based upon disapproval coming from outside, from other persons."[22] It should not be overlooked that parents frequently have negative feelings toward normal children but usually the positive feelings are strong enough to prevent outward expression. In the case of the handicapped child, however, the strength of these negative feelings is more intense, for reasons of reality as well as on rational basis. Satisfactions on the part of parents are fewer, opportunities for bolstering the ego are rarer, and aggressive feelings reach sufficient height to evoke extreme guilt.

THE CHILD IN THE FAMILY

Each child has his symbolic significance within the family. The handicapped child, however, requires a different kind of understanding from that which the family gives the normal child. The mentally retarded child needs more than the usual amount of help, guidance, and understanding in living that permits him happiness and contributes to the development of the potential he possesses. Nevertheless, personality needs of the mentally retarded child are no different than the normal child. These basic needs are love, recognition, feeling of belongingness, security, independence.

The human being tends to identify himself with someone he loves and admires. The mentally retarded child is no exception. He identifies himself with an adult who cares for him, shows interest in him, protects him, in short, loves him. The parent, too, identifies himself with the child and feels the child's handicap with its accompanying disadvantages. When the parent suffers too deeply, he finds it difficult to be objective and helpful, yet if he does not become too concerned, he cannot appreciate the difficulties of the handicapped youngster.

---

[22] Walter Baily: Casework with parents of a mentally retarded child. 1961, unpublished manuscript.

Identification is akin to a fundamental need of childhood because it is the basis of sympathy and cooperation. Participation in
the family group is dependent upon the child's ability to identify
himself with the desires, goals, and behavior of the family. First
of all the child identifies with the mother. To a certain degree, he
adopts her feelings, attitudes, and even her way of doing things.
Later his identification extends to father and to brothers and sisters. His motives eventually should become socialized by the requirements laid down by the family configuration with which he
identifies himself. Eventually the "me" and "self" becomes the
sum of all the identification he makes with the personalities around
him, and in so doing he slowly adopts the broader culture patterns
of our society.

The physiological needs of mentally retarded children are primarily satisfied in the home, although many educators are accepting responsibility, too, and are doing something about meeting
these needs when indications of home failure are found. The
physiological needs most frequently unsatisfied are food, rest, and
activity.

Closely related to the need of affection is the need for a feeling
of belongingness. The feeling develops only after the child is accepted by his family. The ego-integrative needs of *all* children are
intimately concerned with their need to believe in themselves and
to have self-respect. Children need to feel adequate in capacity
and skill to meet a fair degree of success in solving the problems
which constantly come before them. Notwithstanding, children
must obtain a balance of failure with success in the realization of
their hopes and desires.

The feeling of security and self-assurance are needs embracing
identification and belongingness as cited above. In fact, personality (social) needs are all "over-lapping" in meaning and defy
boundaries in definition. Notwithstanding, it is helpful to discuss
them separately. The feeling of security is based on stability of
expectancy. In the interaction between the child and his family
there is established a feeling of predictability of the type of response difficult patterns of behavior will produce. The feeling of
security or insecurity begins early in life, normally in expected
and predictable patterns of interaction between mother and child.
The mother expects certain behavior from the child and the child

expects certain behavior on the part of the mother. In other words, there appears to be an adjustment and personality reorganization in meeting the requirements of other people. Any child who does not know what to expect may eventually develop into anxious, neurotic, and fearsome individuals. A child who is loved, has friends, and belongs has an unassailable feeling of his own value; in the absence of such love, however, a child's life is marked by strong feelings of insecurity.

The teacher should endeavor to discover the child who has no warm, close friend and help him have a variety of real contacts with the most likely chum.

The mentally retarded child needs to have a feeling of worth (self-esteem). Practically, this can frequently be done by teaching him physical skills; e.g., to ride a bicycle, to skate, to throw a baseball, or to shoot marbles. Discover what the child can do best, help him use what assets he has, and give him recognition, self-esteem is bolstered by feelings of success regardless how little it may be.

THE EFFECT OF SIBLING RELATIONSHIPS

Siblings of a mentally retarded child may be deeply hurt by the presence of an exceptional child in the family. Children are frequently quite primitive in their feelings about the one that is different. They may reject the odd one or accept an abnormal overprotective attitude toward him—or themselves. These attitudes must be understood, not merely condemned.

The healthy children of a family often are made to suffer because of parental insistence that the exceptional child should be considered first, i.e., money for special medical fees, for special care, for special tutoring. For example, all children experience a certain amount of jealousy of one another; for they may be jealous when the mother must necessarily give more time and attention to the handicapped child. Love and acceptance, freedom to develop, control to protect, and good family relationships are the foundations for healthy personality development of any child.

Some parents give the other children responsibility beyond their capacity in sharing the care of the retarded child. The sister is frequently delegated duties concerning the child and housework. It has been found, for example, that on the average, the normal sister is helped by placing the retarded child in an institution. Many points of conflict between mother and daughter are removed. On the other hand, institutionalized retarded children did not appear to help the normal brothers. It was found, too, that younger retarded children affected the adjustment of their siblings more than did older retarded children.[23]

COUNSELING PARENTS OF A MENTALLY RETARDED CHILD

If the mentally retarded child is to be assisted, it is essential to understand fully the attitudes and emotional reactions of the parents. In a survey of the attitude of six hundred parents, Thurston[24] found that virtually all parents experienced emotional upset and anxiety when they learned that they had a handicapped child. While they differed in their initial reaction, most displayed helplessness, grief, or guilt in varying degrees.

QUALIFICATIONS OF THE COUNSELOR

Because the mentally retarded child can be identified only by specific circumstances and purposes, the counselor must be well qualified. A child mentally retarded can be diagnosed for purposes of medicine, social work, psychology, and vocational rehabilitation. For school purposes the mentally retarded child is one who cannot perform at a level, or above, of normal children in educational tasks. Such a child cannot profit from special instruction; he is socially inadequate, yet with special assistance he can become adequate eventually.

Historically, the mentally retarded child has been one to receive a low score on a psychological test. That is, he has been traditionally described in a quantitative fashion. No child is unique in all characteristics to be diagnosed as mentally retarded. Quantitative measures do not show the underlying modes of intellectual processes, thus mental retardation cannot be rigidly defined in terms of test scores. Consideration must also be given to developmental factors, current life situations, and the quality of functioning of the individual. The presence or absence of central nervous system impairment is also important, thus identification must

---

[23] Bernard Farber: Effects of a severely mentally retarded child on family integration. *Monographs of the Society for Research in Child and Development*, Serial No. 71, 24:2:76-81, 1959.

[24] John R. Thurston: Counseling the parents of the severely handicapped. *Exceptional Children*, 26:351-355, March 1960.

be made in terms of the judgment of the psychologist, physician, social worker, or psychiatrist. Any one of these specialists may find it necessary to counsel the parent in terms of his own competencies. When and if the child attends the public school the teacher, too, must counsel the parent.

THE NEEDS OF THE PARENT

It is essential for the parent to be informed about the condition of her child as soon as possible. Blodgett[25] suggests that parents need to be counseled about: a) the acceptance of the disability; b) attitudes and feelings, and c) making short and long term plans. It should be noted that more specifically these areas of counseling should include information about the nature and needs of mentally retarded children, their potentials in learning essential social and academic skills, and competence in healthful living.

THE ACCEPTANCE OF THE DISABILITY

The first procedure followed by most parents who suspect retardation, if they have not been informed at the child's birth, is to take the child to a physician for physical examination. The physician usually makes referrals for further diagnosis for possible abnormalities in physical, visual, auditory, and intellectual development. The parent is then informed about the child's condition and the extent of retardation.

"A diagnosis is communicated to parents whose lives have been, are, and will be affected by the fact that they have a defective or retarded child. Since in *every case*—be it a mentally defective, or maladjusted, or cerebral palsied, or cardiac child—the parents have played an important role in the child's development, just as the child has been an important factor in their lives, the communication of the diagnosis cannot be perfunctorily handled. Parental attitudes and behavior are data which are taken into account in arriving at a diagnosis, and the subsequent communication of the diagnosis to the parents—the *manner* in which the communication is handled—requires skill as well as psychological insight if the parents are expected to obtain a realistic conception of the condition of their child."[26]

[25] H. E. Blodgett: Helping parents in the community setting. *The 33rd Spring Conference of the Woods Schools*, Minneapolis, Minn., May 2-3, 1958.
[26] William M. Cruickshank: *Psychology of Exceptional Children and Youth.* Englewood Cliffs, N. J., Prentice-Hall, Inc., 1956.

The imparting of facts requires considerable skill in counseling. Under stressful conditions, most parents are unable to understand the significance of the situation at the time of the initial impact. If the facts are given in obstruse medical terminology, comprehension may be even more difficult. Some physicians may well use some assistance if counseling is to function adequately.

The cause, nature, and implications of mental retardation may be discussed with parents by the professional counselor, clinical psychologist, or social worker. When working with parents of mentally retarded children, it should be kept in mind that they have experienced keen frustration, family anxiety—even financial hardship. Some parents have never had the opportunity to unburden their anguish and disappointment. It isn't unusual for some parents to disbelieve the physician. Believing that the child will outgrow the condition, they waste time, energy, and money searching for some person who will tell them the diagnosis has been faulty. It follows, therefore, that the initial purpose of parent counseling is to develop necessary and positive adjustments and maintain desirable foundations for the child's personality. *Attitudes and feelings:* The parent needs help in meeting the dismay, the fear of the child's future, and the feeling of helplessness existent in most parents. "When parents can understand that first of all their child is a child, and that the handicap is but one of many factors in his life situation, they can begin to rally their forces to deal with it. . . . Sharing of responsibility and achieving togetherness in goals and methods by a mother and father are essential in meeting a primary need to obtain scientific information about the child's handicap."[27]

Counseling is essential in assisting parents to overcome their feelings of guilt. Parents who feel guilty sometimes try to keep the neighbors from knowing, neglect to seek assistance, refuse to believe the diagnosis, and spend useless time in trying to find someone who will tell them that the situation is not as bad as they fear. The emotional impact of parents may be more serious than the handicap of the youngster. In any case the counselor should recognize the sensitiveness of parents and make allowances for their tendencies to be tense, worried, depressed, and even suspicious.

[27] L. B. Carr: Problems confronting parents of children with handicaps. *Exceptional Children*, 25:251-255, Feb. 1959.

COUNSELING TO GIVE INFORMATION ABOUT THE NEEDS OF THE CHILD

Parents have the problem of learning to know how much can be expected and at what rate their child can achieve. Knowledge, understanding, ingenuity, and imagination must be utilized to help the child do things for himself. Patience and desire to see the child develop are essential traits of parental character. Most mentally retarded children will learn but at a later age than the average child. There is a correct time for assisting the child with a particular task. This time depends upon both maturation of the body and the successful accomplishment of previous learning tasks. Just as with any child, tasks presented before a state of readiness may make later learning more difficult. On the other hand, the child may lose interest if he is not permitted to learn a task when he is ready and willing.

Retarded children need help in learning how to feed themselves, how to talk, walk, and use the bathroom. In many cases long hours of patient guidance will be more necessary than with a normal youngster. Learning in the mentally retarded is accomplished through perfecting skills rather than developing them all at once. If a child is made to feel uncomfortable and unsuccessful when he has not learned a task perfectly, he is not likely to be motivated sufficiently to try again. Even though the child makes mistakes, he should be praised for small amounts of progress.

COUNSELING FOR MAKING PLANS FOR THE CHILD

Planning for the future of a mentally retarded child should begin as soon as the parent has been informed of the child's condition. Parents may be extremely hostile and defensive or very cooperative or somewhere in between these extremes. Emotional status may fluctuate from day to day, thus to deal with parents' feelings requires a mature, highly trained and experienced counselor. Planning with a parent is an individual matter and dependent upon the particular parent and child involved. Too much inquiry and interest, too much sympathy, too much offering of help, may be viewed as an act of helpfulness or as an act of hostility. Parents may be extremely sensitive and defensive and regard as offensive any effort by others to assist. The first step in planning has been taken when parents have come to accept the child as he really is, with full knowledge of his strengths and weaknesses.

The importance of making decisions by the parents themselves of long range plans cannot be overemphasized. Decisions should be made only after parents have made a thorough appraisal of the entire situation. Many counseling interviews may be necessary.

Early in the plans for the child's future should be the possibility of placing the child in an institution. Only a total picture of family and community can determine the correct answer. The total picture must include the kind and degree of disability, family attitudes and the welfare of the other children in the family. For reasons of incompetence, indigence, or illness, or degree of the handicap of the child, it may be well to place the child in another home. The provision for parents to make frequent visits and to give them opportunity to observe the child's progress may be helpful. Parents often need the help of social workers in becoming willing to relinquish the child.

If the child is to remain in the family the mother must consider herself physically capable of assuming her responsibilities. Strain and overwork in caring for and adjusting to a retarded child may affect the physical well-being of the mother. If the mother perceives her child as making great demands on her, which she cannot satisfy regardless of her effort, she may identify herself as a person in poor health. If she considers herself a sick person, the mother will consider herself incapable for caring for the child.

The prospect of long term care of a M. R. child in the home may cause frustration; the mother with a severely retarded child faces a prolonged infancy period and the prospect that socially the child will never achieve adulthood. According to Kohn (1959), working-class mothers emphasize obedience and responsiveness to parental authority as values in the socialization of children. With the prospect that the M. R. child will not be responsive to such obedience is an unhappy prospect for these mothers.[28]

Mothers who are in poor health are more willing to institutionalize their child than are retarded child mothers in good health. Generally the higher the social status of the family, the greater is the willingness of the parents (especially the husband) to place the retarded child in an institution.

---

[28] M. L. Kohn: Social class and parental values. *American Journal of Sociology,* *64*:337-351, 1959.

In a study of family integration, Farber[29] discovered that mothers who had been treated for a nervous condition reported that the reports of the original diagnosis of retardation had a great impact. They perceived the child as making great demands upon them; they were willing to institutionalize the offspring. As compared to other mothers, the mother of a M. R. child attended church less frequently, belonged to fewer organizations, and were less motivated toward upward social mobility.

Of course it is difficult for parents *and professional people* to predict the future of a mentally retarded child. Farber concludes that parents can expect that a retarded boy, especially after the age of nine, will probably have a disruptive effect on marital relations. If sister is in the family she may have personality problems because of her many responsibilities for the child. It is the degree of helplessness of the retarded child rather than his mere presence that will affect the personality of normal siblings adversely.

GROUP COUNSELING AND GROUP STUDY

Insights into their own behavior and the behavior of their child can be accomplished by parents if they talk and study with people who, too, have mentally retarded children. Group participation helps parents to see their child as a separate human being and his handicap as an unfortunate accident of nature. Issues can be seen more clearly and necessary decisions made more wisely.

Every parent brings something to the group which represents his feelings and experiences. This includes his own unique set of values and patterns of expectation. Learning to adjust calls for a basic change in the parent himself—changes which rarely occur through the accretion of facts or even through skillful use of parliamentary rules.

The personality maladjustments of mentally retarded children can sometimes be traced to the emotional environment and personalities of parents. In group conferences and discussions, topics may range from theoretical parent-child problems to practical matters of housing and play space. By means of group participation, the mother may realize that her feelings and behavior influence the feelings and behavior of the child; she may recognize the sig-

---

[29] B. Farber: Effects of a severely mentally retarded child on family integration. *Monographs of Social Research Child Development, 24*:2, Serial 71, 1959.

nificance of sibling rivalry, rejection, child's need of love, child's need of independence and self-determination; release of guilt through verbal sharing of experiences; and increase of parental self-confidence as group participation continues.

Suggestions for leaders of parent-group counseling have been given by Ohlsen and DeWitt.[30] According to these writers, the success of group counseling depends upon these variables:

1. Group climate; e.g., each parent should feel that he has the privilege of talking to the counselor alone, that he may withdraw from the group at will, that he may say anything he wishes without fear of reprisal, that he has a voice in planning what will be discussed.
2. Problems chosen for discussion; e.g., success is most likely to occur with a group that has ordinary, everyday problems. It is unwise to consider problems which have caused a serious case of emotional upset; nevertheless, each problem selected should have sufficient depth to stimulate a desire for its solution.
3. The leader or counselor; e.g., the counselor must recognize his own strengths and weaknesses. Rather than assume the responsibility of giving answers, he should help the group reach its own decisions. The counselor should not depress his approval or disapproval concerning the progress of individual members. Furthermore, the counselor should be willing to relinquish his leadership to group members occasionally. In other words, the group must be "group centered" not "leadership centered."
4. Composition of the group; e.g., better results are obtained if the members are homogeneous in their interest in common problems. Parents who have ten-year-old children who cannot read, for example, should be a congenial group.
5. The size of the group; e.g., the number should not exceed seven or eight.

Once a mentally retarded child is in school, and no preliminary conferences with the parent has been held, the typical questions asked of principal and teacher are: "Is my child feeble-minded? How severely retarded is my child? What kind of a person will he be? Can he ever earn a living for his family? Is he some particular

---

[30] M. M. Ohlsen and A. F. DeWitt: Group counseling: a report on ways and means. *Clearing House*, 24:335-339, Feb. 1950.

clinical type? What is the cause of mental deficiency? How long will it take him to get over it?"

The parent may be filled with anxiety, hostility, guilt, shame, and feelings of rejection. Parents of the mentally retarded child are characterized by their intense resistance to any realistic recognition of the limitations or capacities of their children; by their withdrawal from social activities; and by their overprotection of children. The effects of antisocialism are already beginning to be alleviated when parents have recognized the problem and have joined a group of other parents.

After group counseling, parents often realize that it is not a kindness to the child to protect him to the point that he does not learn to achieve to his fullest capacity. They discover that giving a child the opportunity to carry out tasks in accordance with his ability is the only way independence and initiative can develop. They learn that with supporting love and affection and good judgment in controls, encouragement toward independence will strengthen the child's sense of feeling that he has a place in the world, that he is a useful person.

One group of parents discovered the following facts about its members.[31]

1. Parents often exhibit fierce resistance to any realistic recognition of the limitations or capacities of the retarded individual.
2. Most parents are afraid to permit their handicapped children to do the things they are capable of doing (overprotection).
3. The presence of the child in the home accentuates any personality difficulties which exist in members of the family.
4. Nonacceptance by the community and family groups is translated to the individual parent and then to the child.
5. The knowledge of a parent who has lived through the phases of development of his handicapped child can be used by other parents.
6. Parents in need of guidance extend a more cordial welcome to the specialists.

Homes and schools have a partnership in the rearing and edu-

---

[31] J. T. Weingold and R. P. Hermuth: Group guidance of parents of mentally retarded children. *Journal of Clinical Psychology, 9*:118-124, April 1953.

cation of children. Parents who identify their ambitions, frustrations, and dreams in the lives of their children do the children more harm than good. Group guidance procedures which are proving effective in schools include parent-teacher activities, parent visits to the schools, parent-child study groups, group-parent counseling, and group-teacher participation for professional growth. For example, in some communities groups of parents of mentally retarded children have started their own classes for child study. These classes are aimed at assisting parents to share common concerns; to obtain needed information from speakers and professional resource persons; to make the community aware of particular needs of mentally retarded children; and to contribute to an acceptance of the child with the handicap.

SELECTED REFERENCES

Anderson, Richard J.: A social worker looks at the parent-teacher conference. *Exceptional Children, 28:8:433*, April 1962.

Auerbach, A. B.: Group education for parents of the handicapped. *Children, 8:135-140*, July 1961.

Baum, M. H.: Some dynamic factors affecting family adjustment to the handicapped child. *Exceptional Children, 28:387-392*, April 1962.

Carr, L. B.: Problems confronting parents of children with handicaps. *Exceptional Children, 25:251-255*, Feb. 1959.

Denhoff, E.: Impact of parents on the growth of exceptional children. *Exceptional Children, 26:271-274*, Jan. 1960.

Education of exceptional children: reviews the literature for the six-year period since Dec. 1953. *Review of Educational Research, 79:391-570*, Dec. 1959.

Essex, M.: How can parents and special educators best cooperate for the education of exceptional children? *Exceptional Children, 28:478-482*, May 1962.

Smart, Euzelia C.: Social services in the treatment of cerebral palsy. *American Journal of Physical Medicine, 32:159-164*, June 1955.

Farber, B.: Effects of a severely retarded child on family integration. *Monographs Research in Child Development, 24:2*, 1959.

Frasure, K.: Parent and teacher partnership. *Education, 82:406-409*, March 1962.

Hersh, A.: Casework with parents of retarded children. *Social Work,* 1961.

Holt, K. S.: The home care of mentally retarded children. *Pediatrics, 22:744-755*, 1958.

Hallowitz, D.: Consultation with parents of disturbed children. *Children, 8:22-27*, Jan. 1961.

Justison, G. G.: Parents in programs for the severely retarded. *Exceptional Children, 25:99-100*, Nov. 1958.

Kogan, J. and Moss, H. A.: Personality and social development: family and peer influence, family influences on personality development. *Review of Education Research,* 31:465-467, Dec. 1961.

Kozier, A.: Casework with parents of children born with severe brain defects. *Social Casework,* 1957.

Lerrigo, M. O.: Mentally retarded and the church. *Journal of Religious Education,* 35:20-22, Dec. 1951.

Lowe, R. N.: Parent-teacher education and child development. *Education,* 81:28-31, Sept. 1960.

Lynd, H. M.: *On Shame and the Search for Identity.* New York, Harcourt, Brace & Co., 1958.

Major, J.: How do we accept the handicapped? *Elementary School Journal,* 61:328-330, Mar. 1961.

Innis, J. M.: Selected references from the literature on exceptional children; mentally retarded. *Elementary School Journal,* 62:336-338, March 1962.

Mullen, J. A.: Teacher works with the parent of the exceptional child. *Education,* 80:329-332, Feb. 1960.

Peterson, D. R.: Child behavior problems and parental attitudes. *Child Development,* 32:151-162, Mar. 1961.

Reid, S.: Helping parents of handicapped children. *Children,* 5:15-19, Jan. 1958.

Ross, Helen: The handicapped child and his family. *Crippled Child,* 4:11-59, 1953.

Rose, J. A.: Factors in the development of mentally handicapped children, counseling parents of children with mental handicaps. *Proceedings of the 1958 Woods School Conference,* May 2-3, 1958.

Saenger, G.: The adjustment of severely retarded adults in the community. Albany, N. Y., Report to the New York State Interdepartmental Health Resources Board, 1957.

Sarason, S. B.: *Psychological Problems in Mental Deficiency.* Sec. Ed. New York, Harper & Bros., 1953, p. 368.

Serot, N. M. and Teevan, R. C.: Perception of the parent-child relationship and its relation to child adjustment. *Child Development,* 32:373-378, June 1961.

Silver, D. J.: Retarded child and religious education, a case study. *Religious Education,* 52:361-364, Sept. 1957.

Spock, B., Rheinhart, J. and Miller, W.: *A Baby's First Year.* New York, Duell, Sloan, and Pierce, 1955.

Thurston, John R.: Counseling the parents of the severely handicapped. *Exceptional Children,* 26:7-351-355, March 1960.

Trisdall, W. J. and Moss, J. W.: Total program for the severely retarded. *Exceptional Children,* 28:357-362, March 1962.

Wellin, E.: Social and cultural aspects of mental retardation. *Proceedings of the Institute for Nurses on Mental Retardation.* Trenton, N. J., State Dept. of Health, 1960.

Wright, B. A.: New look at overprotection and dependency. *Exceptional Children, 26*:115-122, Nov. 1959.

Zuk, G. H.: Autistic distortions in parents of retarded children. *Journal of Consulting Psychology, 23*:171-176, April 1959.

Zuk, G. H.: The religious factor and the role of guilt in parental acceptance of the retarded child. *American Journal of Mental Deficiency, 63*:139-147, 1959.

CHAPTER IX

The Mentally Retarded Child and His Community

THE COMMUNITY AS THE CHILD'S SOCIETY

MENTAL retardation can be understood only as the society and culture in which the child lives is understood. It is important to recognize that society defines, perceives, reacts to, and attempts to cope with mental subnormality in terms of cultural factors of belief, customs, taboos, and mores. In reality, the degree to which a child is mentally defective is in terms of social standards only. Mental deficiency currently is applied to mentally retarded persons, who as adults are likely to be socially incompetent. Rather than use a test score alone, mental retardation and mental deficiency should be defined operationally.

In our American society are found conflicting values and attitudes reflected in rules and regulations regarding the relationships between parents and children, regarding attitudes toward individuals who cannot maintain standards, and regarding expectations of children at various ages. Child-rearing practices and the socio-economic level of the home has some effect on accelerating or depressing the child's intelligence. In the United States we do not have a classless society. It may be possible that the social values of lower-class culture are an inversion of middle-class standards and are derived from the disadvantageous position in which the members of the lower class find themselves. The mentally retarded child may be functioning at a lower level of intelligence because of his social economic status. In fact, the results of certain studies appear to support this point of view.

Strong evidence that mentally retarded children from lower socio-economic areas and cultural levels may be functioning at a low intellectual level because of cultural deprivation is found in the studies of Skeels[1] and Kirk.[2] Preschool education is especially needed by these children because of cultural deprivation, yet they

---

[1] Harold M. Skeels: A study of the effects of differentiated stimulation on men-

212

comprise a group who do not get it. Those from the higher cultural and economic levels have a maximum nurture at home yet this group receives the benefit from preschool activities.

Social values and attitudes of the mentally retarded generally correspond to those of the home and neighborhood associates and in many instances typical of low socioeconomic areas and areas of substandard housing. There are more behavior problems and slightly more delinquency among the retarded in proportion to their numbers than among children of average intelligence.[3] The substandard environment in which a large percentage of these children live may account, at least partially, for this.

"The feeble-minded (educable mentally retarded) however, more than any other group in western culture have been reared in most adverse circumstances, followed in many cases by further lengthy periods of residential schools and institutions, with all that this implies. Thus the feeble-minded in such conditions seem likely to be functioning towards the lower end of the spectrum of potentialities, while normals under ordinary conditions of life, approximate more closely to their upper limits."[4]

Mental subnormality occurs in larger numbers in the lowest social classes or in culturally distinct minority groups or from regions with conspicuously poor educational facilities or standards. Unfortunately, there have been no systematic studies of how social and cultural factors operate so as to have an interfering effect on development.[5] After making a longitudinal study of the effects of preschool education on the development of educable mentally retarded children, Kirk[6] came to the following conclusions:

1. Preschool training tended to increase the developmental rate of retarded children. . . .

---

[3] S. A. Kirk: *Educating Exceptional Children.* Boston, Houghton Mifflin Co., 1962, p. 111.

[4] Ann M. Clarke and A. D. B. Clarke: *Mental Deficiency: The Changing Outlook.* Glencoe, Ill., The Free Press, 1958, p. 119.

[5] Seymour B. Sarason: *Psychological Problems in Mental Deficiency.* 3rd Ed. New York, Harper & Bros., 1959, p. 644.

[6] S. A. Kirk: *Early Education of the Mentally Retarded.* Urbana, Univ. of Ill. Press, 1958, p. 100.

---

tally retarded children: a follow up report. *American Journal of Mental Deficiency, 46:*340-350, Jan. 1942.

[2] S. A. Kirk: *Early Education of the Mentally Retarded.* Urbana, Univ. of Ill. Press, 1958.

2. Children from psychosocially deprived homes tended to either retain their rate of development or increase the rate during and after the preschool period, while those who did not receive preschool experience tended to drop or remain the same in rate of development.

3. Children in the institution who received training at the preschool level showed marked gains in rate of growth, while those who were not given preschool experience and remained on the wards tended to drop in rate of growth.

4. Children placed in foster homes and also in preschool changed markedly in rate of growth.

5. Children from relatively adequate homes, not given preschool experience, tended to hold their rate of growth during the preschool period but increased their rate when they entered school at the age of six. This indicated that the age of six is not too late for increasing developmental rate, provided the children come from relatively adequate homes.

The concern, care and education of mentally retarded children is reflected in the basic concepts of public responsibility for all its children and is expressed, in turn, in the legal and judicial protection of the individual and in the types of services which may be provided by law at public expense. Zuk,[7] for example, thinks that culturally speaking, the attitude of American society toward the handicapped child is one of ambivalence. This ambivalence raises feelings in the parent of frustration, anger, and guilt.

SPECIFIC INFLUENCE OF CULTURE

Specific differences in attitude toward the mentally retarded child can be noted in rural and urban areas of our own nation and in differences between our own nation and other nations. In the literature of both European and American countries, discussing the handicapped child, it may be noted that in earlier days the educationally sub-normal were officially described as the mentally defective. At times these people were treated as outcasts from the educational system. Now most of the individuals are considered as a group which can and should be taught in the ordinary schools.

Because of attitudes, specialized personnel, and facilities, the city has become a mecca for the mentally, physically, and emotionally handicapped child.

---

[7] C. H. Zuk: The cultural dilemma and spiritual crisis of the family with a handicapped child. *Exceptional Children, 28*:405-408, April 1962.

In most non-European societies, the incidence of mental retardation is inconsequential; cases are cared for as long as they live, with a minimum of distress or dislocation. The difference lies in culturally determined attitudes, behavior, and criteria of social acceptability.

In Sweden, a child should not be placed in an institution unless there is no possibility of his remaining in his own home or in a suitable foster home. For the child who cannot remain in his own home, the "Central Board" is required to secure foster family placement if at all possible. A strong distinction exists between the educational program and the protective care program.[8]

In Denmark, there is considerably more emphasis on work training than on education; for example, weaving.

"In the Netherlands, it is an established tradition that social and educational work, which is so closely linked with spiritual convictions and views of life, should be the concern of the group having the same conviction as the persons to be assisted. The public authorities are called in to help only when their own group falls short in providing the necessary assistance. In general, the actual work is carried out by voluntary organizations and institutions, largely of denominational character, but under the supervision and financial support of the government. This produces the peculiar Dutch phenomenon, not found anywhere else in the world, of the social service, to a very large extent, being split up on denominational lines.[9]

The dynamic nature of our United States subjects its inhabitants to extreme contrasts and abrupt changes during a lifetime. Attitudes and treatment of exceptional children have been no exception. Several states have legislative commissions studying status of the individual who is mentally retarded and in need of either special training or guardianship.

BIAS IN THE COMMUNITY

School personnel and interested parents have an obligation to inform the community about what has been accomplished and about what can be accomplished with sufficient manpower and

---

[8] S. Boggs and G. Nordfors: Care of mentally retarded in Sweden. *Children,* 7:150-151, July 1960.

[9] D. A. Hindman: Programs for the mentally retarded in Denmark and Holland. *Exceptional Children,* 28:19-22, Sept. 1961.

resources. Required is a broadened concept of the total educational needs of mentally retarded children. The community needs to know that mentally retarded children have to learn how to live in a world beyond their home. Only as the community accepts these children can they learn how to protect themselves, how to manage their own impulses and their consideration for others, how to conform socially through good habit patterns, and how to support themselves at least partially. Constructive community experience is one part of a well-rounded life for a child. Community tolerance of the mentally retarded child may be a factor in the institutionalization of a child. The influence is not as great if the parents care little for the maintenance of the family's status in the community. Presumably, the higher the socioeconomic status, the greater is the importance of a mentally retarded child in the home.

Most important to the parents of mentally retarded community people are mothers and mother-in-laws. A review of case material by Farber[10] showed much sympathy and understanding by the wife's mother whereas the husband's mother generally blamed the wife for the retarded child. Sometimes, there was implication that the mother-in-law regarded the retarded child as punishment for her daughter-in-law's wrong doing.

Parents are well-aware that there are many community prejudices. Often parents, themselves, must reduce their own prejudices; in any case, they must cooperate in some way to reduce a handicap-centered community approach. Many parents expect a great deal from the community and the individuals who comprise it. Most parents want acceptance and assurance from others either by way of positive, comforting acts or by the elimination of unfavorable reactions. In other words, parents feel that other people should act naturally or be sympathetic and understanding when around the handicapped. In many cases parents are highly sensitive, suspicious, anxious, and unhappy individuals; that is, the opposite of what might be desired. In such cases, parents are themselves so handicapped emotionally that they find it difficult to adjust to community attitude.

The changes in community attitude that are being brought about are largely a result of economical rather than humanitarian

---

[10] B. Farber: Effects of a severely mentally retarded child on family integration. *Monographs of Soc. Research Child Development, 24*:2, Serial 17, 1959.

reasons. Currently, there is a tendency in most communities to consider the exceptional child, including the mentally retarded, as being considered a positive national asset; with potential that must be mobilized, rather than a liability that must be tolerated for sentimental reasons. The nation cannot ignore the possible contributions of major segments of the populations who have hitherto been largely ignored.

THE RESPONSIBILITY OF THE COMMUNITY

One of the ideals of the United States has been the equality of opportunity to all regardless of nationality, cultural background, race, or religion. This ideal extends to every child no matter what his talents, capacity, or handicap may be. The founding fathers of this nation agreed that "all men are created equal" before the law. This phrase has been interpreted also to mean equality of opportunity and when applied to education, it refers to the right of each child to receive help in learning to the limits of his capacity. This is the philosophy reflected by the society in which a child lives. "Society" as used here refers to the child's family, community, and nation. Inasmuch as the child's family was discussed in the preceding chapter, the community, including the larger community of State and Nation, shall be considered in this chapter.

"Historically, three stages in the development of attitudes toward the handicapped child can be recognized. First, during the pre-Christian era, the handicapped were persecuted, neglected, and mistreated. Second, during the spread of Christianity, they were protected and pitied. Third, in very recent years, there has been a movement toward accepting the handicapped and integrating them into society to the fullest extent possible. In education, *integration* denotes a trend toward educating the exceptional child with his normal peers to whatever extent is compatible with his fullest potential development."[11]

The movement to provide education for the exceptional child in the local community, as well as in institutions, began in this nation in the early part of the twentieth century. On a nationwide basis, greater emphasis is being placed currently upon spe-

---

[11] Samuel A. Kirk: *Educating Exceptional Children.* Boston, Houghton Mifflin Co., 1962, p. 4.

cial education than in any other period in our educational history.

Because of the influences from the community at large which help determine the course of a child's social and emotional development, the responsibility of the community to the mentally retarded child is great. Community influences impinge upon children and are reflected in attitudes and values held. When the child is exceptional, teamwork between the home and community is basic for effective service to any child.

Basic, especially, to the success of parents and child to community adjustment are the professional resources. The physician, the psychologist, the counselor, the social worker, and the teacher each has a significant role to play. Community institutions such as the child-guidance clinic, the church, the school, the community recreational program can all be of value. State and local agencies provide pertinent information and the sharing of mutual problems.

As an illustration, the community's recreational facilities may be cited. Retarded children need supervised play-experiences just as do all children. Recreation is needed throughout life for some of the same purposes it serves in childhood. Recreation serves as a release from strong emotion, as a means of healthful and satisfying association with friends, and as desirable pursuit of a hobby. Parks and other recreational areas need to be staffed with responsible persons who understand the limitations of retarded children.

COMMUNITY RESOURCES

Included in the community resources for the education of the mentally retarded are: professional individuals such as the physician and nurse, psychologist, social worker, counselor, and teacher; child-guidance and/or community clinics; welfare agencies; citizen's organizations such as parent-teacher associations, Council for the Education of the Exceptional Child; Progress for Retarded Children, Inc.; and the church.

The physician is the key person when the condition of the child is first known. It is he who should inform the parents of the child's handicap either at the time of birth or during some subsequent medical examination. Annual or periodic physical examinations should be made under the direction of the physician. The physician or nurse determines the physical fitness of each child for school work, recommends changes in the school's program in light of the child's physical condition, and brings needs of special medical and dental services to the attention of the school doctor or school nurse. Even the diagnosis of a psychological problem should always begin with a diagnosis of present or past physical condition.

The psychologist administers and interprets test results, analyzes psychological problems, and assists in referral. He may enter the home to assess psychological status. When the child remains home, psychological examinations are usually made when the child is five, six, eight, and ten years old. Diagnosis should be made as early as possible because the passage of time makes it harder to accept reality. When the child is in school, the psychologist is charged with diagnosing children's problems and assisting with remediation in the form of play therapy, supportive or interpretative therapy and counseling. The psychologist often serves as a consultant to the teacher, explaining to her the diagnosis and suggesting ways in which she can manage the child in the classroom.

The social worker assumes the responsibility for the adjustment of the child to the home and school. She (he) obtains information about the child's behavior at home, evaluates the status and attitudes of the parents on the appropriate ways of managing the child, and often deals with the child in individual or group conferences. It is usually the social worker who assumes responsibility for referral of children and their families to service agencies. She (he) acts in a liaison capacity for any community agency interested in a specific pupil or his family and to modify whatever conditions are necessary to meet the individual needs.

It is the counselor who assists the parent who is emotionally disturbed about her child. Usually the mentally retarded child makes the parent feel guilty and ashamed. Although not typical, some parents scream that "no one is going to call my child crazy" when a special school or child-guidance clinic is mentioned. Then, too, ambivalence in attitude toward the child is common. In all of these cases the counseling of parents is a long-term project.

The teacher assumes responsibility of teaching the child, always being careful to assure success in achievement, building good self-concepts, and helping the child to react normally without resorting to deviant behavior. Because of her daily contact with the pupil, the teacher can provide data from daily observation made under a great variety of conditions. This data reported in the form of anecdotes, summaries of pupil or parent interviews, or products of pupil's work can make a valuable contribution.

THE COMMUNITY CLINIC

The community clinic is a generalized phrase which can be used to include more specific organizations such as community mental health clinics, child-guidance clinics, speech clinics, community guidance bureaus, and remedial reading clinics. These clinics are increasing in number but because of the extreme shortage of child psychiatrists, counselors, pediatricians and nurses, and specially trained teachers, many of them have not been able to meet the demands for diagnosis and treatment. The pioneer guidance clinic was the Chicago Juvenile Psychopathic Institute founded by Dr. William Healy in 1909 under the sponsorship of Mrs. W. F. Dummer. This clinic, having the aim of "bettering the adjustment of children to their immediate environment, with special reference to their emotional and social relationships, to the end that they may be free to develop to the limit of their individual capacities for well-balanced maturity" has set the goal for child-guidance clinics today.

The history of the child-guidance is in part the development of the specialities of psychiatric social work, clinical psychology, and child psychiatry. Although most child-guidance clinics select for intensive study and treatment only those children within the wide range of what is called normal intelligence, mentally retarded children are accepted for diagnosis and referral. Clinic teams frequently include a neurologist, pediatrician, psychologist, psychiatric social worker, speech therapist, remedial reading specialist, and even a music therapist.[12]

The modern child-guidance clinic of today correlates its activities. In a highly developed organization it is not unusual to find summer camps, hospital schools, ranch-schools, private schools, boarding homes, and other agencies to enable the staff to supervise and to some extent control the child's life. In most clinics, parents are included as clients, because without cooperation of parents, children cannot receive maximum assistance. Parents are taught

---

[12] These are the personnel in the Morris J. Solomon Clinic for the Rehabilitation of Retarded Children and Division of Pediatric Psychiatry, Jewish Hospital of Brooklyn, Brooklyn, N. Y.

to teach the skills of socially acceptable behavior, or in other ways to increase self-reliance.

The values of the clinic are difficult to determine directly because the results do not lend themselves to statistical treatment. The case history is the most fruitful approach for etiological diagnosis, prediction of outcome, and development of a plan of action. In the case of the mentally retarded, teaching has become the core of the therapeutic approach thus the teacher's role has become increasingly significant.

SPECIAL SCHOOLS AND CLASSES

Many parents do not want to send their retarded children to institutions. In these cases there is need for some kind of group activity including an organized training program. Historically, parents organized their own classes for their children and employed their own teachers. Usually with insufficient equipment and supplies, classes were held in homes, basements, and churches, or wherever they could find space. Because of the influence of parent groups, communities finally accepted the responsibility for helping to support these classes. Currently, many communities have incorporated these exceptional groups into the school system. The statutes of most states were formulated before the concept of the IQ originated, thus it is practically mandatory for schools to admit the mentally retarded and provide adequate training for them.

When classes for the trainable child are organized, the patterns of organizations and procedure vary according to geographical location and to composition of classes. The admission requirements for school classes for trainable children have been formulated in many states. According to Kirk,[13] the following represent those most generally in effect.

1. The age of admission for trainable retarded children in the public school classes is generally the same as for other children. In most instances this age is six.

2. The objective criterion which appears to be the most valid for admission is the IQ based on individual psychometric tests administered by a psychologist trained and experienced in the diagnosis of mental retardation. The usual IQ range for these

[13] Samuel A. Kirk: *Educating Exceptional Children.* Boston, Mass., Houghton Mifflin Co., 1962, p. 140.

classes is between 30 or 35 and 50 and 55 and IQ's are derived from such tests as the Stanford-Binet Intelligence Scale, the Minnesota Preschool Scale, the Merrill-Palmer Scale, and the Kuhlmann Tests of Mental Development.

3. Most children admitted into the classes are required to have a medical examination to determine their physical ability to participate in the program.

4. Not all children with IQ's between 35 and 50 are admitted. Other criteria include ability to get along in the class and a minimum ability to take care of their needs, such as toileting, partial dressing, and so forth. Schools tend to exclude children who are a danger to themselves or others and those whose behavior is likely to disrupt the classroom program.

5. Children admitted to these classes must have some minimum communication ability in the form of either speech or gestures. Most trainable children above the age of six with IQ's over 30 have these abilities.

6. The general procedure for admission is to have a committee composed of a psychologist, a social worker, teachers, and other school personnel accept or reject the children.

The maximum for trainable classes is fifteen after children are adjusted to school routine. At first classes should be small and increased in size according to rapidity of learning routine, to age, and to ability. Transportation should be provided for all trainable children because of geographic distribution and inability to go to school unattended.

Regardless of whether special schools and classes are benefitcial to all children, most people would agree that they have special value for the parents. Once relieved of the constant care of the child, the parent may become more objective by having an opportunity to see what the child can learn outside of her influence. Studies have shown that after the children were in classes for awhile, parents reduced their expectations for the children's learning of academic subjects.[14] In an Illinois study,[15] the parents tended to become more realistic about their children's abilities and limitations. They realized, for example, that although their chil-

---

[14] Marcella H. Lorenz: Follow-up studies of the severely retarded. Reynolds, M. C., Kiland, J. R. and Ellis, R. E., Eds.: *Research Projects*, No. 6, St. Paul, Minn., Statistical Div., State Dept. of Ed., 1953.

[15] *Report on Study Projects for Trainable Mentally Handicapped Children.* Springfield, Ill., Off. of the Superintendent of Pub. Instruction, Nov. 1954.

dren improved in self-care skills, they would not become self-supporting.

RESIDENTIAL SCHOOLS

Oldest of the provisions for caring for exceptional children, the residential school is still found in all states of the Union. The impetus for residential schools was given through the influence of such leaders as Horace Mann, Samuel G. Howe, and Dorothea Dix.[16] These schools offered training, but equally important was the protective environment, often covering the life span of the individual. The prediction of Samuel G. Howe in 1871 that the education of exceptional children would be toward integrating them into the "common" schools with a decrease in residential schools has been realized.

No longer, however, in the United States are the newer schools of this type being built away from population centers to become segregated, sheltered asylums with little community contact. Although of necessity some children have to be removed from home and neighborhood contact because of sparsely populated areas and need for professional attention. There may be situations within the child's home which require that for the welfare of the family and the child he must be placed in a residential school. As public school special education programs provide for the most able of exceptional children, the residential schools will provide programs only for the severely and multiple handicapped children.

As adults, some individuals who have been rehabilitated or educated to do useful work in society, will still need careful supervision and a home to which to return after their daily work hours are finished.

CITIZEN AND PROFESSIONAL ORGANIZATIONS

Powerful national organizations and local citizens organizations are bringing before the public the needs of atypical children. In 1957 alone, there was a 22 per cent increase in the number of special education consultants at the state level.[17] At the present time all states provide some legislative assistance for exceptional children and most states use public funds to support educational pro-

---

[16] Samuel A. Kirk: *Educating Exceptional Children.* Boston, Mass., Houghton-Mifflin Co., 1962, p. 6.

[17] R. Mackie: Exceptional years for exceptional children. *School Life,* 40 Jan. 1958.

grams. Money for research in the education of exceptional children has become available through Federal legislation.[18] Federal fellowships exist for the providing of leadership personnel and advanced training of personnel in the field of mental retardation.[19]

In many states, piecemeal legislation over the decades interspersed programs for the mentally retarded and other handicapped children throughout state departments of mental health, welfare, health, education, and/or institutions.

At the federal level, provisions for programs for exceptional children have been shifted from the Department of the Interior to the Federal Security Agency and hence (where the responsibility currently lies) to the Department of Health, Education, and Welfare. Provision for present programs concerning exceptional children are found in the Section on Exceptional Children and Youth of the Office of Education. Major responsibilities are also found in other sections of the Office of Education, in the Children's Bureau, and in the Office of Vocational Rehabilitation.

"In the eighty years that groups of special educators have been organized for national objectives, their scope has gradually widened to include all the exceptional children recognized currently. . . . Today the Council for Exceptional Children is the main organization in this country for all personnel interested in the education of exceptional children. With its National headquarters in Washington, D. C., an executive secretary and staff available for information and help, and local chapters set up in every state, it numbers over 14,000 members and forms a strong, unifying force for an improved special education."[20]

Of the many national professional or voluntary groups devoted to the welfare of the mentally retarded, the following are important. Inasmuch as each publishes a professional newsletter or periodical, retains a national headquarters staff to answer inquiries, and conducts an annual meeting of interest to its members, they have strong influence:

American Association for Mental Deficiency

---

[18] R. Mackie, H. Williams and A. Scates: *Cooperative Research Projects 1957.* Bull. No. 5, 1958. D. Clark and A. Scates: *Cooperative Research Projects, 1958.* Bull. No. 18, 1959, Washington, D. C., Government Printing Office.

[19] Public Law 85-926 and T. Carlson: Guide to National Defense Education Act of 1958. Circular No. 553, Washington, D. C., Government Printing Office, 1959.

[20] L. E. Connor: *Administration of Special Education Programs.* New York, Teachers College, Columbia Univ., 1961, p. 8.

American Association of Social Workers
American Occupational Therapy Association
American Psychological Association
International Society for the Rehabilitation of the Disabled
National Association for Retarded Children
National Conference of Jewish Communal Service
National Catholic Welfare Council
National Foundation
President's Committee on Employment of the Handicapped
United Nations World Health Organization

Not to be overlooked are the strong parent groups organized to strengthen the schools and special education in particular. Such agencies are the National Parent-Teacher Association, National Association for Retarded Children, and Progress for Retarded Children, Inc.

Community organizations have had strong influence on state legislatures, on local school boards, on Congress, in obtaining assistance for the mentally retarded child. These organizations have undertaken vast programs of fund raising and direct action. Largely the result of parent influence, a large national program of research in mental retardation initiated by Congress and placed under the United States Department of Health, Education, and Welfare, has been launched. Parent groups have not waited for educators to lead. Most of these organizations are well-informed about the appropriate type of educational program for mentally retarded children and will cooperate with any organization interested in medical research, psychological research, legislation, teacher education, finance, and community health.

THE CHURCH AS PART OF THE CHILD'S COMMUNITY

The rise of Christianity marked a gradual change in the attitude of civilized peoples towards exceptional children. Before the onset of Christianity, the Spartans and Romans, striving for a superior race, used the direct and decisive method of deliberate destruction of obviously defective children. It is said that children were thrown into the river or left to perish on the mountainside. During the Christian area, individuals with physical deformity, epilepsy, psychotic states, deaf mutism, and mental incapacity were given humane treatment in sheltered abodes. During the twentieth century all trainable and educable handicapped children should be assisted in special education programs.

The Christian influence has been strong in the United States. In colonial Puritan New England, parents were delegated the responsibility to educate their children with sufficient ability to read the Scriptures and to conduct their own affairs.[21] Later public spirited parents organized such groups as the Society for the Propagation of the Gospel in Foreign Parts. This was a missionary effort mainly for the poor and underprivileged. Sunday Schools were organized for the same purpose. By the middle of the nineteenth century the principle of free public education was establishing itself in the state legislatures.

Religious belief is determined largely by the family and community into which a child is born. It can be a distinct influence in shaping the attitudes of parents and the community toward the exceptional child and serve as a guide toward establishing standards of moral conduct. The church can frequently serve as an intermediary between home and institution when the parent is embarrassed or refuse to cooperate for society's benefit. Church, school, and home working together can often succeed in bringing maximum benefit to a mentally retarded child. The doctrine of original sin still current in many theologies[22] which claims that a child's innate tendencies are evil because he inherits the original sin committed by Adam in the Garden of Eden may be detrimental to some exceptional children. The parent may even look upon the misfortune of having such a child as a rebuke from God for some parental sin. Then, too, because formal acceptance of salvation as provided by the church is impossible because of the lack of the child's intelligence, the parent frequently undergoes further mental anguish. Many theologians today now reject the view that the child is inherently evil and believe instead that children are born neither good nor evil, but rather with potentialities that society may direct into either good or evil channels.

Religion is generally recognized as a necessary factor in an individual's all-round development. Religion can provide a valuable source of motivation and assist in good adjustment by contributing to the individual's feeling of security and belongingness.[23] "Religion should make an individual feel at home in his universe by

[21] N. Edwards and H. G. Richey: *The School in the American Social Order.* Cambridge, Mass., The Riverside Press, 1947.

[22] U. S. churches, their practices. *Life, 39*:104-105, Dec. 26, 1955.

[23] H. S. Tuttle: Religion as motivation. *Journal of Social Psychology, 15*:255-264, 1942.

causing him to recognize some relationship between his personal ideals and goals and the ongoing process of nature as a whole."[24]

VOCATIONAL OPPORTUNITY OF THE MENTALLY RETARDED IN HIS COMMUNITY

"The ultimate objective in the area of social adjustment is complete independence in society at large . . . the objective can be achieved by teaching the child to make adjustments compatible with his developmental level. Continued social experiences and expansion of self-direction as the child matures will enable him to grow in this area as in the areas of physical and intellectual growth. As he learns to adjust to social situations requiring greater social maturity and understanding, he also learns to make the necessary adjustments that will be required of him as an adult."[25]

Economic independence requires vocational competence. Such competence has its beginnings in the elementary school and is reflected in objectives of achieving emotional stability, personal adequacy, and social competency. Note the objectives of social competency as listed in "A curriculum guide for the education of the trainable mentally retarded" by the Nevada State Dept. of Education:

1. To help the child make an acceptable adjustment to the group.
2. To teach good manners and consideration.
3. To teach respect, rather than fear, for authority.
4. To cultivate respect for the property of others.
5. To help child develop a willingness to share.
6. To provide opportunities for child to assume some minor responsibilities to group.
7. To teach acceptable social behavior in classroom and elsewhere.
8. To teach right from wrong in environment.
9. To develop attitudes of tolerance.
10. To encourage cooperation.[26]

---

[24] F. K. Merry and R. V. Merry: *The First Two Decades of Life.* 2nd Ed. New York, Harper & Bros., Publishers, 1958, p. 531.

[25] G. Orville Johnson: The education of mentally handicapped children. In W. M. Cruickshank and G. Orville Johnson: *Education of Exceptional Children and Youth.* Englewood Cliffs, N. J., Prentice-Hall, Inc., 1958, p. 194.

[26] *A Curriculum Guide for the Trainable Mentally Retarded.* Carson City, Nev. State Dept. of Ed., p. 14.

That these social adjustment objectives are important is indicated by studies[27] which show that the majority of mentally handicapped people lose their jobs for non-manual reasons such as poor attitudes, lack of conscientious effort, and inability to get along with their employer and fellow employees.

Early experiences in the manual skills should be provided at the primary and elementary levels in relation to the activities and experiences of the children. The vocational goals for mentally retarded children are much different than for those of normal youngsters. For example, experiences with tools and materials should be of a general rather than a specific nature. The large majority of the mentally retarded capable of employment will earn their living in unskilled and semi-skilled jobs requiring little specific training.

The attitude that mentally retarded children should go only to a technical or vocational school is changing, thus there is a marked increase of enrollment of mentally retarded in the public high school. The high school must, therefore, be concerned with the important problems of vocational guidance, occupational guidance, and work experience of a pre-vocational nature.

A number of community agencies are at work in providing some postschool training and counseling for the mentally retarded. These agencies are the adult education program of the public schools, the Smith-Hughes vocational school program, and the vocational rehabilitation program.

In 1945, the War Manpower Commission printed the following information:[28]

1. Close and constant supervision may be a necessary factor in the proper adjustment of the individual on the job.
   a) Mentally retarded do their best work when working immediately under the supervision of a patient, tolerant person whom they can respect.
   b) In some instances, it may help the supervisor to know that some mentally retarded people learn better by observing

---

[27] Samuel A. Kirk and G. Orville Johnson: *Educating the Retarded Child.* Boston, Mass., Houghton Mifflin Co., 1951, p. 232.

[28] Selective Placement for the Handicapped. War Manpower Commission, U. S. Employment Service, Washington, D. C. Revised, Feb. 1945.

a demonstration of the job than by following only verbal or written instructions.

2. Placement officers (interviewers) will want to check:
    a) Working with or around others, or alone.
    b) Mechanical or electrical hazards which the applicant can understand.
    c) Working speed.
3. Because some mentally retarded people verbalize easily, a place should be found in which "glibness" is an asset. "Glibness" should not be used as the criterion for recommendations for continuing formal education.
4. Those mentally retarded individuals who have had the following specialized training usually fare best:
    a) Awareness of limitations so that realistic job choices can be made.
    b) Training in occupational skills within suitable job areas such as food preparation and serving, building maintenance, personal services in beauty parlor, barber shop, domestic service, cleaning and pressing.
    c) Encouragement in development of character traits that facilitate job holding.
    d) Drilling in methods of job getting and holding.

The status of mentally retarded youth and adults as found in numerous investigations may be summarized as follows:

EXTENT TO WHICH EMPLOYED

The unemployment of mentally handicapped adults is slightly greater than that of unselected groups of workers.[29] Of a group of normal workers matched with mentally handicapped workers on factors other than mentality, it was found that among the mentally retarded are more unskilled laborers, and poorer work ratings.[30]

KINDS OF WORK

Although there appears to be no general occupational or industrial field in which there are no jobs for the mentally handicapped,

---

[29] John A. Smith: Areas of occupational opportunity for the mentally handicapped. Unpublished study, L. A. Harbor Jr. College, no date.

[30] Ruby R. Kennedy: *The Social Adjustment of Morons in a Connecticut City.* Hartford, Conn., Mansfield-Southburg Training Schools, Social Service Dept. State Office Bldg., 1948.

mentally retarded people are predominantly employed as un-skilled and semi-skilled labor.[31] The rapid transition of manual unskilled and semi-skilled tasks to automation is decreasing the demand for manpower. Only the best of the unskilled and semi-skilled people will be employed in the future. Even in non-automation industries, the mentally retarded are costly employees and they do not continue in employment when the need is not great. Then too, many industries hesitate to employ handicapped persons because of supposed safety hazards. Modern conditions, there-

Boys	Girls	Both
Automobile maintenance	Garment (e.g., seamstress)	Shoe (e.g., packing, stock
Drivers (e.g., delivery	Food handlers	room)
service)	Chemical (e.g., cleaning)	Paper box factory helper
Driver's helpers	Furniture (e.g., construc-	Button (e.g., seamstress,
Newsboys	tion and finishing)	packing)
Peddlers	Printing (e.g., cleaning,	Candy (e.g., packing,
Agricultural workers	stocking)	dipping)
Washing cars	Maids	Tobacco (e.g., sorting,
Gas station helpers	General housework	grading)
	Caring for children	Woodworking (e.g., fin-
	Ironing	ishing, sanding)
	Restaurant work	Helpers in stores and
	Elevator operators	markets
	Dishwashers	Scrubbing and waxing
	General cleaning in	floors
	hospitals	Sorting objects
	Laundry	

fore, make it imperative that the mentally retarded need the best of training and assistance in finding jobs. As long as national prosperity is high, the mentally retarded can usually find self-supporting employment but if the economic condition of the nation is low, the mentally retarded will be the first to lose their jobs.

Of the mentally retarded group it has been found that factories employ the largest group.[32] Mentally retarded boys are commonly employed in transportation[33] and the majority of girls are em-

---

[31] Alice Channing: *Employment of Mentally Deficient Boys and Girls.* U. S. Dept. of Labor, Bur. of Pub., No. 210, Washington, D. C., Government Printing Office, 1932.

[32] John A. Smith: Areas of occupational opportunity for the mentally handicapped. Unpublished study, L. A. Harbor Jr. College, no date.

[33] S. G. DiMichael: *Vocational Rehabilitation of the Mentally Retarded.* Rehabilitation Service Series, No. 123, Fed. Security Agency, Off. of Vocational Rehabilitation. Washington, D. C., Government Printing Office, 1950, p. 86.

ployed in personal and domestic service.[34] Both boys and girls are employed in clerical tasks. Reasonable success can be expected in occupations in which there is a well-defined routine and which require physical strength, endurance, and simple manipulation.[35]

More specifically the kinds of work in which the mentally retarded have succeeded appear in the table on page 230.[36]

NON-MANUAL QUALIFICATIONS

Traits other than intelligence are influential in determining success of the mentally retarded in employment; for example, character, personality, and type of intelligence. It has been found that when a mentally handicapped person fails to obtain a job or hold one, it is usually because of lack of punctuality, absenteeism, failure to adjust to fellow employees or to the employer, inability to take responsibility, indifference, unreliability, and various other types of personality handicaps.[37] Factors enabling the mentally retarded to make an economic adjustment are: 1) the ability to get along with co-workers, 2) job interest, 3) desire for more than adequacy of performance, 4) dependability, and 5) cheerful acceptance of criticism.

Communities are changing their attitudes toward the retarded from preoccupation with their limitations to recognition of their capabilities when provisions are made for their development. The task of assisting the educable mentally retarded child now rests with the home, school, and community rather than with a special institution. However, the persons within a community who are in a position to provide employment need to know what jobs the retarded can do, even do better, than the normal worker.

The Vocational Rehabilitation program both State and Federal has never realized its potential in developing a postschool program for the mentally retarded. In vocational training, there should be an opportunity for mentally retarded persons to learn some of the

---

[34] Alice Channing: *Employment of Mentally Deficient Boys and Girls*. U. S. Dept. of Labor, Bur. Pub., No. 210, Washington, D. C., Government Printing Office, 1932.

[35] Ruby R. Kennedy: *The Social Adjustment of Morons in a Connecticut City*. Hartford, Conn., Mansfield-Southbury Training Schools, Social Service Dept. State Office Bldg., 1948.

[36] M. F. Baer: Mentally retarded youth: training and employment. *Personnel and Guidance Journal, 38*:456-457, Feb. 1960.

[37] Samuel A. Kirk and Orville Johnson: *Educating the Retarded Child*. Boston, Mass., Houghton Mifflin Co., 1951, p. 232.

specific skills required in a trade. Vocational rehabilitation, employment services, family agencies should all be part of the mentally retarded's community and culture.

SUMMARY

Next to the home, the mentally retarded child's community is the most important factor in his life. The community represents the culture in which the child and his parents must live. Community interaction in which the parents are given sympathetic understanding and reassurance will affect the parents' role in handling the child. Parents can directly influence, favorably or adversely, an exceptional child's ability to adjust into society.

More community agencies are now active. Many organizations of professional workers, parents, civic groups et al. are now devoting their full energies to the provision of needed services for exceptional children, i.e. raising funds, conducting research and pilot studies, demonstrating new approaches, influencing local, state and federal groups involved in public education to add needed services, and, possibly most influential of all, encouraging legislative bodies to mandate, or in other cases to make permissive the supplying of educational and correlated services.

SELECTED REFERENCES

A Curriculum Guide for the Trainable Mentally Retarded. Carson City, Nevada, State Dept. of Ed., p. 14.

Amacher, P.: Church school and the handicapped child. *International Journal of Religious Ed., 38*:14-15, Dec. 1961.

Anderson, A. V.: Orienting parents to a clinic for the retarded. *Children, 9*:178-182, Sept. 1962.

Appell, M. and Kinsella, B.: Coordinating group on mental retardation of Monroe County, N. J.: a study of a coordinated community effort. *American Journal of Mental Deficiency, 67*:14-20, July 1962.

Baer, M. F.: Mentally retarded youth: training and employment. *Personnel and Guidance Journal, 38*:456-457, Feb. 1960.

Baldini, J. T.: Importance of professional standards as viewed by a parent and his organization. *Exceptional Children, 28*:507-508, May 1962.

Beck, H. L.: Advantages of a multi-purpose clinic for the mentally retarded. *American Journal of Mental Deficiency, 66*:789-794, Mar. 1962.

Begab, M. J. and Goldberg, H. L.: Guardianship for the mentally retarded. *Children, 9*:21-25, Jan. 1962.

Berryman, D.: Leisure time and mental retardation. *Training School Bulletin, 58*:136-143, Feb. 1962.

Blodgett, H. E.: Helping parents in the community setting. 33rd Spring Conference of the Woods Schools, held in Minn. May 2-3, 1958.

Boggs, E. and Nordfors, G.: Care of the mentally retarded in Sweden. *Children,* 7:150-154, July 1960.

Channing, Alice: *Employment of Mentally Deficient Boys and Girls.* U. S. Dept. of Labor, Bur. of Pub., No. 210, Washington, D. C., Gov't Printing Office, 1932.

Clarke, Ann M. and Clarke, A. D. B.: *Mental Deficiency: the Changing Outlook.* Glencoe, Ill., The Free Press, 1958.

Cohen, J. S. and Williams, C. E.: Five phase vocational training program in a residential school. *American Journal of Mental Deficiency, 65*:230-237, Sept. 1961.

Connor, L. E.: *Administration of Special Education Programs.* New York, Teachers College, Columbia Univ., 1961, p. 8.

Cromwell, R. L.: Mental retardation and some current dilemmas in the profession of psychology. *Training School Bulletin, 58*:83-91, Nov. 1961.

Cromwell, R. L.: Selected aspects of personality development of mentally retarded children. *Exceptional Children, 28*:44-51, Sept. 1961.

Crozier, M.: Ineducable? New attitudes. *Times Education Supplement, 2355*: 47, July 8, 1960.

Dybwad, G.: Administrative and legislative problems in the care of the adult and aged mental retardate. *American Journal of Mental Deficiency, 66*:716-722, Mar. 1962.

Developing new state program for mentally retarded children. *Ill. Education, 50*:353-356, Apr. 1962.

DiMichael, S. G.: *Vocational Rehabilitation of the Mentally Retarded.* Rehabilitation Service Series, No. 123. Federal Security Agency, Office of Vocational Rehabilitation. Washington, D. C., Government Printing Office, 1950, p. 86.

Dubrow, M.: Sheltered workshops for the mentally retarded as an educational and vocational experience. *Personal and Guidance Journal, 38*:392-395, Jan. 1960.

Edwards, N. and Rickey, H. G.: *The School in the American Social Order.* Cambridge, Mass., The Riverside Press, 1947.

Erikson, E.: *Childhood and Society.* New York, Norton, 1950.

Essex, M.: How can parents and special educators best cooperate for the education of exceptional children? *Exceptional Children, 28*:478-482, May 1962.

Farber, B.: Effects of a severely mentally retarded child on family integration. *Monographs of Social Research Child Development, 24*:2, Serial 17, 1959.

Gardner, W. J. and Nisonger, H. W.: Manual on program development in mental retardation; guidelines for planning, development, and coordination of programs for the mentally retarded at state and local levels. *American Journal of Mental Deficiency Monographs Supplement, 66*:1-192, Jan. 1962.

Goddard, A. L.: Action on many fronts. *International Journal of Religious Education, 38*:22, Feb. 1962.

Gordon, O. B.: Finding and training leaders. *International Journal of Religious Education, 38*:14-15, Feb. 1962.

Handman, D. A.: Programs for the mentally retarded in Denmark and Holland. *Exceptional Children, 28*:19-22, Sept. 1961.

Hill, A. S.: The status of mental retardation today—with emphasis on services. *Exceptional Children, 25*:205-216, Jan. 1959.

Johnson, G. Orville: The education of mentally handicapped children. In W. M. Cruickshank and G. Orville Johnson: *Education of Exceptional Children and Youth.* Englewood Cliffs, New Jersey, Prentice-Hall, Inc.

Kemp. C. F.: Who are the persons with special needs? *International Journal of Religious Education, 38*:4-6, Feb. 1962.

Kennedy, Ruby R.: *The Social Adjustments of Morons in a Connecticut City.* Hartford, Conn., Mansfield-Southbury Training Schools, Social Service Dept., State Office Bldg., 1948.

Kirk, S. A.: *Early Education of the Mentally Retarded.* Urbana, Ill., Univ. of Ill. Press, 1958.

Kirk, S. A.: *Educating Exceptional Children.* Boston, Mass., Houghton-Mifflin Co., 1962, p. 111.

Kolstoe, O. P.: Examination of some characteristics which discriminate between employed and not-employed mentally retarded males. *American Journal of Mental Deficiency, 66*:472-482, Nov. 1961.

Lombardo, A. and Gootzeit, J. M.: Can retarded adults be treated? *Journal of Educational Sociology, 33*:326-332, March 1960.

Lorenz, M. H.: Follow-up studies of the severely retarded. In M. C. Reynolds, J. R. Kiland and R. E. Ellis, Editors: *Research Projects.* No. 6, St. Paul, Minn., Statistical Division, State Dept. of Ed., 1953.

Mackie, R.: Exceptional years for exceptional children. *School Life,* 40 Jan. 1958.

Mackie, R., Williams, H. and Scates, A.: *Cooperative Research Projects, 1957.* Bull. No. 5, 1958. And Clark, D. and Scates, A.: *Cooperative Research Projects 1958.* Bull. No. 18, 1959, Washington, D. C., Gov't Printing Office.

Magnifico, L. X. and Doll, E. E.: Out of school and self-supporting. *Overview, 3*:32-34, Sept, 1962.

McGinnis, I. M.: Selected references from the literature on exceptional children; mentally retarded. *Elementary School Journal, 62*:336-338, Mar. 1962.

Merry, F. K. and Merry, R. V.: *The First Two Decades of Life.* 2nd Ed. New York, Harper & Bros., Publishers, 1958.

Mullen, F. A. and Itken, W.: Value of special classes for the mentally handicapped. *Education Digest, 27*:46-49, Oct. 1961.

Murray, W.: Outcasts no longer; the sub-normal since 1944. *Times Education Supplement, 2458*:1345, June 29, 1962.

Niehm, B. and Kradel, J.: Program for adjustment and habilitation of retarded young adult males. *Training School Bull., 58*:23-29, May 1961.

Nisonger, H. W.: Changing concepts in mental retardation. *American Journal of Mental Deficiency, 67*:4-13, July 1961.

Olshansky, S.: Mentally retarded or culturally different? *Training School Bulletin, 59*:18-21, May 1962.

Palmer, C. E.: They need a chance to grow. *International Journal of Religious Education, 38*:10-11, Feb. 1962.

Peterson, L. and Smith, L. L.: Comparison of post-school adjustment of educable mentally retarded adults with that of adults of normal intelligence. *Exceptional Children, 26*:404-408, Apr. 1960.

Preparation of mentally retarded youth for gainful employment. U. S. Office for Education, Bull. No. 28, 1959, Rehabilitation service series, No. 507, Washington, D. C., Sup't of Documents.

Public Law 85-926 and Carlson, T.: Guide to National Defense Education Act of 1958. Government Printing Office, 1959.

Report on Study Projects for Trainable Mentally Handicapped Children. Springfield, Ill., Office of the Sup't of Public Instruction, Nov. 1954.

Rockwell, J.: Ministry to parents of the retarded. *Journal of Religious Education, 38*:16-17, April 1962.

Rubinstein, J. H.: Role of the diagnostic clinic in the care of the mentally retarded child. *American Journal of Mental Deficiency, 66*:544-550, Jan. 1962.

Sarason, S. B.: *Psychological Problems in Mental Deficiency.* 3rd ed. New York, Harper and Bros., 1959, p. 644.

Skeels, H. M.: A study of the effects of differentiated stimulation on mentally retarded children: a follow-up report. *American Journal of Mental Deficiency, 46*:340-350, Jan. 1942.

Smith, John A.: Areas of occupational opportunity for the mentally handicapped. Unpub. Study, L. A. Harbor Jr. College, no date.

Stevenson, H. W. and Fahel, L. S.: Effect of social reinforcement on the performance of institutionalized and noninstitutionalized normal and feebleminded children. *Journal of Personality, 29*:136-147, June 1961.

Tisdall, W. J. and Moss, J. W.: Total program for the severely mentally retarded. *Exceptional Children, 28*:357-362, Mar. 1962.

Tabias, J.: Evaluation of vocational potential of mentally retarded young adults. *Training School Bulletin, 56*:122-135, Feb. 1960.

Tramburg, J. W.: Future aspects of state governmental programs. *American Journal of Mental Deficiency, 66*:205-212, Sept. 1961.

Tuttle, H. S.: Religion as motivation. *Journal of Social Psychology, 15*:255-264, 1942.

U. S. churches, their practices. *Life, 39*:104-105, Dec. 26, 1955.

Wakefield, R.: Work experience for the mentally retarded in Santa Monica. *National Association Secondary School Principals Bulletin, 46*:217-219, April 1962.

Wilke, H. H.: They need a place in church. *International Journal of Religious Education, 38*:9-10, Feb. 1962.

Wille, B. M.: Role of the social worker. *American Journal of Mental Deficiency, 66*:464-471, Nov. 1961.

Wallin, J. E. W.: Sheltered workshops for older adolescents and adult mental retardates. *Training School Bulletin, 56*:111-121; *57*:24-30, Feb.-May, 1960.

War Manpower Commission: *Selective Placement for the Handicapped.* Washington, D. C., U. S. Employment Service, Rev. Feb. 1945.

Zuk, G. H.: Cultural dilemma and spiritual crisis of the family with a handicapped child. *Exceptional Children, 28*:405-408, April 1962.

Name Index

237

Subject Index

243